D1707384

European Monographs in Social Psychology
National characteristics

European Monographs in Social Psychology

Executive Editors:
J. RICHARD EISER, JOSEPH M. JASPARS, KLAUS R. SCHERER
Sponsored by the European Association of Experimental Social Psychology

This series, first published by Academic Press (who will continue to distribute the numbered volumes), appears under the joint imprint of Cambridge University Press and the Maison des Sciences de l'Homme in 1985 as an amalgamation of the Academic Press series and the European Studies in Social Psychology, published by Cambridge and the Maison in collaboration with the Laboratoire Européen de Psychologie Sociale of the Maison.

The original aims of the two series still very much apply today: to provide a forum for the best European research in different fields of social psychology and to foster the interchange of ideas between different developments and different traditions. The Executive Editors also expect that it will have an important role to play as a European forum for international work.

Other titles in this series:

Unemployment: its social psychological effects by Peter Kelvin and Joanna E. Jarrett.

National
characteristics

Dean Peabody

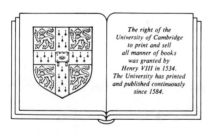

Cambridge University Press

Cambridge

London   New York   New Rochelle

Melbourne   Sydney

Editions de la Maison des Sciences de l'Homme

Paris

Published by the Press Syndicate of the University of Cambridge
The Pitt Building, Trumpington Street, Cambridge CB2 1RP
32 East 57th Street, New York, NY 10022, USA
10 Stamford Road, Oakleigh, Melbourne 3166, Australia
and Editions de la Maison des Sciences de l'Homme
54 Boulevard Raspail, 75270 Paris Cedex 06

First published 1985

Printed in Great Britain by The University Press, Cambridge

Library of Congress catalogue card number: 84–29221

British Library cataloguing in publication data

Peabody, Dean
National characteristics.—(European monographs in social psychology)
1. National characteristics
I. Title   II. Series
155.8'9   BF753

ISBN 0 521 30449 0
ISBN 0 7351 0108 8 (France only)

UP

Contents

Preface

Sometimes a college student who has been talked out of his
stereotypes in a psychology course is amazed to discover, on his first
trip abroad, that the Germans really are different from the Italians.

Brown, 1958, p. 365

It may be helpful to outline briefly my own background that led me to this
problem. I grew up at a time when traditional American liberal values were
more universally accepted than they are today. In particular, the equalitarian
premise of the American creed, "All men are created equal," shifts easily,
but not logically, to the corollary that "All people are pretty much alike."
And this shift was reinforced in the World War II period of opposition to
fascism. A specific intellectual influence was Hayakawa's *Language in action*
– a more manageable version of the ideas of general semanticists than the
formulations of Korzybski. This book became a best-seller in 1941 and was
used as a text in a class at my secondary school. The emphasis was strongly
on the dangers of abstraction and of neglecting the differences between
members of a category. The slogan "COW_1 is not COW_2," was extended at
once to ethnic membership: "JEW_1 is not JEW_2," was a particularly relevant
extension for the period 1941–5.

With this background I later spent four years during 1949–54 living in
western Europe and working with refugees from eastern Europe. My reaction
was much like that of the Harvard students described by Roger Brown in the
quotation above. I was overwhelmed by the obvious differences between
different European groups, whether taking the historic route south from
Munich across the Brenner pass to Italy, or the other route west to Paris.
Moreover, educated Europeans who were not fascists took it for granted that
important differences existed (just as educated Americans took it for granted
that they did not). An extreme example occurred in my refugee work which
brought me in contact with people from the three small Baltic nationalities
– Estonians, Latvians, and Lithuanians. My previous knowledge would have
permitted me to name the three nationalities, but not to order them correctly
on a map. But now I was told that even these three nationalities were very
different! These years began a lasting interest in group differences, which
continued in later visits to Europe.

This personal interest in group differences was combined only later with a theoretical viewpoint. My undergraduate college years at Swarthmore (and much later as a faculty member) brought me in contact with the viewpoint of Gestalt psychology and the related cognitive views of Tolman and Lewin. This viewpoint emphasized that human perception and judgment were determined by the organization of information from the outside world. This cognitive viewpoint, more atypical of American psychology then than now, was opposed to the more typical influences of reinforcement theory and psychoanalysis – an opposition that was emphasized, if not exaggerated, by the "anti-establishment" traditions of Gestalt psychology.

Later, in graduate school, I began to study social psychology. Gordon Allport, a teacher there, and Otto Klineberg, a senior colleague later at my first academic position, both represented a long-term interest in attitudes and judgments about groups. An extension to social psychology of the Gestalt and cognitive viewpoint was represented by Asch and Roger Brown. Their writings suggested the extension of such a viewpoint to judgments about groups – that these judgments may be analyzed like other cognitions, and not simply written off as irrational and evil.

In discussions with Asch during my early years on the Swarthmore faculty, we returned to the problem of impression formation, which he had begun in 1946. This led me into problems involving trait-adjectives (e.g., Peabody, 1967, 1970, 1978): using trait-adjectives to represent the possible personality characteristics of people; analyzing judgments using trait-adjectives to separate their evaluative and descriptive aspects; and examining the relations between trait-adjectives – the results suggested three large factors: evaluation and two descriptive factors. It was soon apparent that these points could be applied to national characteristics and judgments about them. An initial study was carried out in the Philippines (Peabody, 1968). The present work is a much larger extension to Europe.

Acknowledgments

This book is dedicated to the Europeans. They have contributed in different ways both to its more remote and to its more immediate origins. They have provided the interesting variety of national characteristics that seemed to call for some account. They have generally accepted calmly the possibility of national characteristics and so provided encouragement for an American who was uneasy about this point. More immediately, they have served as student "judges" in the empirical part of the present study.

Most of all I am indebted to my European professional colleagues. They have not only arranged for the collection of data from the student "judges," but in many cases helped in additional ways, for example, in translating the scales and gathering evaluative norms for these. They may properly be considered co-authors of the present work. But they should not be considered responsible for the many opinions expressed. Their names follow:

Dora Capozza, *University of Padua, Italy*
Willem Doise, *University of Geneva, Switzerland*
Gustavo Iacono, *University of Naples, Italy*
Jorma Kuusinen, *University of Jyväskylä, Finland*
Helmut Lamm, *University of Cologne, Germany*
Ezio Ponzo, *University of Rome, Italy*
Manfred Sader, *University of Munster, Germany*
Georg Wieser, *University of Vienna, Austria*

Introduction

This book is relevant to an old question: do nationalities have definite psychological characteristics? This question is obviously interesting and important, but it is usually avoided as being too controversial.

The issue has taken two forms: first, when judgments about national characteristics are made by ordinary people – in practice by university students – social scientists traditionally call them "national stereotypes"; on the other hand, "national character" refers to what national characteristics "really" are.

This book goes beyond previous treatments in considering both forms of the issue: an extensive empirical study of judgments by students, and reports on national character.[1] There are several special features: (a) the empirical study improved in several ways on previous studies of "national stereotypes"; (b) there is a systematic comparison between these results and reports on national character;[2] (c) the analysis of national character consistently aims at a comparative point of view.

Part I considers general questions regarding judgments about groups. Chapter 1 considers assumptions that would rule out such judgments in advance; Chapter 2 considers the psychological characteristics to be measured, and Chapter 3 the judgment principles that could apply. Chapter 4 summarizes the design of the empirical study, and Chapter 5 the overall results, relevant to the judgment principles. (Specific results for the separate nationalities are considered in Part II for comparison with national character.)

Part II begins (Chapter 6) with a consideration of existing schemes that permit a comparative approach toward different nationalities (as opposed to considering each on its own terms). Chapters 7 to 12 analyze reports on national character for each of the "standard" nationalities and then compare this with the results from the empirical study. Chapters 13 to 16 summarize the empirical results regarding other nationalities, with briefer consideration of national character.

Part III presents conclusions regarding national character (Chapter 17) and judgments about national characteristics (Chapter 18).

[1] The empirical study was carried out first, and was the main emphasis of an earlier manuscript circulated in 1975–6. The present version represents a major revision, with the main emphasis shifted to national character.

[2] Both of these approaches focused primarily (but not exclusively) on six "standard" nationalities: four large nationalities in western Europe (English, Germans, French, and Italians) and two world powers (Russians and Americans).

Part I
Judgments about national characteristics

1 National characteristics and group judgments

> ...the term [stereotypes] is usually applied to *someone else's* generalization.
>
> Brigham, 1971, p. 31

This book considers the psychological characteristics of nationalities ("national characteristics") and judgments about them ("group judgments"). There have been many objections to these topics as a matter of principle. Therefore, it is necessary to begin by examining these objections, since if they were wholly valid they might seem to rule out in advance any serious consideration of these topics.

The problem of national characteristics has appeared in two forms: when judgments about national characteristics are made by ordinary people – in practice by students – these are traditionally called "national stereotypes"; when the possibility of real national characteristics is considered, this is traditionally called "national character."

Social scientists traditionally assume that national stereotypes are generally "irrational" and more specifically that they are false in fact and evil in their consequences. These assumptions may be true of the judgments by many people, but they are not really proved by traditional stereotypes research, where the initial studies of Katz and Braly (1933, 1935)[1] with Princeton University students have been repeated many times. The term "stereotype" suggests in advance that any judgment about group characteristics is irrational, false, and evil.[2] To avoid such circular argument, judgments about group characteristics will be simply called "group judgments" here. Whether a "group judgment" is a "stereotype" (false and evil) is then not established by definition.

Before and besides social scientists, national character has been considered by informed observers from Tacitus to Madame de Stael. A modern social science version appeared in anthropology with Ruth Benedict and Margaret Mead, who proposed generalizations about personality characteristics for the small, preindustrialized cultures which anthropologists traditionally study.

---

[1] The main criticism of these studies is not to the pioneering work of Katz and Braly, but that their design has been slavishly repeated without any further advance.

[2] Brigham's (1971) review defines "stereotype" as "a generalization about an ethnic group, concerning a trait attribution, which is considered to be unjustified by an observer" (p. 31).

But both of them went on to make comparable generalizations about the "national character" of larger industrial societies:

Many who object to "national stereotypes" would not object to the possibility of "national character" in principle. (There may be objections to particular generalizations, as indeed there have been to both kinds proposed by Benedict and Mead – e.g., that the Samoans had a trouble-free adolescence, or that the Japanese had a predominantly "anal" national character.)

This chapter considers 13 specific objections, divided into three groups. Probably most of these come from discussion of "national stereotypes." However, some of these objections are to the very possibility of generalizations about the psychological characteristics of nationalities. Hence they would rule out the possibility of "national character" as well.

Other objections are concerned more specifically with *judgments* about group characteristics. Even here, one should recognize that most of the proposals about national character are also judgments – more-or-less informed judgments by more-or-less expert observers. (Only rarely is more clearly objective evidence available.) One should avoid an elitist assumption that there is a qualitative difference between judgments by ordinary people (false and evil) and judgments by experts (possibly correct).

It will be argued that most of the objections are basically invalid, as regards ruling out in principle the possibility of national characteristics and judgments about them. Some of the objections seem partially valid – e.g., to the extent that the objection applied it would be valid. These objections are grouped at the end.

In sum, the objections are arranged in three sections as follows: I, general objections to national characteristics (1–4); II, objections primarily directed at *judgments* about national characteristics (5–9); III, objections that seem partially cogent (10–13).

These objections have all been encountered in discussions of national characteristics, but they are often only implicit and not openly stated in the published literature. An earlier review by Roger Brown (1965) included many of the present ones, and the present chapter could be considered a revision and expansion of his discussion, which will be cited where relevant.

I. General objections

1. *Generalizations*

The most basic objection is that *any* generalization ignores what is specific and unique. This danger was developed systematically by the general semanticists such as Korzybski and Hayakawa. Within academic circles, such a position is often taken – usually implicitly – by some of the humanities faculty: an artistic work (or historical event) should not be interpreted using generalizations, but can somehow be understood in more specific or unique terms. This position has been questioned by some philosophers (e.g., Hemphill with regard to history) who argue that "explanation" always involves a least implicit reference to a generalization.

In any case, the basic answer to this objection is that while generalizations may involve the danger of ignoring what is specific and unique, they may also be powerfully effective and even unavoidable. All science assumes that generalizations about its subject matter are possible, even though specific and unique features are ignored. Every snowflake may be unique. But the success of physics comes from ignoring such features, abstracting some very general features (such as "mass"), and relating these in powerful generalizations.

If this answer is accepted, it follows that one cannot object to generalizations about national characteristics simply because they are generalizations. Roger Brown (1958, p. 365) makes the same point this way:

> It has been said, for instance, that a stereotype is a generalization; it overlooks individual differences. To react to a person as a German is to forget that no two Germans are exactly alike. Stereotypes are "bad" because they are indiscriminate. This characterization is insufficient because it does not distinguish stereotypes from any other categories. The notion of a right triangle is also a generalization; it overlooks differences of size and color and location. And so are all categories generalizations that overlook differences. However, this is not necessarily a bad business. Right triangles are all equivalent in that they satisfy the Pythagorean theorem.

Another, less direct answer to this objection is that generalization or categorization is an unavoidable psychological tendency (cf. Asch, 1952; Brown, 1958, 1965). The world may be in continual flux, like Heraclitus' river, no event may ever repeat itself, and each individual may be unique. Still, in order to learn anything from experience, a human (or any animal) must be prepared to bypass such differences and respond to similarities of events and people.

2. *Generalizations about people*

Another possibility is not to object to all generalizations but only to generalizations about people. Not surprisingly such a position may be taken – often implicitly – by natural scientists who assume that generalizations are possible about things (their own subject matter) but not about people. On academic committees I have often encountered a kind of alliance – I considered it an "unholy" alliance – between those natural scientists who assumed that generalizations were possible about things but not about people, and those from the humanities who may really have assumed that no generalizations were possible of any kind. Both agreed in assuming (implicitly) that no generalizations were possible about people.

On the other hand, psychology and the social sciences must necessarily assume that generalizations are possible about *their* subject matter (people). Admittedly the evidence for the success of this assumption is less overwhelming than for the natural sciences. But unless one argues that such generalizations are impossible in principle, the assumption stands.

3. *Generalizations about the psychological characteristics of nationalities*

If one accepts that generalizations about people are possible in principle, one could still object to – either or both of – the following: (a) generalizations about national differences or (b) generalizations about psychological characteristics. In general, neither of these objections, taken separately, seems to be made too seriously. As regards (a), within the social sciences there do not seem to be special objections to studying national differences in comparative economics, comparative politics, or comparative sociology. As regards (b), within psychology (especially American psychology) there are periodic objections that to analyze individuals in terms of traits is to attribute more consistency than is factually justified. However, these objections do not argue that people could not in principle have the consistency implied by traits, but only that in fact the consistency is much less than traits imply.

Hence, serious objections in principle are made only to the *combination* of the preceding: i.e., to generalizations about the psychological characteristics of nationalities.[1] The remaining objections are generally different versions of this.

4. *Variability within national groups*

An objection, that appears in several different forms, is to point to the variability within national groups, and from this to argue against generalization about such groups. This objection can be dealt with most directly by considering the possible forms of group differences. Allport (1954) remains one of the few explicit considerations of this. The several types of differences discussed by Allport can be related to two basic types of difference, which he sometimes treats as continuous distributions and sometimes as categorical percentages. Figure 1.1 shows as continuous distributions these two types, which are called here simply (a) "complete" differences, and (b) "partial" differences.

A situation approaching "complete" differences can, according to Allport (1954, p. 97), occur for the "essential attributes of the group – those characteristics that define the group." Examples would be language and skin color. However, the evidence suggests that for the personality characteristics

---

[1] "National characteristics" will be used here as an abbreviation for "modal psychological characteristics of members of a nationality" and not for other possible "characteristics" of a nation (e.g., gross national product, etc.).

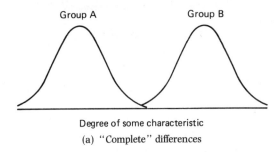

Degree of some characteristic

(a) "Complete" differences

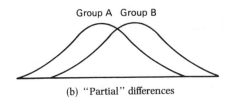

(b) "Partial" differences

Figure 1.1 Two types of group differences

of interest, differences between groups tend to be "partial" ones, with the differences within groups typically greater than those between groups.

One clear conclusion follows from this: it *would* be a mistake *if* anyone interpreted group differences on psychological characteristics as if they were complete differences.

Can one also conclude that one should reject the possibility of partial differences between groups because there is variability within them? It seems fair to say that such a conclusion would not be seriously proposed for any other topic. In psychology or the social sciences any effective variation between conditions is virtually always accompanied by variation within conditions. Indeed, in psychologists' favorite methodology – the analysis of variance – the existence of variation within groups is taken for granted and used to test the significance of differences between them. In fact, the distributions in Figure 1.1 were taken from an elementary statistics book illustrating such points.

It would be absurd to bring up considerations from elementary statistics, except that one repeatedly encounters the argument that national characteristics need not be considered because there is variation within the nationality. For Europeans a favorite version of this argument is to point to regional and ethnic differences within the nation – examples of which appeared to some surprise prominently again after World War II (e.g., Belgium, Canada). Such an argument seems to be contained, for example, within the otherwise informed review by Duijker and Frijda (1960), where the existence of regional differences within a nationality is taken as a presumptive argument against the concept of "national character."

It should be illuminating to compare national differences with social class differences – since the same social scientists who are against the first are typically in favor of the second (and would not accept the argument that social class differences are ruled out because there is variation *within* social classes). This seems a clear case not of scientific reasoning but of the values of scientists. National differences are felt to be somehow fascistic; to oppose them is to be on the side of the angels. On the other hand, to favor social class differences is to be progressive and on the side of Engels and his co-author.[1]

II. Objections to group judgments

The next block of objections comes from the stereotypes studies and is directed particularly at *judgments* about national characteristics: in general one can say that everyday observation suggests that the objections *do* apply to the judgments about groups by many ordinary people. The problem is that the research does not present relevant evidence. Hence, the thesis that the objection applies to all group judgments by ordinary people is based only on assumptions, not on any actual data.

5. *Group judgments are "irrational"*

The most general objection – that group judgments are "irrational" – may be expressed rather vaguely. However, a more specific interpretation can be offered as to what is meant: group judgments primarily represent the projection of affect, rather than any cognitive principles involving "information processing." This view is implied by Katz and Braly and their successors, although not actually shown by their results.

A small minority of psychologists (Asch, Brown, Campbell) suggested earlier that judgments about groups must involve general cognitive principles such as categorization. Only very recently have a larger number of American psychologists begun to propose that cognitive principles are involved in "stereotypes" (e.g., Hamilton, 1979).

We will discuss separately below a milder form of the present objection – as objection 13 on the "ethnocentrism of evaluation." This latter proposes that group judgments involve differing evaluations that reflect the norms of the judge. This version becomes central to the design of the present empirical

---

[1] The suggested pun is more successful in other Germanic languages and recalls that of Pope Gregory I who – on being told that the blond captives were Angles – commented "Non angli, sed angeli" (not Angles, but angels). Indeed, a triple pun is possible in Dutch, where "Engel(s)" can refer to (a) the collaborator of Marx, (b) angels, and (c) English.

study, which systematically compares the relative importance of the evaluative and descriptive aspects of judgment.

Of course, affect is not identical with the evaluative aspects of judgment, although they should generally be related to each other. Actually, in stereotypes research the data concern evaluation more than affect and are primarily of two kinds: for each nationality target there is (a) the percentage of subjects checking each adjective, and (b) an evaluative index based on the evaluative aspects of these traits. However, no real argument is made from the evaluative index to the irrationality of the judgments. Instead the latter is simply assumed on other grounds.

6. *Group judgments are inaccurate*

The stereotypes literature certainly implies a more specific objection: that group judgments are inaccurate or false generalizations.

It may well be that group judgments are often inaccurate, but there is little evidence to support this assumption. Allport (1954, p. 84) commented on the evidence in the following terms: "...we find social scientists who overhastily reject the very possibility of racial, national, or group differences of any appreciable or fundamental order. Some of them do so on the basis of charitable motives, but the evidence they offer is usually fragmentary." Later, Brown (1965, p. 177) speaks of the same evidence as "just scattered fragments." More often than not, these fragments seem to correspond to popular judgments – e.g., Jews and Negroes score relatively high and low on intelligence tests. On the other hand, there are cases that seem to contain no "kernel of truth."[1]

Brown concludes (1965, p. 179): "For most of the popular generalizations about ethnic groups there is no evidence with respect to validity or invalidity, nothing to tell us whether the facts confirm the expectancies. We cannot then say that the objection to ethnic stereotypes is their demonstrated falsity."

Thus the empirical evidence is inconclusive regarding the objection that group judgments are inaccurate. However, this objection does not disappear. Instead, it remains in the background for several of the further objections – if these objections were valid, it might follow logically that group judgments must be inaccurate.

---

[1] However, just as with perceptual illusions, one should expect at least a "kernel of stimulus" to explain how they arose. For example, the belief that Jews are prominent in international banking is refuted by Allport (1954) with evidence from the United States in 1946, but has a plausible origin earlier in history with such salient cases as the Rothschild family.

7. *Agreement between judges*

Such an argument is implied by Katz and Braly from their main data index: the percentage of subjects who agree in checking a trait for some national group – often called the actual index of "stereotyping." The degree of agreement is typically fairly high for some traits and it is implied that this is a major objection to group judgments.

Any objection based on a *direct* argument from high agreement can be disposed of quickly. Agreement between judges is normally called reliability, and is a necessary but not sufficient condition for accuracy (validity). This point would be clear if several anthropologists agreed about the characteristics of an ethnic group, where this would be taken as evidence for, rather than against, their possible validity.

Moreover, in this case there is some evidence available, and this evidence does not support the implications about agreement. Brigham's (1971) review shows that degree of agreement ("uniformity") has a relation (sometimes high) with choosing favorable rather than unfavorable traits, and with the degree of familiarity of the groups judged. Neither of these results supports the idea that agreement about group judgments makes them false or evil.

Although any objection directly based on judges' agreement would seem untenable, Katz and Braly may have intended a more indirect argument in two stages: (a) agreement implies a lack of personal experience by the judges, (b) lack of personal experience implies that group judgments are false and evil. Such an argument is suggested by the following quotation:

The degree of agreement among students...seems too great to be the sole result of the students' contacts with members of these races. If for example the Germans are more scientifically minded on the whole than other peoples, this characteristic would be distributed in more or less degree among Germans and the distribution would overlap tremendously with a similar distribution of scientific-mindedness among Americans. Hence, many American students judging Germans from those whom they know might find their German acquaintances belonged to the great part of the curve which overlapped with that of the Americans. Their idea of Germans, therefore, would not emphasize the German love for science. Yet we find 78 per cent of 100 students agreeing that one of the most typical characteristics of Germans is their scientific-mindedness.

Katz and Braly, 1933, p. 288

This objection implies that agreement should vary inversely with familiarity, and hence is contradicted by the evidence cited by Brigham (1971). In any case, it reduces to an argument from lack of personal experience, to be considered next.

8. *Lack of direct experience*

It is clear that group judgments are not limited to cases of direct experience with members of the group. Does it follow that judgments not based on direct experience are false and evil? One could begin a reply with the preceding quotation from Katz and Braly which shows that it may be rational not to rely only on direct experience. If, as the quotation assumes, "Germans are more scientifically minded on the whole than other peoples," it would be rational for 100% of the students to make this judgment, although, in the example, only a small percentage could do so from direct experience with German acquaintances.

More generally, it *is* a principle underlying empirical science to prefer direct experience to received opinion. However, if this principle were carried to the extreme of trusting only direct experience, one could not benefit at all from the experience of others. Each individual would have to begin over again not only with science, but with most of civilization. Brown (1965, p. 180) put the point this way:

> Most of our beliefs are acquired from the talk and writing of others. For most of our beliefs, we do not have adequate direct evidence. How do we know that the world is round, that Columbus discovered America in 1492, that Australia exists? If it were to be required of us that we give up any belief that is not based on our own induction from our own experience, we should have to give up most of our beliefs, including many that are valid and powerful. Much of what we pick up uncritically from other people's talk is true, and so it does not discredit ethnic stereotypes to demonstrate that they have been acquired in this way. Perhaps these reputations represent the distilled wisdom of many generations.

If this objection has a "kernel of truth," it is that attitudes and judgments are typically learned from others rather than from direct experiences. This fact does not prove that they are false and evil.

9. *Judgments that are exceptionless, undifferentiated, or inflexible*

In connection with Figure 1.1, it was already seen that any relevant group differences are likely to be "partial" ones. Any group judgments that assumed "complete" differences would be known a priori to be inaccurate. Certainly many people in making group judgments *have* made this assumption and so were inaccurate. The problem is that the Katz and Braly tradition does not provide any relevant evidence.

More specifically, if group judgments had certain properties, one could object to them a priori. These properties will be discussed under three related headings.

Probability. As we have seen, groups may be nearly exceptionless in certain of their defining characteristics, but the psychological characteristics of interest will tend to be probabilistic ones. Hence, if group judgments represented exceptionless generalizations, one could object in advance.

Subjects in the Katz and Braly tradition, however, were given no opportunity to show whether their judgments were probabilistic or exceptionless (but could only choose to check or not to check a trait-adjective). Brigham (1971) reports that in more recent investigations where subjects were permitted to show the probability or degree of their judgments, few extreme judgments were made. Brown (1958, p. 366) comments as follows:

There is no reason to suppose that Princeton men in 1933 thought that the traits they ascribed to a group were true of all members. There is every reason to suppose from work done since 1933 that people seldom believe in the exceptionless ethnic generalization. The popular notion is not that all Germans are militaristic but that Germans *tend to be militaristic*.

The falsity of such a qualified belief cannot be presumed in advance.

Differentiation. An exceptionless generalization would also be one that did not allow for differentiation into subcategories – for example, "pacifistic Germans." Bruner and Perlmutter (1957) provide an example: subjects (American, French, German) were given varying information about occupation (professor, businessman, unspecified) as well as nationality for hypothetical stimulus persons. Of interest here is one result (not emphasized in the original report). Consider only those subjects given a single stimulus person and both occupation and nationality (e.g., a French businessman). These subjects reported that their impression was influenced by occupation at least as often as by nationality, more often in the case of their own nationality. We can infer that their nationality judgments were differentiated into subcategories for occupation, and relatively more so for their own nationality.

Obviously, we can no more assume without evidence that group judgments are undifferentiated into subcategories than that they are exceptionless in terms of probability.

Inflexibility. A third and related consideration is whether the judgment about nationality is modifiable on the basis of other information. This property of "inflexibility" is often included in definitions of "stereotypes" and "prejudice." Thus, Katz and Braly defined "stereotype" as a "fixed impression."

The properties of modifiability and differentiation can easily be related. The subjects of Bruner and Perlmutter (1957) were university students, who might have had initial presumptions that people are like professors, which would have to be modified by the information that the stimulus person was a businessman. This would be equivalent to shifting to an occupational subcategory.

In general, all three of these related properties *would* be highly relevant to whether a group judgment was objectionable. They should have been important topics for research. However, the Katz and Braly design provides no evidence about any of these relevant properties, although it may seem to presume them. The tradition has tended to delay research on these relevant properties of group judgments.

III. Partially cogent objections

With the last objection we have come to the first of those which clearly could have some merit. These objections still do not succeed in ruling out in principle the possibility of national characteristics and judgments about them. But they do present some relevant considerations – to the extent that these *do* apply, the objections would be cogent.

10. *Change*

A common objection is that national characteristics can change over time. To the extent that this occurs, yesterday's generalizations would no longer be valid today, nor today's generalizations tomorrow.

Into the nineteenth century national characteristics were often considered unchanging – contemporary German characteristics were related directly to those described by Tacitus, and French characteristics directly to those of Vercingetorix. This assumption is not made in the present book, which assumes instead that national characteristics are due to historical developments and therefore can and will change.

Thus the objection has merit in principle. The problem becomes one of degree: to the extent that change is more or less rapid, generalizations have lesser or greater importance. National characteristics are not the only feature of the world subject to historical change. If the social observers who say that we are now in a post-industrial society are correct, then industrial society lasted only something like 200 years. But it may nevertheless be of very great importance.

Thus it will be relevant to consider the rate of change of national characteristics. The evidence suggests that they may sometimes change rapidly, but generally show a considerable inertia even in the face of other changes in a nation. In particular, one should be careful as regards theories of "economic determinism" or "sociological determinism." Some versions of these theories might suggest that changes in the economy or the social system of a nation can be instituted without much regard for the psychological characteristics of the individuals, and, further, such changes would cause any existing psychological characteristics to change fairly rapidly. A different alternative is suggested by Inkeles and Levinson's (1969) discussion of national character: the mutual relations between society and its members are likely to induce "congruence" between them in the long run, but "incongruence" between them (and tendencies to change) can in principle be either "societally induced" or "characterologically induced." As evidence that a policy of institutional change may not produce basic changes in national character in the short or medium run, a striking case in point is the Russian national character, discussed in Chapter 11.

In any case, it is clear that the national characteristics considered below are subject to change sooner or later, and it is appropriate to specify the time period considered here: in general, it is limited at least to the present century, and primarily for the period before the late 1960s (when change seemed to be rapid), but secondarily for the period since then.[1]

11. *National characteristics as innate and racial*

Related to the preceding is objection to the belief that ethnic groups have inborn psychological characteristics. Roger Brown (1965) cites the study of Buchanan and Cantril (1953) where subjects were asked whether their own national characteristics were mainly inborn or due to the way they had been brought up. The belief that their national characteristics were mainly inborn was expressed by 59% of the West Germans, 39% of the British, and 15% of the Americans.

It *would* be relevant to investigate the differences between those who do or do not believe that national differences are mainly inborn. It is plausible that this belief would be more likely to make group judgments evil. Brown (1965, p. 184) comments:

Most people in the United States know that "national characters" can be transformed in a generation, but many people are not sure that the characters of such supposed races as the Jews and the Negroes can be changed in a generation. The notion that Negroes are innately inferior to whites in intelligence has been very widely held and has been used to justify the vicious institution of segregation.

12. *Discrimination*

As the previous sentence suggests, it is discrimination – giving worse treatment to individuals because of their group membership – that seems most objectionable. The relation to the preceding objection – the belief that group characteristics are racially inherited – is not strictly a logical one. One could

---

[1] The empirical study of group judgments was largely carried out in 1969–70, and the judgments should have referred primarily to those whose characteristics were formed before the late 1960s. The literature on national character refers primarily to the same period.

believe in innate group differences and not discriminate against individuals (e.g., on the basis of a pluralistic view that accepts the differences). Alternatively, one could disbelieve in innate differences and discriminate against individuals because of their group membership (e.g., simply on opportunistic grounds). It is not the belief in innate differences itself, but the punishment of individuals because of their group membership that has provided the tragic examples in this century.

Nevertheless, there is enough *psychological* congruence between the two that the belief in innate differences has been used to support discrimination. This seems the most strongly felt objection to national characteristics. In this objection, the possibility of national characteristics is combined with two additional assumed beliefs: that national characteristics are innate, and that the innateness justifies discrimination.[1] It should be clear that the position taken here is to accept the possibility of national characteristics, but to reject both of the additional beliefs (and indeed that there is any logical connection linking them).

However, this sequence of beliefs existed historically. One may nevertheless ask how general is this sequence leading from group judgments to discrimination. Stereotypes research has generally not provided evidence on this. What evidence there is shows that the relationship is far from simple between discriminatory behavior and verbally expressed judgments or attitudes. The classic example is La Piere's (1934) trip across the United States with an Oriental couple, where the proprietors of the public accommodations generally accepted them in practice, but stated in reply to a subsequent letter that they would not accept Orientals. On the international level, Brigham (1971) cites several studies as indicating that "stereotypes are not determiners of national policy, but tend rather to reflect this policy." More generally, Brigham concludes that "there is not a simple relationship between the expression of ethnic stereotypes and their 'use' in behavior toward specific ethnic group members" (pp. 28, 29).

13. The "ethnocentrism of evaluation"

We will add here a further objection. This might have been included as a milder form of the earlier objection that group judgments are irrational and represent primarily the projection of affect. It is treated separately here because in this milder form it is relatively cogent, and moreover it will be dealt with as a central part of the design of the empirical study below.

We begin with Brown's (1965) presentation: the traits used in stereotypes studies are mixtures of empirical content (which could conceivably be checked against the facts) and evaluative prescriptions reflecting the norms of the

---

[1] A further assumption is that the reaction (affective or evaluative) to the outgroup is negative, if we are concerned with discrimination *against* the outgroup.

judge. For example, Brown asks what the difference is when the Katz and Braly subjects call the Chinese "superstitious" and the Italians "religious."

In both cases one is saying that a nationality subscribes to a set of supernatural beliefs, beliefs outside the province of natural science and not testable by science. Surely one set of beliefs is called "superstitious" because that set of beliefs is not accepted in our culture. The other set of beliefs is called "religious" because it is accepted and institutionalized among ourselves.

(1965, p. 181)

Brown concludes:

To think of the norms of one's own group as right for men everywhere is called, in social science, "ethnocentrism." It is a frame of mind directly opposed to cultural relativism. In earlier centuries unlike cultures were seldom in contact and the peoples having such cultures had no great need to cooperate. Orientals could think of us as ugly barbarian "white devils" and we could think of them as wily, superstitious "heathen." Today when Africans, Orientals, Europeans, and Americans must often meet and must somehow avoid conflict, it is recognized that ethnocentrism is an inadequate and dangerous world-view.

(1965, p. 183)

The point made by Brown was made as a more specific hypothesis comparing outgroup and ingroup judgments by Campbell (1967; Levine and Campbell, 1972) and in the earlier work of Peabody (1967, 1978). The empirical study reported here is designed to provide systematic evidence relevant to this general problem. As described in detail in Chapter 2, the trait-adjectives were carefully selected so as to permit the separation of the evaluative and descriptive aspects of group judgments. The results provide evidence as to the relative importance of evaluation and descriptive judgment.

Conclusion

Although the last several points have some cogency, the general conclusion of this review must be a negative one. In general, the objections are assumptions made independently of any evidence or any sound arguments. Indeed, seldom in intellectual history have so many poor arguments been based on so little relevant evidence.

If one asks why so many unsound arguments have been made on just this topic, one is led to the hypothesis that this is due to the liberal values of those – including social scientists – who have made them. Struck by the evil consequences of discrimination, and its possible relation to national characteristics, they have accepted arguments whose weaknesses would not be accepted on any other topic.

The stereotypes research asks students to check characteristics for national groups, and if they do so this is interpreted as false and evil, and a sign of fascistic tendencies. While this may be true of some respondents, there is no evidence to prove this. Under these circumstances, what are the students to do? The Katz and Braly (1933) study was repeated at Princeton by Gilbert (1951) and by Karlins *et al.* (1969). These three studies – which may be called the "Princeton" studies – provide a useful comparison over time. Already in Gilbert's (1951) replication, many of the students objected, and even refused to participate. This reaction probably reflected an extension to the students of the same values as the social scientists. However, for the present point of view, this refusal was also wholly rational: in the Katz and Braly tradition, any judgments students made would be assumed to be false and evil, without regard to the actual views of the subjects.

This leads us to an ironic conclusion: the social scientists have assumed without adequate evidence the irrationality of judgments by ordinary people about national groups. Thus, the social scientists themselves fit one of Allport's (1954) many definitions of prejudice: "Thinking ill of others without sufficient warrant." This suggests a special form of equalitarianism: the judgments of ordinary people (about national groups) may be less irrational than had been thought, but the judgments of social scientists (about ordinary people) may be more irrational. This conclusion should be sobering, but not surprising: social scientists are people, and should be expected to follow their own social psychological principles; strongly held values may affect judgments in the absence of adequate evidence. One cannot assume a qualitative difference between social scientists and ordinary people. Getting rid of such an assumption has not only negative, but also positive, implications: the social scientists may in part make irrational judgments of the kind traditionally assumed for ordinary people, but ordinary people may in part make less irrational judgments of the kind traditionally assumed for social scientists. The present study attempts to provide some evidence as to what extent the judgments of ordinary people are more rational or more irrational.

2 Characteristics of persons[1]

The purpose of this book is to compare the characteristics of nationalities as judged by ordinary people (traditionally called "national stereotypes"), with the characteristics of nationalities derived from other sources (traditionally called "national character"). The previous chapter served a necessary preliminary purpose: before proceeding, it was necessary to answer the claim that judgments about national characteristics by ordinary people are necessarily false and evil – in which case they could hardly deserve serious consideration or comparison with anything.

We are now free to ask: what are the possible characteristics of nationalities? This leads at once to the more general question: what are the possible characteristics of persons – without regard to whether they are considered as members of national groups? This question is easily stated, but it has no easy answer.

What is needed is to define the "domain" of the possible personality characteristics of persons, so that any empirical work can try to represent this domain, however selectively. Unfortunately there is no generally accepted solution to the definition of this domain.

Noting that we are in part concerned with *judgments* by ordinary people about personality characteristics, a strong case could be made that these *judgments* can be represented by trait-adjectives in ordinary language.

Can a case be made that trait-adjectives – used for *judgments* about persons – also provide a basis for defining the domain of personality characteristics themselves? It is clear that we should not expect trait-adjectives to represent the *entire* domain of possible personality characteristics. Most obviously omitted are characteristics that are not prominent in manifest behavior but are inferred as latent characteristics especially by psycho-pathologists. With these exceptions, however, a case can be made that trait-adjectives provide as good a representation as any alternative of the manifest characteristics of persons. This argument makes a plausible linguistic assumption: that the

[1] Some readers may have only a limited interest in the technical details of representing trait-adjectives and analyzing the relations between them. Accordingly the text of this chapter includes only a summary overview of these questions. More technical treatment is given in the appendices. Appendix B gives a more recent account of the problem of selecting trait-adjectives to represent the characteristics of people. Appendix A includes several basic statistical analyses of the relations between the scales selected and their evaluative and descriptive components.

important manifest characteristics will tend to be coded as single terms in the natural language. Norman (1967, p. 2) puts the case more eloquently for the use of trait-adjectives as

the set of *all perceptible variations in performance and appearance between persons or within individuals over time and varying situations* that are of *sufficient social significance, of sufficiently widespread occurrence,* and of *sufficient distinctiveness* to have been encoded and retained as a subset of descriptive predicates in the natural language during the course of its development, growth and refinement.

We shall accept as an adequate definition of the trait domain the set of trait-adjectives in ordinary language. We are then immediately confronted with two problems: a practical problem, and a theoretical problem in interpretation.

The Allport and Odbert problem

The practical problem may be called the Allport and Odbert problem. It can be stated briefly: the number of trait-adjectives in English is unmanageably large. Using the unabridged dictionary, Allport and Odbert (1936) listed about 16,000 adjectives altogether that had some application to persons, of which around 4,000 represented permanent personality traits. If one inspects this list, it is apparent that a large proportion of these are of infrequent usage. But the number that remains is clearly of the order of many hundreds. For most purposes, this number is still unmanageably large. Accordingly some preliminary method of condensation is necessary.

It would be encouraging to have some rationale as a basis for making such a condensation. A possible rationale emerged from the theoretical problem to be considered next.

A basic theoretical problem

Evaluative and descriptive aspects of trait-adjectives

Leaving the Allport and Odbert problem aside for the moment, we confront a basic theoretical problem in interpretation: trait-adjectives are seldom neutral, but generally have a clear evaluative aspect as favorable or unfavorable. However, trait-adjectives are generally not *simply* evaluative, but also have a non-evaluative (or "descriptive") aspect. Thus, "X is thrifty" implies not only the evaluative judgment "X is good" (or, alternatively, the affective reaction "I like X"), but also "X tends not to spend money."

The problem is how to interpret the use of any trait-adjective. To what extent is the judgment an evaluative or affective one, as opposed to a descriptive one? This question is part of an old and more general question:

to what extent is human nature rational or irrational? More specifically, to what extent does human judgment and cognition involve some representation of the world, however imperfect, or – on the other hand – the expression of motives and emotions? Within psychology, the latter emphasis on the importance of affective aspects of judgment is strongly represented. Moving to the still more specific problem of judgments about persons, there are major theoretical positions[1] within contemporary psychology that emphasize the importance of evaluative or affective aspects of such judgments.

An investigation of trait-adjectives was undertaken (Peabody, 1967) to question this emphasis by examining the relative importance in judgments about persons of descriptive aspects as opposed to evaluative ones.

A method for separating evaluative and descriptive aspects

The problem – as developed thus far – is to try to represent the domain of possible characteristics of people, and in such a way as to separate the evaluative and descriptive aspects.

Actually, the logic of a method for separating evaluative and descriptive aspects is fairly simple. As we have seen, a single trait-adjective (e.g., *thrifty*) combines a descriptive aspect (tends not to spend) and an evaluative aspect (good). In the terminology of research design, the two aspects are "confounded" – one does not know whether to interpret any result as representing one aspect or the other.

Moreover, if one considers two trait-adjectives that are opposites (e.g. *thrifty* vs. *extravagant*) the problem remains: the contrast between the two traits combines a descriptive contrast (not spending vs. spending) and an evaluative contrast (good vs. bad). It would remain unclear to what extent any result should be attributed to one contrast or the other.

The logic of a solution becomes clear if the problem is represented as in Table 2.1. The situation just considered would be represented by two traits that are diagonally opposite in Table 2.1. What is needed to unconfound the descriptive and evaluative contrasts is to find a term to represent at least one (or preferably both) of the remaining combinations. An example of such a solution is given in Table 2.2.

The logic of this procedure is straightforward enough. Unfortunately, trait-adjectives do not necessarily come adapted to this scheme, and for various reasons almost never fit it perfectly.[2] (We shall not try to explain here more than a very few of these reasons.) Even in the set in Table 2.2, selected as one of the best examples, the fit is not perfect. While the implications of

---

[1] To question these theoretical positions was the original motivation for the investigation of trait-adjectives. However, these theoretical issues are not of primary importance for the present study. They are discussed elsewhere (e.g., Peabody, 1967).

[2] The general problem is discussed by linguists as the existence of "semantic gaps."

Table 2.1. *A general scheme for unconfounding evaluative and descriptive aspects*

Evaluative contrast	Descriptive contrast	
	A	B
Good (+)		
Bad (−)		

Table 2.2. *An example of unconfounded traits*

Evaluative contrast	Descriptive contrast	
	A	B
Good (+)	thrifty	generous
Bad (−)	stingy	extravagant

"thrifty" tend to be limited relatively narrowly to spending money, the implications of "generous" tend to extend further to include general interpersonal unselfishness.

One reason why trait-adjectives cannot be classified neatly is suggested by philosophers who have considered the relation between the evaluative and descriptive aspects of judgment (e.g. Brandt, 1959) – in the special case of ethical evaluation, this is often called the relation of "ought" to "is." In contrast to many psychologists' assumptions that evaluative aspects deserve primary attention without regard to the descriptive aspects, philosophers generally argue that evaluation is derived from descriptive judgment. In particular, they argue that the descriptive aspects of judgments must differ, if there is a difference in evaluation. As regards the classification scheme, this means that the terms in the same column that differ in evaluation (e.g., *thrifty* and *stingy*) cannot be descriptively the *same*, but only similar. Following Aristotle, Peabody (1967) proposed that the descriptive difference relevant to evaluation was typically the *degree of extremeness*, with the positive trait representing a more moderate and the negative trait a more extreme degree.

The preceding point provided a rationale for taking courage in the face of the Allport and Odbert problem. If the schema is to be used, it is necessary to accept a degree of descriptive similarity (between positive and negative terms) that falls short of near-synonyms. It then becomes consistent to require no more than this same degree of similarity in classifying other terms. For example, if we will have to treat *thrifty* and *stingy* as descriptively similar, it would be inconsistent to quibble with the more subtle differences between, say, *thrifty* and *economical*. Consequently, there is a rationale for reducing the

Table 2.3. *An alternative scheme using opposites*

Pair	Descriptive contrast A	vs.	B
a.	thrifty (+)		extravagant (−)
b.	stingy (−)		generous (+)

Table 2.4. *A marginal case of descriptive similarity*

Pair	Descriptive contrast A	vs.	B
a.	peaceful (+)		aggressive (−)
b.	passive (−)		forceful (+)

Allport and Odbert problem into a manageable number of sets of trait-adjectives.

In several respects, it is more realistic to represent the problem in an alternative way from the schema already presented. Starting with a particular trait-adjective, it is generally[1] relatively easy to find another that is more or less its opposite – and so represents a contrast for both evaluative and descriptive aspects. The question then becomes whether one can find another trait-adjective (or, generally, another pair of opposites) that reverses the evaluative aspects, but is sufficiently similar regarding the descriptive aspects. This alternative scheme is illustrated in Table 2.3.

What is "sufficiently similar" ultimately becomes a judgmental decision[2] that is potentially open to debate. The example used thus far represents a relatively easy case, since all four terms share implications about a central theme of non-spending vs. spending. If the method is to be applied broadly, it is necessary to consider lower degrees of similarity. To illustrate the opposite limit, Table 2.4 presents a marginal case of descriptive similarity.

Here the descriptive contrast for pair (a) has implications for a theme of belligerence, while those for pair (b) concern a more general theme of self-assertiveness. It seems a marginal decision whether these themes should be kept separate, or considered sufficiently similar to be combined.[3]

On the basis of the preceding analysis, the "trait inference" study – described in more detail in Peabody (1967) – attempted a systematic

[1] For exceptions, see the case of "sets of three" below pp. 25–6.
[2] In principle, it might be possible to set up a linguistic "frame" to operationalize this decision.
[3] In fact – in view of the different purposes of the original trait-inference study and the present study of group judgments – the two themes were separated in the first study and combined here.

Table 2.5. *Example of an initial adjective set*

	Descriptive contrast	
A	vs.	B
+ *thrifty, economical, frugal*		*generous* *altruistic*
− *stingy,* parsimonious, miserly *selfish?* possessive greedy mercenary		*extravagant,* wasteful

Note: italicized terms were among the 289 terms selected for evaluative ratings.

Table 2.6. *Example of a "set of three"*

	Descriptive contrast		
Pair	A	vs.	B
a.	intelligent (+)		stupid (−)
b.	crafty (−)		? (+)

classification of trait-adjectives. This "trait inference" study forms a necessary background for the selection of trait-adjectives used in the present study of group judgments.

The trait inference study: procedure

Classification into tentative sets

Some 700 of the more common trait-adjectives were classified into about 45 tentative sets. An example of such a tentative set is shown in Table 2.5. These tentative sets were of three kinds:

Complete sets (sets of four). About half of these sets included terms for all four of the combinations, as illustrated in the preceding tables.

Sets of three. Some of the sets included terms for three of the four combinations. Typically, what was missing was a term for one of the positive combinations. An example is given in Table 2.6.

As in several sets dealing with intellectual performance, one can find terms involving a negative form of intelligence, but no single term for a positive form of stupidity.

These sets are puzzling, and many explanations might be proposed. Perhaps the simplest is to regard them as transitional cases where one can only partly unconfound evaluative and descriptive aspects. One descriptive direction is generally good, and the other is generally bad. The remaining combinations may be conceived of, but are improbable. They may therefore be represented in English either by infrequent terms or by no term at all. As another example of the former, consider the opposites *polite* vs. *rude*. There are possible terms for negative forms of politeness, but they tend to be low frequency words: *ingratiating, obsequious, sycophantic*. On the other hand, a positive form of rudeness can be conceived of, but there are no adequate terms (*blunt* is evaluated negatively; adjectives like *frank* have a much broader reference). Hence *polite* (+)/ *ingratiating* (−) vs. *rude* (−) became a "set of three."

Sets of two. The remaining sets included only two opposite combinations. Examples would be *warm* vs. *cold*; *hard-working* vs. *lazy*. Pursuing the previous argument, these cases would represent a still higher degree of confounding. Both the missing combinations are so unlikely as to be represented by no single term in English.

How do these different sets relate to the problem of unconfounding evaluative and descriptive aspects? The "sets of two" involve two opposite categories of trait-adjectives. As argued earlier, in such a situation the evaluative and descriptive aspects are confounded with each other. To unconfound these aspects, it would be necessary to have one or both of the additional combinations of these aspects represented in the schemas presented earlier. These correspond to the "sets of three" and the complete "sets of four." Accordingly, the "sets of two" were omitted from further consideration in the trait inference study. (The possible consequences of this omission are considered in Appendix B.) The "sets of four" and "sets of three" were retained for the further stages of the trait inference study.

Selection of specific terms. The trait inference study continued with the sets that represented four or three of the combinations in the classification schemes. As potential representatives of each of these combinations, trait-adjectives were selected (typically two for each combination of evaluative and descriptive aspects). The resulting 289 terms were rated by 20 student judges on each of two primarily evaluative scales (*favorable–unfavorable* and *desirable–undesirable*).[1]

A final selection was then made of sets and trait-adjectives to represent them. The criteria used for this selection were that the adjectives should have relatively clear evaluative ratings, that they should be of relatively common usage, and that the several adjectives from a set should share a common

[1] Examples are the italicized terms in Table 2.5.

descriptive contrast. Adjectives were finally selected for 15 sets of four and 10 sets of three, a total of 90 single trait-adjectives. Since each set of four provided two bipolar scales, and each set of three provided one such scale, there were a total of 40 scales.

Trait inferences. Each item consisted of an inference from one of the single trait-adjectives to a seven-step semantic differential scale, defined by one of the pairs of adjectives. Thus, one of the items was essentially: "Assume a person who is THRIFTY. How likely is it that the person has one or the other of the traits given by the scale: *generous* vs. *stingy?*" The basic data consisted of the means on each item for 20 subjects.

Results

In general, this method made it possible to show that both descriptive and evaluative aspects are important in judgments about people, the descriptive aspects being generally more important. Of particular interest were the results of analyses of the relationships *between* the different sets. Somewhat surprisingly, since the selection had been designed to include a broad representation of the domain of trait-adjectives, a variety of analyses indicated that much of these relationships could be summarized by two large, descriptive dimensions plus a dimension of general evaluation.

(1) A descriptive dimension which was called "Tight vs. Loose control over impulse-expression" represented[1] about 43% of the total variance. This dimension was represented by such sets as: Thrifty (+) and Stingy (−) vs. Generous (+) and Extravagant (−); Serious (+) and Grim (−) vs. Gay (+) and Frivolous (−); Firm (+) and Severe (−) vs. Lenient (+) and Lax (−). Similar dimensions, most often called Introversion vs. Extraversion, have been found frequently by others.

(2) A descriptive dimension which was called "Self-assertiveness vs. Unassertiveness" represented about 23% of the total variance. This dimension was represented by such sets as: Confident (+) and Conceited (−) vs. Modest (+) and Self-disparaging (−); Individualistic (+) and Uncooperative (−) vs. Cooperative (+) and Conforming (−). Similar dimensions, often called Dominance vs. Submission, have been found repeatedly in studies of interpersonal traits.

(3) A dimension of general evaluation, representing about 17% of the total variance. This dimension is represented generally across the evaluative aspects of the sets.

There were, of course, some sets that were not strongly related to these

---

[1] These percentages are taken from *re*analyses using 14 complete sets as described in Appendix A.

major dimensions but appeared as relatively "specific" and on additional smaller factors. An example was the set: Pragmatic (+) and Opportunistic (−) vs. Idealistic (+) and Unrealistic (−).

It may seem implausible that, with an extensive representation of the domain of trait-adjectives, so much of the relationships should be represented by a very few dimensions. This question is considered in Appendix B.

Revised scales used in the present study of group judgments

The trait inference study was unusual in that the same trait-adjectives were used both as "measures" – pairs of opposite adjectives were used to define the scales – and as "objects of measurement" – the single adjectives from which the inferences were made. This situation affects the theoretical problem of unconfounding evaluative and descriptive aspects. For the complete "sets of four," the method for unconfounding could be applied in two ways: one could compare results for the two scales from a set (e.g., *thrifty* vs. *extravagant* and *stingy* vs. *generous*) or, alternatively, one could compare results for the four separate traits (e.g., THRIFTY; GENEROUS; STINGY; EXTRAVAGANT).

The first comparison could not be used with the "sets of three" which were used to define only one scale (e.g., *intelligent* vs. *stupid*). However, the method for unconfounding could still be applied by comparing results for the three single traits (INTELLIGENT; CRAFTY; STUPID).[1] This second comparison is no longer possible in the more usual situation where the "objects of measurement" are not trait-adjectives, but something else (e.g., a person, or – here – a nationality). In this situation, the method for unconfounding can only be applied by comparing two scales, and so to sets that provided two scales – i.e., to the complete "sets of four," and not to the "sets of three." Accordingly, the present study of group judgments omits the sets of three as well as the sets of two. (Exceptions were a few single scales used as "filler" items.) Nevertheless the complete sets represent about half of the domain of possible trait-adjectives.

The 15 pairs of scales used in the trait inference study were reexamined for possible revision. The criteria were much the same as before. In addition there was further information available, particularly about the actual strength of the descriptive relations within a set. Moreover, there was evidence that some of the adjectives used previously were relatively unfamiliar even to highly selected college students. (For example, on this basis, "pragmatic" was replaced by "practical.") Additional data were gathered with evaluative ratings of possible substitute adjectives. This evidence was combined with a reconsideration on conceptual grounds of entire sets and of possible substitutions within sets. The revision resulted in the selection of 14 sets of

---

[1] Neither comparison would of course be possible for the "sets of two," which was the reason for their omission from the trait inference study. See above, p. 26.

Table 2.7. *Basic scales and their descriptive relations* (*used in the study of group judgments*)

			Tight vs. Loose	Assertive vs. Unassertive	Other
A	vs.	B			
1a. Thrifty (+)		Extravagant (−)	+		
b. Stingy (−)		Generous (+)	−		
2a. Self-controlled (+)		Impulsive (−)	+		
b. Inhibited (−)		Spontaneous (+)	−		
3a. Serious (+)		Frivolous (−)	+		
b. Grim (−)		Gay (+)	−		
4a. Skeptical (+)		Gullible (−)	+		
b. Distrustful (−)		Trusting (+)	−		
5a. Firm (+)		Lax (−)	+		
b. Severe (−)		Lenient (+)	−		
6a. Persistent (+)		Vacillating (−)	+		
b. Inflexible (−)		Flexible (+)	−		
7a. Selective (+)		Undiscriminating (−)	+		
b. Choosy (−)		Broad-minded (+)	−		
8a. Cautious (+)		Rash (−)	+		
b. Timid (−)		Bold (+)		+	
9a. Calm (+)		Agitated (−)	+		
b. Inactive (−)		Active (+)		+	
10a. Peaceful (+)		Aggressive (−)		−	
b. Passive (−)		Forceful (+)		+	
11a. Modest (+)		Conceited (−)		−	
b. Unassured (−)		Self-confident (+)		+	
12a. Cooperative (+)		Uncooperative (−)			X
b. Conforming (−)		Independent (+)		(+)	(X)
13a. Tactful (+)		Tactless (−)	(+)		
b. Devious (−)		Frank (+)			X
14a. Practical (+)		Impractical (−)	(+)		
b. Opportunistic (−)		Idealistic (+)			X

Note: for the first two dimensions, plus and minus signs indicate the *direction* of the relationship. (In the analyses of results, each scale is scored according to the *evaluative* sign shown in parentheses next to each adjective. Thus scale 1a is scored with *thrifty* positive, and scale 1b is scored with *generous* positive. Hence, for an *evaluative* dimension the sign for every scale would be plus, indicating a positive relationship. In contrast, the alternating signs in the first column show the direction of the relation of each scale to this *descriptive* dimension.)

In the third column, the letter "X" indicates the *presence* of a relationship to some other smaller factor.

For column entries *without* parentheses, the relationship is consistently large across the several analyses described in Appendix A. For entries *with* parentheses, there is a large relationship in some of these analyses.

trait-adjectives, yielding 14 pairs of scales. These scales will be called the "basic" scales in the present study.

The procedure and results of the empirical study of group judgments are presented in the later chapters below. Details of several overall analyses of the relations between the different scales are presented in Appendix A. At the

moment, we need only anticipate one conclusion of these analyses: the three
dimensions already mentioned can again be identified in the overall results:[1]
(1) a descriptive dimension called "Tight vs. Loose control over impulse-
expression"; (2) a descriptive dimension called "Self-assertiveness vs. Unassertiveness"; (3) a dimension of general evaluation. These dimensions are
used to organize the presentation of the 28 basic scales in Table 2.7.

Table 2.7 lists the revised scales and their largest descriptive relations. For
the first seven sets, various analyses consistently indicate that all scales have
their largest relationship to a descriptive dimension which we have previously
labelled "Tight vs. Loose control over impulse-expression." Adjectives in the
left-hand column (A) represent Tight impulse-control, and those in the
right-hand column (B) represent Loose impulse-expression. As explained in
the note to Table 2.7, the alternating plus and minus signs in the column
labelled "Tight vs. Loose" show the relation of each scale to this descriptive
dimension.

For sets 10 and 11 both scales consistently have their strongest relations
to a second dimension, which we have called Self-Assertiveness. In this case,
the adjectives in column A represent Unassertiveness, and those in column
B Assertiveness.

Sets 8 and 9 represent both dimensions, with the two scales tending to split
between them. Thus the scale *cautious* vs. *rash* is most strongly related to the
Tight vs. Loose dimension, while the companion scale *timid* vs. *bold* represents
most strongly the Unassertive vs. Assertive dimension.

The remaining sets 12 to 14 do not have consistently strong relations to
the two major descriptive dimensions, but may appear on smaller, more
specific factors.

Discussion

Our selection of characteristics of persons had two objectives: to clarify
theoretical interpretation by separating evaluative and descriptive aspects,
and to represent broadly the possible characteristics of persons (the trait
domain). The first objective placed some limits on the second one. Nevertheless,
we would claim that our representation of the trait domain is better than most.

It may seem fantastic to claim that the apparent great variety of
characteristics of persons can, with any adequacy, be summarized using three
broad dimensions. We will consider the relevant issues separately in the
appendices. In particular, Appendix B considers the implications of omitting
the "incomplete sets" of trait-adjectives.

---

[1] However, as might have been anticipated, these dimensions were less pervasive in the present
study. For example, as regards revised set 12 – *cooperative* (+) vs. *uncooperative* (−) and
conforming (−) vs. *independent* (+) – the comparable set in the trait inference study had a strong
relation to the Assertiveness dimension, as is no longer true.

The present section discusses two other questions: (1) the situationist argument that personality traits exaggerate the consistency of people's behavior, which is better ascribed to situational rules (this argument must be given considerable justice); (2) comparison is made with the trait-adjectives used in previous major studies of judgments about national characteristics. It is clear that these selections are not superior to the present one.

The situationist argument

Early in this chapter, we argued that a strong case can be made that *judgments* by ordinary people about personality characteristics can be represented by trait-adjectives in the ordinary language, and that a case can be made that trait-adjectives provide as good a representation as any alternative of the (actual) manifest characteristics of persons.

A situationist argument has appeared repeatedly. It is congenial both to behaviorism and to sociology. Its recent prominence can be traced particularly to the American psychologist Mischel (1968). Situationism might accept both the arguments above, but the second only because no adequate analysis of situations has been worked out to provide a better alternative. The situationist argument is that while people may *judge* others in terms of the relatively consistent personality dispositions represented by trait-adjectives, these judgments greatly exaggerate the degree of actual consistency, which is much more variable between situations.

The issues will remain controversial for some time. Some of the claims for the importance of situational variables were clearly themselves exaggerated. The outcome of the controversy may be that personality variables are equally or even more important than situational ones. (A current favorite as a proposed resolution is the *combination* – "interaction" – of personality and situation.) In any case, we may accept the *direction* of the situationist argument: as compared with the relatively high consistency implied by ordinary judgments which typically are formulated using trait-adjectives, people actually are much less consistent across situations.

Note that this controversy has concerned the consistency of individuals, rather than those of national groups. The issues are much the same when applied to the problem of national characteristics. Indeed, we shall find some very clear examples where various nationalities show variability across situations. Nevertheless, the following point is worth noting: it is generally thought that the rules for action in a situation are in large part cultural. The situationist emphasis will then reduce the importance of individual differences within a culture, but it need not reduce the importance of differences between nationalities, who may have different situational rules.

Previous studies of judgments about national characteristics

Whatever the limitations on the present study of judgments about groups, these are relatively minor compared with those of most previous investigations. In particular these studies generally do not deal with the problems of representing the trait-adjective domain and the confounding of evaluative and descriptive aspects of judgment. We will deal here only with two major lines of investigation.

The Katz and Braly tradition

Most important is the Katz and Braly tradition. The criticisms here should be considered as directed not so much at the original pioneering study in 1933, but at the continued repetition of the same design without any improvement over the intervening years.

The selection of trait-adjectives. In the Katz and Braly tradition the 84 trait-adjectives were selected from those provided by a preliminary sample of Princeton students using an open-ended form to write in adjectives to describe 10 nationality groups; in the main study, students checked adjectives from the resulting "closed" list – the primary measure was the percentage choosing particular adjectives for each nationality.

This method of selecting adjectives at least had the advantage that some adjectives from the list were likely to be seen as applicable to the national groups. However, it does not attempt to be representative of trait-adjectives. (One consequence is to make relatively meaningless the primary measure. The percentage of subjects choosing a particular adjective clearly depends on the similarity among the 10 nationalities: for similar nationalities, a larger number of similar adjectives will tend to be produced on the open-ended form, and so appear on the list of 84. This will tend to lead to a scattering of selections in the main study, and lower indices of "uniformity" or "stereotyping.")

Jones and Ashmore (1973) may have been the first to examine the relationships *between* the trait-adjectives from the Katz and Braly list, when they included 45 of the 84 along with other adjectives in a multiple-scaling procedure. They propose a two-dimensional solution, which bears some resemblance to the dimensions discussed here of Tight vs. Loose impulse-control, Self-assertive vs. Unassertive, and general evaluation. A definitive comparison is hardly possible, given the different bases of selection of adjectives.

The confounding of evaluative and descriptive aspects. The Katz and Braly procedure includes no method for unconfounding evaluative and descriptive aspects. In contrast to the more recent explicit claims for the importance of evaluation, it is only fair to say that the interpretations by Katz and Braly did not especially emphasize evaluation or affect. Instead they simply treat judgments about groups as *generally* "irrational."

However, in the absence of any other basis for data analysis, it was natural to calculate an evaluative index, based on the evaluative aspects of the traits chosen for each nationality. Indeed, in the Katz and Braly tradition, the presentation of data consists largely of simply listing the adjectives that were frequently chosen for each nationality, and then using some evaluative index based on these adjectives. In summary, for the Katz and Braly tradition, evaluation is not emphasized theoretically, but in practice plays a major part in presentation of the results, by default of any other theoretical analysis.

A great many studies have essentially repeated the Katz and Braly design without any change or progress. (For a review, see Brigham, 1971.)

The Buchanan and Cantril study

One other study that deserves attention is that of Buchanan and Cantril (1953), if only because of its magnitude. They had samples from eight countries that were large (around 1,000 each) and selected to be representative. (The eight groups of judges were from Australia, Britain, Germany, France, Italy, Netherlands, Norway and the United States. All judges had as targets for judgment AMERICANS, RUSSIANS, and themselves. In addition, the following targets were each judged by three other groups of judges: the BRITISH, the FRENCH, the CHINESE.)

In view of this investment, the selection of trait-adjectives is distressing and even tragic. The respondents were asked to choose from a list of 12 characteristics those that best described several nationalities. As in the Katz and Braly tradition, data presentation consisted largely of listing for each nationality those adjectives chosen by a high percentage of judges, and then constructing several evaluative indices based on the evaluative aspects of these adjectives. Since most of their adjectives were related to ones used here, it is possible to classify them in our terms in Table 2.8.

It is obvious from Table 2.8 that this massive investigation did not deal adequately with two problems: the selection of trait-adjectives, and the unconfounding of evaluative and descriptive aspects. As an illustration, consider judgments by three outgroups about the BRITISH and the FRENCH. The BRITISH more than the FRENCH are judged with the trait-adjectives indicating "Tight" impulse-control. Because of the selection of adjectives this necessarily produces more positive adjectives and a more favorable evaluative index for the BRITISH than for the FRENCH.

It should be added that one's impression from the results is that the evaluative aspect of judgment was extremely important with these non-student

Table 2.8. *Classification of characteristics used by Buchanan and Cantril* (*1953*)

Evaluative aspect	Tight	Loose	Assertive	Unassertive	Other
Positive	Self-controlled Hard-working Intelligent Practical	Generous	Brave	Peace-loving	Progressive
Negative			Conceited Domineering Cruel?		Backward

samples of judges, particularly for the main target nationalities, where the AMERICANS received favorable adjectives and the RUSSIANS unfavorable ones. This time was the height of the "cold war" centering around these two nationalities (all the judges were from countries then in military alliances with the United States). However, the inattention to the selection of traits and the confounding of evaluative and descriptive aspects makes it difficult to establish any conclusion.

3   Judgment principles

National characteristics are not necessarily the same as judgments about them. The possibility that there may be important differences between national characteristics does not establish that these are the differences that appear in judgments about them.

The preceding statements are not at all unconventional. Indeed, the conventional assumption is that these considerations have overwhelming weight, so that judgments about groups are treated only as cognitive distortions and projections by the perceiver. What is unconventional is to take judgments about groups seriously as judgmental processes.

As we have seen, it is often assumed that judgments about groups are necessarily inaccurate and irrational. It would also be a mistake to assume that they are accurate and rational. A more balanced approach is to do justice both to what may be irrational and what may be rational in group judgments. Instead of arguing whether judgments are accurate or inaccurate, the objective here is to consider factors that would affect such judgments – and so make them more or less accurate. In order to avoid sheer speculation, we are led to emphasize principles that have some implications for evidence. For our own evidence, this can take two forms: first, we can compare our results for empirical judgments with other statements about national characteristics; secondly, we can make comparisons *within* our results for empirical judgments. These comparisons typically concern differences between ingroup and outgroup judgments.

The main section in this chapter considers nine judgment principles that might plausibly affect group judgments. A final section returns more directly to the question of accuracy, by considering the possible bases people might have for forming judgments about groups.

I. Evaluative and descriptive aspects of judgments

Our basic procedure attempts to separate the evaluative and descriptive aspects of judgments about groups. Obviously we should begin by taking advantage of this. Two obvious hypotheses are that different judges may agree about the descriptive aspects but disagree about the evaluative aspects (Peabody, 1968). We will consider these two hypotheses in turn.

Table 3.1. *Illustration of reciprocal judgments*

Judgments by	Judgments about Yankees	Hidatsa
Yankees	(Good) thrifty, provident	(Bad) spendthrifty, improvident
Hidatsa	(Bad) stingy, selfish, hoarders	(Good) generous, unselfish, share good fortune

1. *Descriptive convergence*

The hypothesis that different judges tend to agree about the descriptive aspects of a nationality is essentially the same as principle 10.4.3 of Levine and Campbell (1972, p. 171). Extending the terminology of Campbell and Fiske (1959), who emphasize the need for "convergence" between different measures of the same characteristic, we will call this "descriptive convergence."

The possible agreement between different judges does not of course establish the accuracy of these judgments, but it does make this a more plausible possibility. (See our discussion in Chapter 1 about "agreement between judges.") Reliability is a necessary but not a sufficient condition for validity.

> 3.1 *Descriptive convergence: different judges tend to agree as to the descriptive aspects of judgments about national characteristics.*

2. *Ingroup/outgroup differences in evaluation*

A hypothesis that is extremely plausible, though not necessarily always true, is that ingroup judgments will be relatively favorable in comparison to those by outgroups. This hypothesis was asserted by the sociologist Sumner (1906),[1] and is what Brown (1965) called the "ethnocentrism of evaluation." It can be combined with the previous hypothesis about agreement regarding descriptive aspects. We begin with an example from Levine and Campbell (1972, p. 172) contrasting judgments in the Dakotas of the United States

---

[1] There is a question whether to include Sumner's assertion in the *definition* of "ingroup" and "outgroup." For convenience, we follow Levine and Campbell in not doing so, and use "ingroup" and "outgroup" judgments as equivalent to "judgments by the membership group" and "judgments by others." It then becomes an empirical question whether Sumner's proposition is true. On the other hand, it should be noted that Merton (e.g., 1957) restricts "ingroup" and "outgroup" to cases where Sumner's assertion is true; the empirical question would then be whether a membership group is an "ingroup" in this sense.

Table 3.2. *A more complex illustration of reciprocal judgments*

Judgments by	Judgments about	
	Group N	Group S
Group N	(a) thrifty, serious, etc. (b) hard-working, reliable, etc. (c) strong, etc.	(a) wasteful, etc. (b) lazy, unreliable, etc. (c) weak, etc.
Group S	(a) stingy, pessimistic, etc. (b) hard-hearted, etc. (d) stupid, etc.	(a) generous, etc. (b) amiable, etc. (d) intelligent, refined, etc.

between the Hidatsa Indians, and the local ranchers of European extraction, whom they call Yankees.

It can be seen that Table 3.1 essentially represents our first pair of scales: *thrifty* (+) vs. *extravagant* (−), and *stingy* (−) vs. *generous* (+). The judges disagree about evaluation, evaluating the ingroup positively and the outgroup negatively. At the same time, they agree about the descriptive aspects: that, in this respect, the Yankees are "Tight" and the Hidatsa "Loose."

It will be useful to generalize this schema. Consider a comparison between two groups, N and S. (a) Group N is judged to show "Tight" impulse-control (thrifty, stingy, etc.) and group S to show "Loose" impulse-expression (wasteful, generous, etc.). (b) Similarly, group N is judged to have what we call in Appendix B "impersonal virtues" (hard-working, reliable, etc.) and group S the corresponding vices (lazy, unreliable, etc.). Conversely, group S is judged to have "interpersonal virtues" (amiable, etc.) and group N the corresponding vices (hard-hearted, etc.). (c) Group N is judged to be more powerful (strong, etc.) and group S less so (weak, etc.). (d) Group S is judged to have greater intelligence and sophistication (intelligent, refined, etc.) and group N less so (stupid, etc.).

Table 3.2 arranges these statements. We can compare this table with the proposals of Ehrenfels as to a recurrent pattern of regional differences between Northerners and Southerners, conveniently summarized by Levine and Campbell (1972, p. 162).[1] It will be seen that Table 3.2 captures much of Ehrenfels' proposals. Actually Table 3.2 represents a more consistent ingroup–outgroup difference in evaluation than Ehrenfels' proposals, where the outgroup judgments include characteristics that are not negative.

In a proposal that self-judgments tend to be relatively favorable, comparison might be made with either judgments *by* outgroups, or judgments *about* outgroups. The Philippines results gave consistent support only to the first version. Filipino self-judgments were consistently more favorable than Chinese judgments about Filipinos, but not generally more favorable than Filipino

[1] We will consider the merits of Ehrenfels' proposals later in Chapter 6. Here we consider it simply as a more complex example of reciprocal judgments.

judgments about the Chinese. However we will state the principle to include both versions:

> 3.2 *Ingroup self-evaluation: ingroup self-judgments tend to be more favorable than those by outgroups or those about outgroups.*

Are there any circumstances where this hypothesis might be false? As regards the individual, it is overwhelmingly likely that there will be a tendency to defend and enhance one's own self-esteem (with atypical exceptions such as masochists, those given to extreme self-effacement, etc.). The comparable principle as regards one's own group seems nearly as likely (with similar exceptions, such as group self-hatred, etc.). Nevertheless, the sociological concept of "reference group" suggests a case where there could be a discrepancy between these two principles: membership groups may not necessarily serve as positive reference groups; our judges may not identify with the "typical" member of their nationality that they are rating. In such a case, judgments about the ingroup will not necessarily be especially favorable.

II. Differences in descriptive judgments

We have thus far proposed principles for (a) similarity between judges for descriptive aspects of judgments and (b) differences between judges for evaluative aspects. We now consider principles that would allow for differences in the descriptive aspects. Of the many principles that could be considered, we will select only a few that have some implications for our empirical results. For the first four principles below, the implications are of possible differences between outgroup and ingroup judgments.

3. Homogeneity

Levine and Campbell (1972, p. 169) claim that groups are wrongly judged as too homogeneous in possessing a characteristic. This follows plausibly from general principles regarding categorization. (However, the relevant data on *actual* homogeneity are generally not available to permit comparison with *judged* homogeneity.)

It is also plausible that this tendency should be reduced for ingroup judgments, where there is more direct information as to the actual heterogeneity between members of a group. One implication for our data (which is not really designed to provide evidence about this principle) is that outgroup judgments would tend to be more extreme or "polarized," and ingroup judgments less so.

> 3.3 *Homogeneity: judgments, especially judgments by outgroups, tend to exaggerate the homogeneity within a group. One implication is that*

outgroup judgments will tend to be more polarized, and ingroup judgments less polarized.

4. Descriptive consistency

Judgments about people may reflect general personality dimensions, such as impulse-control vs. impulse-expression. It is plausible that judges may tend to fill in more specific characteristics, especially if these would otherwise be ambiguous, from these general dimensions and so exaggerate descriptive consistency. In terms of the traditional errors of judgment (Guilford, 1936) this overconsistency of descriptive aspects comes closest to the "logical error," while a comparable overconsistency of evaluation is close to the "halo effect."

It is plausible that descriptive overconsistency should be less for the ingroup, who are in a better position to recognize differentiation between different traits (and presumably more accurate in doing so). As regards judgments about individuals, Jones and Nisbett (1972) have presented evidence that the actor attributes causality to the situation, where the observer attributes it to characteristics of the actor. Self-judgments thus imply less consistency than judgments by others. The present principle could be considered an extension of the Jones–Nisbett principle. (The extension is from judgments about individuals to those about groups, and from situations vs. traits to more specific traits vs. more general dimensions.) Note that we are here concerned about overconsistency between different characteristics, while the previous proposal about "homogeneity" concerned overconsistency in judgments between members of the group being judged.

> 3.4 *Descriptive consistency: judgments may exaggerate the descriptive consistency between different characteristics. Outgroup judgments tend to show more descriptive consistency, and ingroup judgments less.*

5. Perceived change

We said above (in Chapter 1) that national characteristics may change, and that there will tend to be a "perceptual lag," whereby changes may be recognized only after some time interval. This interval will tend to be longer for outgroups. The effect on ingroup–outgroup differences is not always the same, but will depend on how the change relates to the previous *direction* on our bipolar scales. The change may reverse the previous direction (in which case, the ingroup judgments would tend to be *less* polarized, or even reverse the direction of outgroup judgments). Alternatively, the change may move further in the previous direction (in which case, the ingroup judgments would tend to be *more* polarized). Hence it would be necessary to examine each case separately.

3.5 *Perceived change: changes in national characteristics tend to be recognized only after some interval. Perceived change tends to occur later for outgroup judgments, and earlier for ingroup judgments.*

Comment. For some results, the three preceding principles may offer competing explanations. Such a result would occur, for example, if the outgroup judgments for several scales related to a descriptive dimension were descriptively consistent and relatively polarized, and the ingroup judgments were less consistent and/or less polarized. How could one then decide between the various explanations? One relevant consideration is whether the ingroup actually reverses the direction of outgroup judgments – in this case the principle of homogeneity (implying simply less polarization) would not apply. It would then become relevant whether the ingroup direction represented a new characteristic (which would favor the principle of perceived change), or a long-standing exception to the general descriptive direction (which would favor the principle of descriptive consistency). These kinds of considerations would help in choosing an explanation for some results.

6. *Behavior vs. conscious experience*

Behaviorists insist that we know others only from their "behavior," which is to be distinguished from their "private experience." Different evidence is thus available to the ingroup and outgroup as a basis for their judgments: the ingroup has access to their own conscious experience, while the outgroup is more dependent on the ingroup's manifest behavior. (This is not to exclude the possibility that a knowledgeable outgroup observer may be able to infer to the ingroup's conscious experience – to learn "how the ingroup thinks.")

What is intended here is not a subtle point, but an obvious and even old-fashioned one. Note that according to the Jones–Nisbett hypothesis already mentioned, one possible result of the difference in evidence is that the actor or ingroup is more aware of external situational factors, while the observer or outgroup is more likely to attribute behavior to personality characteristics of the actor. This result might seem paradoxical otherwise: for the ingroup, evidence from conscious experience accompanies attribution to external factors; for the outgroup, evidence from behavior is attributed to "internal" characteristics of the ingroup.

3.6 *Behavior vs. conscious experience: ingroup judgments may be based on their conscious experience; outgroup judgments are more dependent on manifest behavior.*

7. Recognized unfamiliarity

The preceding principles are generally consistent with the ingroup judgments being more accurate, and so with several principles of Levine and Campbell which imply that familiarity will relate to accuracy. Where the outgroup judges recognize their unfamiliarity – i.e., that their basis for judgment is inadequate – they will tend to give less polarized judgments (or reject the task altogether).

Such a situation must be distinguished from that of "unrecognized unfamiliarity" – where the outgroup judges do *not* recognize that they have an inadequate basis for judgment. This latter case is of course the classic assumption about inaccuracy.

> 3.7 *Recognized unfamiliarity: outgroup judgments tend to be relatively unpolarized when they recognize their unfamiliarity with the group being judged.*

8. Context effects

A general cognitive principle is that judgments about a particular stimulus are affected by the stimulus context. The effect is typically one of "contrast" – judgments of the stimulus are shifted in the opposite direction from the context. In a classical example the context involves the judgment of relatively heavy (or light) weights, where the typical effect is that an intermediate weight will then be judged relatively light (or heavy).

Similar effects from the context – explicit or implied – are to be expected in judgments about groups. As an example from the present research, in judgments about ITALIANS the context – implied if not explicit – is with other European nationalities, while in judgments about NORTH ITALIANS the implied comparison is with SOUTH ITALIANS. Context effects could lead to ITALIANS being judged impulse-expressive and NORTH ITALIANS as relatively impulse-controlled. The design of our empirical study allows only a minor role for context effects, since most judges had the same "standard" nationalities as "stimuli."

> 3.8 *Context effects: judgments tend to show context effects, typically contrast.*

9. Judges' perspective

The preceding case should be distinguished from a different if related use of "contrast." The classical example is the judgment of weights by weight-lifters and watch repairmen, who judged the same weights as relatively light and heavy (Tresselt, 1948). These different judges have developed different

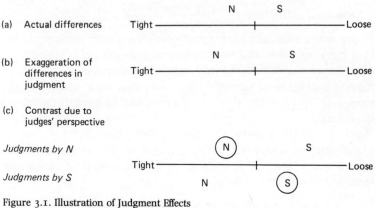

Figure 3.1. Illustration of Judgment Effects

Note: N: judgments about group N
        S: judgments about group S
        Ingroup judgments are circled

"perspectives" (Ostrom and Upshaw, 1968) about the judgmental attribute – (e.g., as to what is a "heavy" or "light" weight) centering around different "adaptation levels" (e.g., as to what is a neutral weight). These different perspectives may derive from the previous principle – past experience with different stimulus contexts.

In principle, differences between judges' "perspectives" might be specified in various ways. In practice, in studies of judgments about attitude statements, the effects are usually related to the judges' "own position" on the attitude dimension. There is less agreement than in the case of context effects that the effect is typically one of contrast (Eiser and Stroebe, 1972; Eiser, 1984). However, this is as plausible a hypothesis as the more complex effects that have been proposed (e.g., Sherif and Hovland, 1960).

Figure 3.1 illustrates several cases. On a dimension of Tight impulse-control vs. Loose impulse-expression, group N is relatively "Tight" and group S is relatively "Loose," as shown in section (a) of the figure.

Levine and Campbell (1972, p. 170) argue that actual differences between groups will tend to be exaggerated in judgments. This principle seems plausible enough, and is shown in section (b) of Figure 3.1. However, to examine this principle empirically would require *separate* evidence about the actual differences and the judged ones. Such evidence is generally not available.

Section (c) of Figure 3.1 illustrates contrast relative to the judges' different "perspectives," as related to the judges' "own positions." In this comparison, group N's greater impulse-control is reflected in a shift of judgments in the direction of impulse-expression. Their own impulse-control is judged relatively

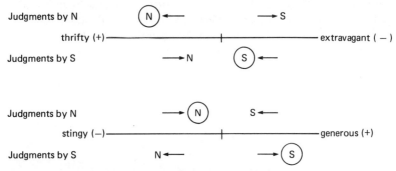

Figure 3.2 Hypothesized effects derived from balance theories. (Effects are shown by arrows. Ingroup judgments are circled)

moderate, but group S's impulse-expression is judged relatively extreme. For group S, the effects are the other way around.

Complications. The preceding discussion suggests an attempt to look in our own results for contrast effects relative to the judges' perspectives. However, any such attempt is complicated by other factors that could obscure any such effects. An important factor is the use of scales with a definite evaluative direction, on which all judges would tend to agree.[1]

With such scales, one might derive the following hypothesis from cognitive balance theories: judges will tend to judge themselves as closer to the favorable end of a scale, and/or opposing others as closer to the unfavorable end of a scale. Generalizing to ingroup and outgroup judgments, the effects are shown in Figure 3.2, which shows the consequences for a pair of our scales. Since the two scales have opposite evaluative directions (relative to the descriptive direction), the hypothesized effects are also opposite on the two scales.

One implication of Figure 3.2 is that judges should show greater variability ("polarization") of judgment on scales where they are in the evaluatively favorable direction. Eiser and Stroebe (1972, Ch. 6) present a series of studies using scales of this type confirming this implication for individuals.

Such effects would, however, tend to obscure any evidence for contrast effects relative to the judges' own perspective. Here one must imagine the effects shown in Figure 3.2 as superimposed on what would have been the results shown in sections (b) and (c) of Figure 3.1. It is clear that it will not

[1] Findings of clear contrast effects have generally involved two other kinds of scales: (a) for the judgment of weights, the two ends of the scale are intended to be evaluatively neutral; (b) for attitude scales, judges should tend to evaluate favorably the end of the scale nearer their "own position," and so disagree with the evaluation of any opposing judges.

be easy to identify which version of Figure 3.1 *would* have been the result underlying the superimposed effects. (Admittedly such an identification *would* be possible if one could assume that the several effects in Figure 3.2 were equal and precise. Such assumptions might be common in physics but tend to be implausible in the social sciences.) Thus, any evidence for contrast effects relative to the judges' perspective may be complicated by other factors. We can only conclude that the contrast effects *may* be found.

> 3.9 *Contrast relative to the judges' perspective: judgments may show contrast effects relative to the judges' perspective.*

III. Bases for judgment

Turning more directly to the question of accuracy, it is obvious that the accuracy of judgments will depend on the information on which they are based. This section considers what these bases may be.

1. *Opinions of others*

There is little doubt that the most important source of individual opinions comes from the opinions of others. However, this factor cannot be generalized to everyone; we must go on to consider other bases for judgment.

2. *Direct contact*

This is a potentially valid basis for judgment. Relevant here is the degree that the contact may be unrepresentative, as regards both the selection of members of the nationality with whom there is contact, and the situation in which interaction occurs. Thus, as regards the former, European travelers traditionally tended to be limited to the aristocracy; American travelers may have been more representative earlier.

Representativeness in both senses would seem to favor the case where the judge visits, rather than is visited by, members of another group. Tourists are generally an unrepresentative selection and may act atypically (e.g., in a way that is more impulse-expressive than normally).

3. *Literature and the media*

Anyone whose views were based on the novels of Dostoevski might have gotten the impression that even the simplest Russians had enormous psychological complexity. But our judges may have little acquaintance with such classics. American films are thought to have given others an impression of affluence that is atypical of average Americans.

4. *Inferences from national policy*

A distinction can be made of the "character of a nation" as opposed to the "national character" of individuals. Inkeles and Levinson (1969) insist on a comparable distinction to avoid confusion, and criticize the application of personality traits to the "nation" or society, implying that it is a form of the group-mind fallacy; an example is Ruth Benedict's (1934) description of the Dobi *culture* as "paranoid." Although this may be a fallacy, it seems to be a natural one. People frequently apply personality traits to national policies. It seems particularly common to apply the assertive–unassertive dimension to a nation's foreign policies.

Especially in the absence of other information, these judgments may be extended to the individual members. Such extensions may be in part not invalid. At times when the nation is relatively strong and assertive, the individual members may as a result feel confident and act assertively (e.g., Germans after 1871 as compared with 1806). However, such extensions can easily be invalid (e.g., did individual Americans become abruptly more assertive after 1945?). In any case, they involve the confusion to which Inkeles and Levinson objected.

Conclusions

The series just given of bases for judgment generally tends to become progressively less accurate. The European judges in our empirical study are more likely to have visited other west European countries. Their bases for judgments about Americans are more likely to be limited to American tourists in Europe and the media. Finally, they are likely to have little contact with representative Russians, and a limited contact with Russian media and literature. We should therefore expect that judgments about Russians are particularly likely to be based on inferences from Soviet policy.

On the whole, the principles considered in this chapter imply that ingroup judgments should have the greatest descriptive accuracy. More generally, there is every reason to support the propositions of Levine and Campbell that accuracy will be greater between groups that have greater proximity and frequency of contact.

4 The empirical study: design and method of analysis

I. Design

The Philippines study. The present study was preceded by one on a smaller scale in the Philippines, reported in Peabody (1968). This study had two groups of judges: Filipinos and the Chinese minority living in the Philippines. The "target" nationalities judged included the same two groups plus Americans and Japanese. The same basic 28 scales were used as in the present study. The Philippines study will be reconsidered in the light of the present larger study in Chapter 16. Results from this study are included in some of our overall analyses.

The present study. There were several reasons for extending the Philippines study into a larger study of European groups. An immediate reason was that the trait inference study had disclosed a large descriptive factor (called "Tight impulse-control vs. Loose impulse-expression") which seemed to correspond to what are often said to be differences between northern and southern Europeans. A more basic reason was that the method of separating evaluative and descriptive aspects seemed promising for the theoretical interpretation of judgments about groups. The present study of national groups in Europe was the main direction for investigation, but happened to be preceded by a preliminary study in the Philippines.

The larger scale of the present study permitted more extensive comparisons, improvements in methods of analyses, and more clear-cut interpretation.

Overview of the design

Groups of "judges" from different countries made ratings of several nationality "targets" on 32 "scales." In the great majority of cases, certain "standard arrangements" were followed regarding (1) judges, (2) targets, and (3) scales; these included six groups of "standard" judges and six "standard" target nationalities. We will first describe the standard arrangements, and then consider the exceptions.

46

Standard arrangements

1. *Judges.* In the standard arrangements a group of judges consisted of 40–50 students in the first year at a university or the last year of secondary school.

As so often, students provided the most available source of subject-judges. One reason for including a second option of using secondary school students in their final year was that just at this time (in general, the academic year 1969–70) there was a world-wide peak of student radicalism, especially among university students.[1] This student radicalism included in its ideology an objection to making any generalizations about people – an objection discussed in Chapter 1. As a result, there was the possibility that students might refuse to answer the questionnaire, like the 1951 Princeton students. Indeed, some refusals did occur in most of our samples, either explicitly, or implicitly by marking the neutral position on a majority of scales.[2]

In the standard arrangements, 48–50 questionnaires were used for each group of judges. From the returned questionnaires there were eliminated (a) foreign students, of a different nationality; (b) those who explicitly refused to respond; and (c) those who either omitted or used the neutral category on a majority of all items. The number of judges that remained varied between 40 and 50 for the standard judges.

Since it is believed that judgments about groups are widely shared within a given culture, we are not critically concerned that the judges are not representative samples from each country.[3] The different sets of judges were generally comparable in age and educational level. Nevertheless, it is necessary to consider that characteristics other than nationality could affect the results. For example, the French judges were from suburbs of Paris, and the Italian judges from a small provincial city.[4] Differences between these judges might not reflect a national difference, but differences in sophistication related to living in a metropolitan area.

It was planned in advance that the judges and targets should both include four nationalities from western Europe: the English, Germans, French and

---

[1] The most dramatic incident occurred when I came to visit one of my Italian colleagues, whose office I had to find through a series of side entrances, since many of the main entrances of the university buildings were closed because of a student strike.

[2] The most striking instance of such refusal occurred with an initial German sample. Of the 48 students from this school, about half refused to respond on grounds of an ideological objection to making any generalizations whatsoever. Accordingly, it was necessary to substitute a second group of German judges. This second group was obtained during the academic year 1970–1, whereas most groups were obtained during the academic year 1969–70. The other exceptions were obtained earlier: the Philippines judges (summer 1967) and the Greek judges (summer 1969).

[3] Indeed, there are obvious advantages in using judges who are relatively articulate.

[4] It was intended that the Italian judges should be from the Rome area which is considered intermediate between "north" and "south" Italy. In the event, they were from east of Rome on the other side of the Italian peninsula, an area technically part of "southern" Italy (the "Mezzogiorno").

Italians. These four groups, plus two additional groups of judges – Austrian and Finnish – made up the six groups of "standard judges."

2. *Targets*. In addition to the four nationalities just mentioned, the two other standard *targets* represented the two world powers since 1945: the RUSSIANS and the AMERICANS.[1] In the standard arrangement, each group judged the six standard targets, plus two to four additional targets,[2] which were smaller nationalities that were culturally adjacent (and typically geographically adjacent).[3]

3. *Scales*. All judges, without exception, used the same 28 basic scales listed previously in Table 2.8. These represented 14 pairs of scales selected to unconfound evaluative and descriptive aspects. Two of the four "extra" scales were also identical in all cases: *hard-working* vs. *lazy*, and *intelligent* vs. *stupid*.

In the standard arrangement, the remaining two scales were: *admirable* vs. *deplorable*, and *likeable* vs. *not likeable*. These scales were expected to be *primarily* evaluative but likely to involve some descriptive aspects related to the dimension of "Tight impulse-control vs. Loose impulse-expression" (e.g., "Tight" traits might be more "admirable," but "Loose" traits more "likeable").

Other arrangements

There were three exceptions to the standard arrangements. One was deliberately planned; the other two were carried out before the arrangements became standardized.

1. *North and south Italians*. A separate regional substudy was carried out in Italy, where north Italians and south Italians were the judges and targets. Aside from this difference in targets, the arrangements were identical with the standard ones.

---

[1] Where relevant, we will follow the convention of Osgood *et al.* (1957), and use capital letters for the objects of measurement (here "targets"), and italics for the measures (here "scales").

[2] In a few cases, two of these extra targets were each judged by half the judges (details are given in Table 4.2 below). In this way, an individual judge never had more than 10 targets (320 items).

[3] This principle was designed to meet the traditional objection that judges are unfamiliar with the nationalities judged. For similar reasons a group of American judges was not used with these European target nationalities.

Several atypical targets were used in relation to the Finnish judges, arranged by Dr Kuusinen. He was interested in including the WEST GERMANS and EAST GERMANS as separate targets, as well as the FINNISH–SWEDISH minority in Finland. To provide an ingroup–outgroup comparison, the FINNS were used as a target for the German judges.

Table 4.1. *Summary information about groups of judges*

Group of judges	N.	Description and location
English	42	Secondary school, Bristol
Germans	43	University students, Mannheim
French	42	Secondary schools, suburb of Paris
Italian	47	University students, L'Aquila
Austrian	40	College of Business, Vienna
Finnish	50	University students, Jyväskylä
Greek	32	Adults, Athens
North Italian	44	University students, Padua
South Italian	46	University students, Naples
Chinese	22	College of Business, Manila
Filipinos	66	College of Business, Manila

Note: the groups above the line are the six "standard" groups of judges.

2. *Greek judges.* Arrangements for the Greek judges compared with the standard ones as follows.

   a. Instead of 40–50 students, the judges were 32 adults.[1]
   b. The targets followed the standard arrangements.
   c. The final two extra scales were *honest* vs. *dishonest*, and *desirable* vs. *undesirable*. This last scale was intended to be a purely evaluative scale.

3. *The Philippines judges.* Arrangements for the Philippines study compared with the standard ones as follows.

   a. The judges were 66 Filipino and 22 Chinese students.
   b. The targets were these same two groups plus the AMERICANS and the JAPANESE. In order to compare ingroup and outgroup judgments, these two groups of judges are kept separate here when judging each other, but combined when judging the AMERICANS and JAPANESE. The results had shown previously that there were important differences between the two groups of judges in the former cases, but not in the latter.
   c. The final two extra scales were the same as for the Greek judges.

Summary

A summary regarding the judges is presented in Table 4.1, and regarding the targets in Table 4.2. For different purposes, the analyses of results made use

[1] They were gathered by my colleague, Stephanie Cooley, through her parents, long-term residents of Athens.

Table 4.2. *Summary of judges and targets*

Judges	No. of targets	Targets[a]
English	8	6 + DUTCH + IRISH
Germans	10	6 + SWISS + AUSTRIANS + DUTCH[b] + FINNS[b]
French	9	6 + SWISS + DUTCH + SPANISH
Italians	9	6 + SWISS + AUSTRIANS + GREEKS
Austrians	10	6 + SWISS + AUSTRIANS + CZECHS[b] + HUNGARIANS[b]
Finnish	10	6 + EAST GERMANS + FINNS + SWEDES + FINNISH–SWEDISH
Greeks	10	6 + GREEKS + TURKS + N. GREEKS + S. GREEKS
North Italians	2	NORTH ITALIANS + SOUTH ITALIANS
South Italians	2	NORTH ITALIANS + SOUTH ITALIANS
Chinese[c]	2	CHINESE + FILIPINOS
Filipinos	2	CHINESE + FILIPINOS
Chinese and Filipinos	2	AMERICANS + JAPANESE
Total	76	

Note: the judges above the line are the six "standard" sets of judges.
[a] The "6" standard targets were: ENGLISH, GERMANS, FRENCH, ITALIANS, AMERICANS, RUSSIANS. Instead of GERMANS, the Finnish sample judged separately WEST GERMANS and EAST GERMANS; WEST GERMANS will be treated as equivalent to GERMANS as judged by the other samples.
[b] Targets judged by one half the group of judges.
[c] The "Chinese" as both judges and targets were "Chinese living in the Philippines."

of three different sets of data: the 36 "cases," representing the six standard judges and the six standard targets; the entire set of 70 European cases; by adding the Philippines results, a total of 76 cases. In each analysis below, it will be made clear which set of data is involved.

Translation of the scales

It is simpler to concede in advance that exact translation may not be generally possible. What was important for present purposes was not that each trait-adjective be perfectly translated, but that the descriptive and evaluative relations be generally preserved between the four terms in a set. Thus, since two trait-adjectives were always used to define the scales, this context would help to resolve any ambiguity about the evaluative or descriptive aspects of a single trait-adjective. What is required is that the two trait-adjectives defining a scale preserve their *relative* evaluative and descriptive contrasts across translation.

This advantage of using pairs of trait-adjectives would not apply to using single trait-adjectives, as advocated by others (e.g., Rosenberg and Sedlak, 1972, p. 136). An example: "aggressive" is generally used by Europeans in a negative sense related to "hostile," but by Americans often in a positive sense, related to "forceful" or "assertive." Our bipolar scales tend to resolve this ambiguity toward the former meaning by pairing *aggressive* vs. *peaceful*, along with *forceful* vs. *passive*.

Accordingly, the translators were instructed to consider not only the translation of each trait-adjective, but also the relationship between the trait-adjectives in each set, as in the schema represented in Table 2.1. Several informants were used in each language; the final selections were made by senior investigators in each language. The translations are considered further in Appendix C.

Procedure

The first page of the questionnaire gave general instructions, adapted from those for the semantic differential by Osgood *et al.* (1957, pp. 82–4). The first two paragraphs of the instructions read as follows:

This is part of a survey of public opinion. The purpose of this survey is to determine, in as scientific a manner as possible, the characteristics of various groups of people as seen by the public. Your answers will be kept anonymous and confidential.

For each group, you are to judge the likelihood of various characteristics. The name of a group is given at the top of each page. The rest of the page contains a series of scales. At each end of a scale, a characteristic is written. Your task is to place a mark on each scale to show *how likely* it is that a member of the group has one of the characteristics.

The remaining instructions copied those of Osgood *et al.* on how to use these seven-step graphic scales. The only change was that the scale steps were defined in terms of "likelihood" – i.e., whether either characteristic was *very likely, quite likely, slightly likely,* or *equally likely*. Osgood *et al.* defined the scale steps in terms of "degree" of relationship – i.e., whether either end of the scale was *very closely related, quite closely related, only slightly related,* etc. This change was to meet the objection to judging groups as *all* having some specified degree of a characteristic.

Following these instructions, for the remainder of the questionnaire, each nationality was given at the top of each of two pages, followed on each page by 16 graphic semantic differential scales:

An ENGLISHMAN is likely to be:

intelligent _ _ _:_ _ _:_ _ _:_ _ _:_ _ _:_ _ _:_ _ _ stupid

etc.

The four "extra" scales were used at the top and the bottom of the two pages as "filler" items. For the 14 basic pairs of scales, the two scales were placed in the corresponding position on the two pages. The order of these scales was arranged to separate those of related content.

The questionnaire was further counterbalanced in a number of ways:

(a) in the sequence of scales, the evaluatively favorable end of the scale alternated from right to left; (b) half of the subjects received an alternative form of the questionnaire that reversed both the sequence and the left–right orientation of the scale; (c) the order of nationality targets within the questionnaire was counterbalanced between different judges.

II. Method of analysis

All analyses of results are based on the mean scores for an entire group of judges. Thus for a group of judges rating a nationality target, the basic data are the scores on the 32 scales averaged across the group of judges (e.g., for the "standard" groups of judges, across 40–50 individuals. A "score" always refers to such an average. A major consequence is to eliminate the unreliability (e.g., the "error of measurement") for individual judges, thus greatly increasing the stability of the results.

Strategy for interpretation: what results are notable?

The general strategy for interpreting results is perhaps obvious: a more specific result can be explained by a more general one, and should be given a separate interpretation only when it is notably different. To consider an example, the average evaluative rating across all scales for all targets is +0.4 – representing an average evaluative component. This result – that judgments tend to be favorable rather than unfavorable – is of interest in itself, and is consistent with many findings of an overall "leniency effect" in judgments about people. Suppose we consider a more specific result: for the English judges the average rating of both AMERICANS and RUSSIANS is +0.4. It should be clear that we do not need a specific interpretation for these results, since they follow from the more general one.

This strategy is followed for all interpretations: results for different judges or different targets should be given a general interpretation if they are similar, a specific one if they are distinctively different. Results for a given set of scales should be given a more general interpretation if they relate to other sets as part of a factor, a specific one if distinctively different. Finally, results on a single scale should always be interpreted in relation to the other scale with which it is paired – which permits an interpretation of the evaluative and descriptive components. Indeed, this point is where the present study began. We are therefore always able to go beyond the listing of separate traits for each nationality used in previous studies.

When is a result "notable" as a distinctive one, and so deserving interpretation? The answer should evidently be related to what is called "statistically significant," but need not be identical with this. Osgood *et al.* (1957) mentions half a scale step (0.5) as the size of a result that is typically significant on a seven-step semantic differential scale. In an initial analysis, we tested the significance (as different from zero) of the means (for each group of judges with each nationality target) on each scale and for the evaluative and descriptive components (explained in the next section). The means generally became significant when they were larger than ± 0.5 for the scales, and somewhat smaller values for the evaluative and descriptive components. When several sets of judges are combined (as in the "consensus" judgments described below) the critical value would tend to become smaller. In the spirit of Kurt Lewin's famous question, "Is it a difference that makes a difference?", we will *generally* consider only differences that are at least 0.5 as "notable" (i.e., deserving comment). Smaller values should receive comment only when they are part of a more general pattern.

Evaluative and descriptive components

A major theoretical objective in designing this study was to separate the evaluative and descriptive aspects of judgment. These aspects are normally confounded in single trait-adjectives or single scales defined by two opposite adjectives; the purpose of selecting trait-adjectives to provide *pairs* of related scales was to allow some way of *unconfounding* the two aspects. It now remains to consider how this might be done quantitatively using scores on the two scales.

Let us begin, however, with a qualitative example. Suppose a northern European nationality (N) is judged "thrifty," in the contrast *thrifty* ($+$) vs. *extravagant* ($-$). This judgment confounds a favorable evaluative aspect and a descriptive aspect reflecting impulse-control over tendencies to spend money. To unconfound these two aspects, the qualitative solution is to present the additional contrast *stingy* ($-$) vs. *generous* ($+$). If nationality N is also judged *stingy* we would say that the descriptive aspects of judgments were more important than the evaluative aspects; if nationality N is judged *generous*, we would say that the evaluative aspects were more important.

The preceding qualitative account treated each judgment as *either* evaluative *or* descriptive, which is surely oversimplified. Accordingly, the qualitative account now needs to be translated into a quantitative one. Scores on the seven-step scales will be presented here[1] on a range from $+3$ to -3, where a positive score always represents the more favorable direction of the scale (e.g., *thrifty*, *generous*). Suppose that nationality N is rated $+3$ (very thrifty) on the scale *thrifty* ($+$) vs. *extravagant* ($-$), and -1 (slightly stingy) on the scale *stingy* ($-$) vs. *generous* ($+$). As before, we would say that the descriptive

---

[1] It is traditional to score such scales 1 to 7 (by adding 4 as a constant) for actual computation (for which it is simpler), and such scores are often used for presentation to the reader (for whom they are *not* simpler). We believe that translation from the computer language should be the responsibility of the writer, not the reader.

Table 4.3. *Schema for scales*

Scales	Descriptive direction		
	A	vs.	B
a.	thrifty (+)		extravagant (−)
b.	stingy (−)		generous (+)

aspect in the direction of impulse-control is more important than the evaluative aspect. But it is also true that on the average the evaluative aspect tends to be favorable for the two judgments combined.

Our scoring system represents a natural way to score the evaluative aspects: a tendency to respond in a favorable (or unfavorable) evaluative direction will contribute toward a positive (or negative) score on both scales of a pair. In contrast, there is an arbitrary choice involved in scoring the descriptive aspects. Consider Table 4.3 which reproduces the schema of Table 2.3.

A tendency to respond in descriptive direction "A" will contribute toward a positive score on scale "a," and toward a negative score on scale "b." A tendency to respond in descriptive direction "B" will contribute toward a negative score on scale "a," and toward a positive score on scale "b." For purposes of calculation, we will designate descriptive direction "A" as corresponding to a positive descriptive component, and descriptive direction "B" as corresponding to a negative descriptive component. An essentially arbitrary choice is involved in this designation,[1] or alternatively, in the choice, for a particular set of trait-adjectives, as to which direction is called "A" or "B."

With this reservation, we can consider scores on scales "a" and "b" as representing combinations of evaluative and descriptive "components."[2] The evaluative component is added into both scales; the descriptive component is added for scale "a" and subtracted for scale "b":

$$a = E + D, \quad \text{and} \tag{4.1}$$
$$b = E - D;$$

where "a" and "b" represent scale scores, and "E" and "D" the evaluative and descriptive components.

The assumption of equations (4.1) – that the two components combine by (algebraic) addition – is mathematically simple, but not the only possible one. Solving equations (4.1) the other way around, for E and D, shows that the

---

[1] For this reason, in reporting results, we will indicate the direction of the descriptive component directly as "A" or "B" rather than as positive or negative. For an illustration see Table 4.4 below.

[2] These "components" are thus quantitative estimates of the evaluative and descriptive "aspects."

Table 4.4. *Illustration of the two components*

| Scales | Descriptive direction | | | Judgments about |
	A	vs.	B	nationality "N"
a.	thrifty (+)		extravagant (−)	3
b.	stingy (−)		generous (+)	−1
	Evaluative component			+1
	Descriptive component			2A[a]

[a] For calculations using equations (4.1) or (4.2), a descriptive component marked "A" is treated as positive, and one marked "B" as negative.

evaluative and descriptive components are estimated from the average of the sum and difference of the two scale scores:

$$E = \tfrac{1}{2}(a+b); \tag{4.2}$$
$$D = \tfrac{1}{2}(a-b).$$

Like the scales, the two components each have a potential range from +3 to −3. For illustration, the earlier example is worked out in Table 4.4.

Table 4.4. illustrates the preceding points. In practice, the evaluative and descriptive components are estimated from the scores on the scales, following equations (4.2). Conversely, the scores on the scales can be interpreted as combinations of the two components, following equations (4.1). Putting it verbally, in this illustration, the scale scores representing "very thrifty" and "slightly stingy" can be interpreted as a combination of an evaluative component ("slightly good") and a descriptive component ("quite impulse-controlled").

Decimal places. A reader of an earlier version of this report complained that there were 'too many numbers." We will attempt to deal with this problem in a number of ways. The whole numbers used for illustration in Table 4.4 are unlikely to appear in the actual data, which represent mean scores typically averaged for 40–50 individuals. The data actually used in the analyses were always carried to two decimal places. For purposes of simpler presentation, the results will be reported here for only one decimal place (i.e., on a possible range from +3.0 to −3.0).

5   Overall results

The present chapter considers certain *overall* results. Results for the separate
nationalities will be considered later in Part II (Chapters 7–16).

The overall results in the present chapter will be presented in two sections.
The first section considers the results of several basic analyses. These analyses
involve technical questions, which will be considered in detail in Appendix A.
The text here will consider only the conclusions of these analyses.

The second section collects those overall results that seem relevant to the
judgment principles proposed earlier in Chapter 3.

I. Conclusions from some basic analyses

The initial data from which all analyses began involved the mean judgments
on 32 scales for 76 "cases" of a group of judges rating a nationality target.
Of the scales, 28 had the special property that they were selected in 14 pairs,
with each pair designed to permit separating evaluative and descriptive
aspects of judgment. Many analyses consider only these 28 "basic" scales.
Similarly, some analyses consider smaller subsets of "cases" – for example,
the 36 cases representing the six standard groups of judges and the six
standard targets.

Starting with this initial data, it is possible to derive, and then analyze, other
data. Thus, the latter part of the previous chapter showed that each pair of
scales could be used to estimate an evaluative component and a descriptive
component. One could then analyze these estimated components.

Several basic analyses are presented in Appendix A. We may summarize
the conclusions under three points:

1. *Differences between nationality targets are much more important than differences
between groups of judges.* The first method of analysis considered the variances
of the 28 basic scales. (For details see Appendix A, pp. 229–38). One version
of this analysis distinguished how much of these variances reflected differences
between nationality targets and how much reflected differences between
groups of judges. For this purpose, it was appropriate to consider the subset
of 36 cases representing the six standard groups of judges and the six standard
targets.

56

The results were clear-cut: 63% of these variances represented differences between targets, 9% differences between judges, and 28% the "interaction" between (i.e., the combinations of) targets and judges. Thus differences between targets are much more important than differences between groups of judges in our results. This result may not seem surprising to common sense. But it is not obvious on the basis of the literature on national "stereotypes" which may seem to imply that such judgments are primarily projections by the perceiver.

Among the several consequences of this result is that we need not give equal attention to the judges and the targets. It is appropriate to organize our presentation according to the characteristics of the several nationality targets, rather than according to the groups of judges.

2. *The descriptive aspects of judgment are more important than the evaluative aspects.* In a further analysis, the variances of the basic scales were separated into evaluative and descriptive components. If we consider all 76 "cases," we find that the descriptive components represent twice as much of the variance (67% of the total) as the evaluative components.

There are however, interesting variations (shown in Table A.2 in Appendix A). For the 36 "cases" involving the six standard targets and the six standard groups of judges, the descriptive components are most predominant, representing 73% of the variance versus 26% for the evaluative components. For the other 34 European cases the main change is a decline for the descriptive components (to 63% of the total). This may reflect the inclusion of smaller nationalities that are less familiar. For the Philippines cases the main change is an increase in the evaluative components to become an actual majority (57%) of the total variance.

3. *Three major dimensions summarize much of the results: a descriptive dimension that we have called "Tight vs. Loose control over impulse-expression"; a descriptive dimension that we have called "Self-assertiveness"; a general evaluative dimension.* The evidence for this conclusion in Appendix A includes a variety of analyses.

Certain analyses tend to emphasize descriptive aspects and leave out any dimension of general evaluation. These include inverse ("Q") analysis of the correlations between the objects of measurement (here, the nationality "targets"), and analysis of the correlations between the descriptive components. These analyses provide clear evidence for two large descriptive dimensions, which we specified earlier in Table 2.7 and labelled "Tight vs. Loose" and "Unassertive vs. Assertive." The loadings in the inverse analysis for the nationality targets will be used in Part II as a convenient summary of the results for each nationality target on these two descriptive dimensions.

On the other hand, one can restrict oneself to the evaluative aspects and leave out the descriptive ones. Thus, analysis of the correlations between the evaluative components indicates that a general evaluative dimension represents a majority of this variance.

Other analyses, such as the traditional factor analysis of the correlations between scales, allow for the appearance of both descriptive and evaluative dimensions. In these analyses, there is evidence for the presence of the three major dimensions, where this would be possible (e.g., in the unrotated factors of the analysis of scales). On the other hand, as anticipated, the rotated factors tend to confound again the evaluative and descriptive aspects that we have painstakingly separated.

The several different analyses tend to converge on similar estimates of the relative size of the three major dimensions: the descriptive dimension called "Tight vs. Loose" represents 30% to 38% of the total variance; the descriptive dimension of "Unassertive vs. Assertive" represents 14% to 15% of the total variance; and the general evaluative dimension represents 15% to 16% of the total variance.

II. Overall results relevant to judgment principles

This section considers overall results that seem relevant to the judgment principles proposed in Chapter 3.

> 3.1 *Descriptive convergence: different judges tend to agree as to the descriptive aspects of judgments about national characteristics.*

This principle is certainly consistent with the results of the basic analyses considered in the previous section: that the important features of the results represent differences between target nationalities (rather than between judges), and descriptive aspects of judgment (rather than evaluative ones).

Evidence more directly relevant to this principle comes from considering the correlations (across the 28 basic scales)[1] between different groups of judges rating the same targets, and different targets rated by the same judges. Here it is again appropriate to consider the six standard judges and the six standard targets.

Different judges, same target. Table 5.1 considers the correlations between different groups of judges rating the same target. (Each entry in Table 5.1 is arrived at as follows: consider two of the standard groups of judges, and the correlation between them for any standard target. The average of the six such correlations for all standard targets is the entry in Table 5.1.) These entries have a grand mean of 0.68 and are all in a narrow range from 0.63

---

[1] These correlations are the ones used for the inverse ("Q") analyses as discussed in Appendix A. They tend to eliminate any general evaluative component, and so overwhelmingly represent descriptive components.

Table 5.1. *Correlations between judges (averaged for standard targets)*

	English	German	French	Italian	Austrian	Finnish
English	—					
Germans	0.66	—				
French	0.68	0.70	—			
Italians	0.68	0.68	0.65	—		
Austrians	0.67	0.82	0.66	0.70	—	
Finnish	0.63	0.68	0.66	0.70	0.67	—

Table 5.2. *Correlations between targets (averaged for standard judges)*

	ENGLISH	RUSSIANS	GERMANS	AMERICANS	FRENCH	ITALIANS
ENGLISH	—					
RUSSIANS	0.52	—				
GERMANS	0.58	0.73	—			
AMERICANS	−0.16	−0.18	0.15	—		
FRENCH	−0.25	−0.28	−0.19	0.70	—	
ITALIANS	−0.45	−0.28	−0.18	0.63	0.86	—

to 0.70, except for a high value of 0.82 between the German and the Austrian judges. This result shows that different judges give similar ratings to the same target.

Same judges, different targets. Table 5.2 considers the correlations between different targets rated by the same judges. (Each entry in Table 5.2 is arrived at as follows: consider two of the standard targets, and the correlation between them for any group of standard judges. The average of the six such correlations for all groups of standard judges is the entry in Table 5.2.) The entries have a grand mean of 0.15. This result shows that different targets are judged differently. Actually, there are two "clusters" of targets (ENGLISH, RUSSIANS, GERMANS; and AMERICANS, FRENCH, ITALIANS). The mean correlation within these clusters is 0.67, but between clusters it is −0.19.

Regarding the measurement of personality characteristics of *individuals*, Campbell and Fiske (1959) have stressed the importance of demonstrating both "convergent" and "discriminant" validity – convergence between different "methods" of measuring what is intended to be the same characteristic, and discrimination between characteristics in using the same method. In a similar spirit, we can say that the preceding results indicate convergence between different judges rating the same target, and divergence between targets rated by the same judges.

We conclude that the results strongly support principle 3.1.

Table 5.3. *Evaluative indices: basic data*

	Basic scales			Evaluative scales		
Nationality	(A) Self-judgments	(B) Judgments by others	(C) Judgments about others	(A) Self-judgments	(B) Judgments by others	(C) Judgments about others
ENGLISH	0.7	0.6 (5)	0.3 (7)	1.2	0.7	0.4
ITALIANS	0.1	−0.1 (5)	0.4 (8)	1.8	0.3	0.4
FRENCH	−0.1	0.3 (5)	0.4 (8)	0.4	1.0	0.9
GERMANS	0.0	0.5 (5)	0.5 (9)	0.0	0.4	0.6
FINNS	0.3	1.0 (1)	0.4 (9)	0.8	1.1	0.6
AUSTRIANS	0.1	0.4 (2)	0.3 (9)	0.8	0.2	0.3
N. ITALIANS	0.5	0.5 (1)	−0.3 (1)	1.0	−0.1	0.6
S. ITALIANS	0.0	−0.3 (1)	0.5 (1)	1.4	−0.1	−0.1
GREEKS	0.6	0.3 (1)	0.3 (7)[a]	1.5[b]	0.6	0.1[b]
CHINESE	1.2	0.6 (1)	−0.3 (1)	1.9[b]	0.1[b]	0.2[b]
FILIPINOS	0.4	−0.3 (1)	0.6 (1)	1.6[b]	0.2[b]	0.1[b]
Means	+0.3	+0.3	+0.4	+1.1	+0.5	+0.4

Note: the numbers in parentheses represent the number of outgroups considered as judges (in column B) or as targets (in column C). For the four standard targets, we have considered (in column B) the 5 other groups of standard judges (omitting the Greek judges).

[a] Omitted from the table are the NORTHERN GREEKS and SOUTHERN GREEKS as targets for the Greek judges.

[b] For the Philippines and the Greek judges, these results are for the scale *desirable* vs. *undesirable*. For all other judges the results represent the mean of the two scales *admirable* vs. *deplorable* and *likeable* vs. *not likeable*.

Table 5.4. *Evaluative indices: ingroup–outgroup differences*

Target nationality	Basic scales		Evaluative scales	
	(A)–(B)	(A)–(C)	(A)–(B)	(A)–(C)
ENGLISH	0.1	0.4	0.5	0.8
ITALIANS	0.2	−0.3	1.5	1.4
FRENCH	−0.4	−0.5	−0.6	−0.5
GERMANS	−0.5	−0.5	−0.4	−0.6
FINNS	−0.7	−0.1	−0.3	0.2
AUSTRIANS	−0.3	−0.2	0.6	0.5
N. ITALIANS	0.0	0.8	1.1	0.4
S. ITALIANS	0.3	−0.5	0.8	1.5
GREEKS	0.3	0.3	(1.0)[a]	1.4
CHINESE	0.6	1.5	1.8	1.7
FILIPINOS	0.7	−0.2	1.4	1.5
Means	0.0	−0.1	+0.6	+0.7
% comparisons (with self-judgments more favorable)	47%	30%	67%	66%

Note: the column labels are for differences between the columns from Table 5.3 (where the same letters are used as labels).
[a] For the Greeks, judgments by ingroup and outgroup used different evaluative scales. See Table 5.3 footnote *b*.

3.2 *Ingroup self-evaluation: ingroup self-judgments tend to be more favorable than those by outgroups or those about outgroups.*

This principle seemed plausible on general grounds. Moreover, the first version was strongly supported by the Philippines results. The second version was not supported for the Filipino self-judgments on the 14 basic scales, but on the "extra" evaluative scale, *desirable* vs. *undesirable*. Accordingly we will consider two comparable measures in the present analysis: the evaluative components for the 14 pairs of basic scales, and the two primarily evaluative scales (*admirable* vs. *deplorable* and *likeable* vs. *not likeable*), or – in the cases of the Filipino and Greek judges – the single evaluative scale, *desirable* vs. *undesirable*.

Table 5.3 presents the mean evaluative indices, and Table 5.4 summarizes the differences relevant to the principle. We will proceed directly to the discussion of Table 5.4. This table shows clearly that the European results are *not* generally consistent with the Philippines results.

1. *Basic scales, outgroup judges.* The relevant Philippines results are shown at the bottom of the first column of Table 5.4. Chinese and Filipino self-judgments were both substantially more favorable than judgments by the outgroup. (Indeed, the self-judgments were more favorable on all 14 pairs of scales.)

In our present data, this situation is only approached by the south Italian and Greek self-judgments, and is reversed for several others – leaving no overall effect.

2. *Basic scales, outgroup targets.* The relevant results are shown in the second column of Table 5.4. The Philippines results supported this version of the principle only for the Chinese self-judgments; the Filipino self-judgments were generally *less* favorable than their judgments about the Chinese. The negative result for the Filipinos is generally supported by the European data, where the overall trend is opposite to the principle.

3. *Evaluative scales.* The relevant results are shown in the last two columns of Table 5.4. The negative result for the Filipinos did not extend to the evaluative scales, where both versions of the principle were strongly supported. And indeed this is true on the average for the European data. Several groups show large increases in favorable self-judgments as between the basic scales and the evaluative scales (see Table 5.3). Some groups where this increase is largest (e.g., the Italians, the south Italians) show a pattern similar to the Filipinos: these groups are judged impulse-expressive and (at least in self-judgments) unassertive. They seem willing to acknowledge the implied deficiencies on the basic scales. But they nevertheless give themselves very favorable self-judgments on the evaluative scales.

Against all such cases are the French and German judges who consistently oppose the principle on all measures, with self-judgments generally *less* favorable than those by or about outgroups. It is not clear how to explain these reversals of the basic psychological principle of ego-enhancement. One possibility was suggested in presenting this judgment principle in Chapter 3: these judges may not treat their nationality as a "reference group," and so may fail to show self-enhancement in judging the average Frenchman or German.

We conclude that our results do not support the principle of self-evaluation for the evaluative components of trait-adjectives, but only for scales that are primarily evaluative.

It is instructive to compare these results with those of Brewer and Campbell (1976). They studied ten ethnic groups in each of the three east African countries of Kenya, Uganda, and Tanzania. The measure they used is somewhat comparable to the evaluative components of our basic scales. Of their 30 groups, 27 had self-judgments more favorable than judgments by *any* outgroup, or about *any* outgroup. Altogether, for 270 ingroup–outgroup comparisons, self-judgments were more favorable than those *by* outgroups in 269 cases, and those *about* any outgroup in 263 cases. In other words, in comparison to our results of 47% and 30% at the bottom of Table 5.4, the comparable figures for Brewer and Campbell would be 99.6% and 97%! This indicates a profound difference between their east African groups and our European ones.

    3.3 *Homogeneity: judgments, especially judgments by outgroups, tend to exaggerate the homogeneity within a group. One implication is that outgroup judgments will tend to be more polarized, and ingroup judgments less polarized.*

The main principle in the first sentence of 3.3 comes from Levine and Campbell (1972, p. 169) and seems plausible enough. Our data do not provide information about judged homogeneity. In any case, in the absence of information about actual homogeneity, this principle cannot be tested. We can, however, examine the implication stated in the second sentence of 3.3.

We consider the relative polarization of ingroup judgments on some index of polarization. The basic result does not vary too much whether we use some simple index of polarization (e.g., the average deviation of scale scores), or a more complex index (e.g., from the variance analysis described in Appendix A).

If we use the latter index, then we find that the Italians, south Italians, and Chinese self-judgments are more polarized than the average for all targets, while self-judgments for the remaining eight groups of judges are less polarized than the average. However, this result reflects the fact that the former three groups (especially the Italians and south Italians) are *generally* well above the overall average for polarization both as judges and as targets. If we apply simple corrections for these two effects, as is done by Brewer and Campbell, then we find that these three self-judgments are no longer *distinctively* higher in polarization. On the other hand, most of the other cases are no longer distinctively low in polarization. We are left with three self-judgments that are distinctively low on polarization both before and after such correction: the English, the Germans and the north Italians. Those cases would support the principle. We conclude that we do not find *consistent* support for a principle of low polarization in ingroup judgments.

    3.4 *Descriptive consistency: judgments may exaggerate the descriptive consistency between different characteristics. Outgroup judgments tend to show more descriptive consistency, and ingroup judgments less.*

We will examine this principle using the two main descriptive dimensions which we have called "Tight vs. Loose" and "Unassertive vs. Assertive." In particular we will consider the factor loadings on these two dimensions in the inverse analysis, listed below in Table 18.1.

The results are quite different if we consider the four standard targets for which self-judgments are available (i.e., the ENGLISH, GERMANS, FRENCH, and ITALIANS), or the other cases of self-judgments (for a listing, see Table

5.3 above). For the four standard targets, we can say that for each of these the self-judgments show a markedly lower loading than outgroup judgments on one or the other of the two descriptive dimensions. Thus, on the dimensions of impulse-control vs. impulse-expression, the English judge themselves relatively less impulse-controlled than outgroup judges (average factor loadings are 0.37 and 0.77); the French judge themselves less impulse-expressive than outgroup judges (factor loadings average −0.23 and −0.58). On the self-assertiveness dimension, self-judgments are less assertive than for outgroup judgments for the Germans (factor loadings average 0.10 and 0.67) and the Italians (factor loadings average 0.04 and 0.42). These standard targets are each judged by six outgroups; in all but one of these 24 cases the relevant factor loading is larger for the outgroup.

In contrast the seven remaining cases of self-judgments involve only eight outgroups. For these cases the results do not systematically support or oppose the principle. Some cases (e.g., the Austrians, north Italians and Filipinos) seem to support the principle (e.g., self-judgments have a markedly smaller loading on one of the two dimensions). Other cases (e.g., The Finns, Greeks and south Italians) go in the opposite direction (e.g., self-judgments have a markedly larger loading on one of the two dimensions).

The overall conclusion depends on how one combines these divergent results. If one considers each outgroup–ingroup comparison separately, the 24 outgroups for the standard targets (supporting the principle) will outweigh the eight remaining outgroups (giving inconclusive results) to provide overall support for the principle. On the other hand if we consider each ingroup as a single case, we have only the four standard ingroups and the seven remaining ingroups, and the overall result would be inconclusive.

Alternatively, one could argue that the standard targets differ in some important way (e.g., perhaps in being generally familiar) from the other cases, particularly those giving results opposed to the principle (e.g., perhaps that these latter are unfamiliar).[1] In any case, the principle has in part an ad hoc quality in that it was not specified in advance which of the two dimensions would have larger loadings for the outgroup. In summary, the support for this principle seems suggestive but inconclusive.

> 3.5 *Perceived change: changes in national characteristics tend to be recognized only after some interval. Perceived change tends to occur later for outgroup judgments, and earlier for ingroup judgments.*

> 3.6 *Behavior vs. conscious experience: ingroup judgments may be based on their conscious experience; outgroup judgments are more dependent on manifest behavior.*

---

[1] Thus, one might consider as cases of "recognized unfamiliarity" (see below p. 65) the Germans judging the FINNS, and the Italians judging the GREEKS.

These principles both imply specific comparisons with information from outside our judgment data. Hence no *overall* analysis here of these data would seem relevant to these principles. They will be considered when relevant to the results for individual nationalities in Part II.

    3.7 *Recognized unfamiliarity: outgroup judgments tend to be relatively unpolarized when they recognize their unfamiliarity with the group being judged.*

The relevant data here are very similar to that considered earlier for the principle of homogeneity. In particular, we consider indices from the analysis of the scale variances (see Appendix A) and of the descriptive and evaluative components.

    It would be misleading to say that we had selected in advance cases of recognized unfamiliarity. However, it is possible to single out a few such cases: the DUTCH (as judged by the English, Germans, and French) where some judges made marginal comments indicating unfamiliarity and some gave entirely or largely neutral ratings on the seven-step scales. Other cases were probably exceptions to the general rule that target nationalities should be culturally, and usually geographically, adjacent to the nation of the judges: e.g., the FINNS as judged by the Germans, perhaps the GREEKS as judged by the Italians. These cases are all below average polarization for the variance of the descriptive components, but three out of five were above average for the evaluative components (the DUTCH judged by the English and French, the FINNS judged by the Germans). The results suggest a somewhat vague, bland, and generally favorable impression. We conclude that there is some weak tentative support for the principle of recognized unfamiliarity, but it would require a much more systematic investigation.

    3.8 *Context effects: judgments tend to show context effects, typically contrast.*

This principle emphasizes effects of the "stimulus context." Most of our design considers a standard set of targets, which does not involve major variations in the stimulus context. Hence no *overall* analysis can usefully be made here. There remain certain exceptions. Thus, the regional substudy between north Italians and south Italians, if compared with the standard results for the Italians, shows very dramatic effects which seem to fit this principle. Such exceptions will be dealt with in Chapters 13–16.

    3.9 *Contrast relative to the judges' perspective: judgments may show contrast effects relative to the judges' perspective.*

Earlier discussion of this principle argued that it had considerable plausibility, but any effects in our data were likely to be particularly or totally obscured by other factors.

Table 5.5. *Mean judgments and judges' "own position" (descriptive components on scale pairs 1–7)*

Judges	Own position as judged by Outgroup[a]	Ingroup	Mean judgment of 6 standard targets[b]
English	0.8A[c]	0.2A	0.2A
Germans	0.9A	0.6A	0.1A
French	0.7B	0.0	0.1A
Italians	0.7B	1.3B	0.2A
Finnish	0.1A	0.9A	0.1B

[a] Outgroup judgments are for the other five standard sets of judges, except for the Finns for whom there is only one outgroup.
[b] The relevant grand mean is 0.1A.
[c] As elsewhere "A" and "B" represent the descriptive directions. On these scales, A: "tight" impulse-control; B: "loose" impulse-expression.

In practice, the only obvious way to specify the judges' "perspective" is to relate this to the judges' "own position" using either outgroup judgments or ingroup self-judgments – a question not well resolved in the comparable attitudinal research. To the extent that there is a rationale for contrast relative to the judges' perspective, it implies that differences in perspective (however caused) should at least be *reflected* in self-judgments. (Thus, in Figure 3.1 (c), judgments about the ingroup are more moderate, and judgments about an opposing outgroup are relatively extreme.)

To examine this principle, we consider the major descriptive dimensions of impulse-control vs. impulse-expression, as reflected on the first seven pairs of scales. Table 5.5 considers the six standard targets and five of the six standard groups of judges.[1]

The striking aspect of the results in Table 5.5 is the failure of any important contrast effect to appear. Despite major differences in the judges' own position (especially in outgroup judgments), the mean judgments show only tiny differences between judgments. Since these results are based on huge numbers of judgments, the result for the Finnish judges would even be significantly different from the others (and – by itself – consistent with the hypothesized contrast effect). The overall result is, however, clearly negative.

An earlier analysis of the Philippines study also showed similar negative results. We note that a major factor (discussed in Chapter 3) that might have obscured any contrast effect was derived from principles of balance theory,

[1] Table 5.5 does not include the two remaining groups who judged the standard targets: the Austrians and the Greeks. For both, the judges' own position is ill-defined: e.g., outgroup judgments are in the direction of "Tight" impulse-control, ingroup judgments are in the direction of "Loose" impulse-expression, and neither notably so. The entries for mean judgments would have been 0.0 for the Austrian judges, and 0.3A for the Greek judges.

assuming more favorable ingroup evaluation. This factor *could* have explained the negative results in the Philippines study, where there was a very clear effect of ingroup evaluation. What is now puzzling is the similar negative result for the present European data, where there is no consistent favorable ingroup evaluation. (Nor does Table 5.5 suggest any encouraging signs of contrast for judges who show a negative ingroup evaluation – e.g. the Germans and the French – vs. those with a relatively positive ingroup evaluation – the English and the Italians.) We must conclude simply that our results give no support to the principle of contrast relative to the judges' perspective.

Part II
National character and results for separate nationalities

6 National character

> The appeal to national character is generally a mere confession of ignorance...
>
> Weber, 1930, p. 88

> It was the power of religious influence, not alone, but more than anything else, which created the [national] differences of which we are conscious today.
>
> Weber, 1930, p. 89

The previous chapters considered judgments by ordinary persons about the characteristics of national groups – traditionally called "national stereotypes." This chapter considers other approaches to national characteristics – traditionally called "national character." Most of this material is concerned with separate nationalities, and consideration of it will be deferred for the chapters on these. The present chapter begins with some general points about national character; it then considers existing approaches that might be used in comparing different nationalities.

Two important points were already included in the discussion in Chapter 1.

1. National differences in the psychological characteristics are not likely to be non-overlapping "complete differences," but overlapping "partial differences," where the differences within groups are at least as large as those between groups.

2. National characteristics are not unchanging ones implicitly due to racial inheritance, but the result of historical developments and so subject to change.[1]

Further discussion here can be abbreviated by taking advantage of the careful analysis of Inkeles and Levinson (1969). Among their conclusions, we can add several in particular.

3. National character should be conceptualized as the average (or central tendency) of the characteristics of individuals. Inkeles and Levinson's suggestion that the measure of central tendency should be considered as "modal" (rather than the mean) has the advantage of allowing in principle for several modes representing subvarieties within the population.

[1] It is clear from the context that the first quotation from Weber at the beginning of this chapter objects to the former usage of "national character."

4. National character as so defined should not be confused with the society or nation. It may be possible in principle to specify the individual characteristics that are "required by," or better (so as not to presume that the causal direction is always from the society to the individuals) "congruent with," the nature of the society. However, it should not be assumed that there is an identity between the two. In a stable situation considerable congruency may be expected in the long run, but because of the possibility of change the degree of congruency should be examined empirically and not assumed.

A corollary of the above two points is that we must avoid many of the traditional accounts of national character that are derived from intellectual history: e.g., nineteenth-century German philosophy is used to characterize the "German mind" (Ginsberg, 1945). Such accounts are unsuitable on two grounds: first, they infer from cultural products of the society to individual characteristics without direct evidence of the latter; secondly, even if these inferences are valid, they refer directly only to a cultural elite, and not necessarily to the population as a whole.

5. We follow Inkeles and Levinson in focusing on *adult* personality characteristics. Though these undoubtedly are affected by child training practices, the latter are not directly relevant to our concern. We will give incidental attention to hypotheses relating to child socialization only where these are central to proposals about adult characteristics – as is true for the historically important "psychocultural" approach represented by Ruth Benedict, Margaret Mead, and Geoffrey Gorer.

Ideally, one would want to specify national character on the basis of evidence that was (a) representative, (b) objective, and (c) comparative.

a. Ideally, one would want evidence that is equivalent to a representative sample of the nationality concerned. Representative national samples are regularly taken for public opinion polling, and this objective would not be impossible to meet in principle. But it has not been met in practice. (Ironically, the closest approach to this objective is for what might have been considered the least accessible of our standard "target" groups – the Russians.)

b. Ideally – especially for comparison with judgments by ordinary people – one would want evidence that is objective, so as to avoid reliance on some other human judgment, however expert. This objective is also not met in practice.

c. Ideally, one would want evidence that is comparative across a variety of nationalities. Whatever the disadvantages of a comparative approach, the advantages are great.

A revealing case in point is Gorer's (1955) study of the English. Gorer, an English anthropologist influenced by psychoanalysis, is capable of making proposals about national characteristics that are provocative if sometimes speculative – as shown in accounts of the Americans and the Russians – the latter based on very limited direct evidence. In his study of the English, he begins with assumptions that are similarly provocative: for example, that three central characteristics of the English are the control of aggression, shyness and fear of strangers, and strong moral principles (especially regarding sex).

However, in this study he also had available data from a questionnaire distributed by a popular Sunday newspaper. The sample was large and not so obviously unrepresentative as not to be taken seriously. The data was also relatively objective, providing statistical tables of results to the different questions. Thus, better than most studies, this one meets two of our three criteria mentioned above. Moreover, one's impression is that many of the results support Gorer's initial hypothesis. For example when asked at what age they started being really interested in the opposite sex, the age nearest the median was 16 (p. 78). One suspects that even in the 1950s this was, in comparative terms, late. With any kind of comparative data from other nationalities, it would be possible to confirm whether this suspicion is correct. But in the absence of such data, Gorer's conclusions are uncharacteristically indecisive; his speculative talents seem to have been inhibited by the availability of data that was relatively representative and objective, but not comparative.

While it is possible to specify the ideal basis for statements about national character, unfortunately such evidence is not generally available. Generally one is driven back to judgments by observers – even if relatively expert judgments by relatively informed observers. We can try to preserve something of the spirit of "representativeness," by avoiding those accounts that seem most likely to refer not to the general population but to some social, cultural or intellectual elite. We will attempt to preserve something of a comparative approach by two methods. (a) In the present chapter we will consider a few approaches that offer some possibility of comparative application, where the same variables can be considered for several nationalities. Later, in considering the separate nationalities, we will try to apply these variables wherever possible. (b) Most accounts relevant to national character do not use a comparative perspective. A particular nationality may simply be described in its own terms. Alternatively, because of the numerical preponderance of American social scientists, Americans often serve as an implicit or explicit standard of comparison. But such an approach still has disadvantages. One could show repeated examples where various nationalities are treated separately as distinctive in comparison to Americans, but actually they share similar characteristics. Often it is the American characteristics that are relatively distinctive, in contrast to the rest of the world. In separate chapters below, we will begin with accounts describing each nationality in its own terms. But we will try to apply a comparative point of view, and induce from these descriptions some issues that can be used for comparative purposes. These issues will be summarized in one of the concluding chapters. This summary could serve to supplement the few existing approaches that we now consider.

Comparative approaches to national character

The remainder of this chapter will consider four such approaches, which suggest some variables that can be used for comparing national character. The last of these approaches can be considered an empirical generalization; the other three are all sociological approaches concerned at least as much with characteristics of societies as with those of the individuals in them.

The relationship between the characteristics of society and those of individuals is of obvious importance. We have insisted that the two must be formulated separately. But we have also assumed that congruence tends to develop between them in the long run.

Much of sociology is concerned with "macro-sociological" analyses of the society, without any direct reference to analysis in terms of individuals. It is possible that such analyses can be translated into the terms of individuals by some kind of translation rules. (Economists refer to "aggregation rules" for the comparable translation between the macroeconomics of society and the microeconomics of the individual.) Rather than inventing such translations here, we naturally prefer proposals about society that themselves have fairly direct implications for analysis in terms of individuals. As an illustration, consider Dahrendorf's (1969) attempt to account for the failure of liberal democracy to develop in Germany. He considers four general aspects of German society: (1) lack of full equality of citizenship; (2) an emphasis on substantive solutions for social conflict, rather than procedural rules that allow conflict to proceed; (3) a lack of diversity among the elites; (4) an emphasis on "private" virtues rather than "public" ones. The first and third aspects can not be easily translated into individual characteristics, while the second and fourth can. Accordingly the latter two aspects are more suitable for present purposes.

The four approaches discussed below are not unrelated to each other. This point is better discussed at the end of this chapter. The remainder of this chapter will consider several comparative approaches.

I. Analysis using "pattern variables"

Attempts to provide a comparative schema that would apply to all societies were made by early German sociologists in the last century. In particular,

Toennies proposed a contrast between *Gemeinschaft* (primary, small, traditional, integrated "communities") and *Gesellschaft* (impersonal, secondary, large, socially differentiated "societies"). This contrast was developed further by Parsons (1951, 1960), and applied to national differences by Lipset (1963).

It was clear that the contrast could be applied not only to societies as a whole, but also to different kinds of relationships within a single society. Classical examples would be the contrast between a "primary" group like the family, and a bureaucratic organization in business or government. As used here, the terms refer *primarily* to relationships, so that a "Gemeinschaft" or "Gesellschaft" nation means one where the relationships are generally of one type or the other.

Another question is whether the terms are to be used to *describe* actual relationships, or as "values" for how relationships should be. Parsons assumed that the correspondence was practically perfect between the descriptive and normative usage, and came to treat the normative usage as the primary one. It seems preferable to assume that the correspondence may be typical but not invariable, and to say that the terms *could* be used either descriptively or normatively.

Parsons, perhaps the leading American sociologist of the preceding generation, was given to such assumptions and generally to highly abstract theorizing about society. One of his most useful contributions was therefore also atypical: he made the Toennies type of dichotomy clearer by specifying several different features, called the "pattern variables."

In listing the Parsons' pattern variables here (in later versions, four pairs), the *Gesellschaft* alternative is always given first:

1. *Universalism vs. particularism.* This concerns whether people are treated according to the same standards. Actually Parsons and Lipset use different definitions. For Parsons, particularism applies to the particular relationships of each individual, such as family and friends. For Lipset, on the other hand, particularism concerns *only* whether some people are given special treatment. Thus, "everybody should give deference to members of the upper class" would be particularistic for Lipset. But it would be universalistic for Parsons since it is not relative to each individual. Thus, Parsons treats the analogous principle "Honor all fathers and mothers" as universalistic, and reserves particularism for "Honor *thy* father and mother."

Note that nationalities with some general acceptance of social class differences – like the English or the Germans – would be considered dissimilar to American universalism by Lipset, but similar by Parsons. For present purposes the problem will be dealt with by allowing for three alternatives instead of two: (a) all people are treated according to the same standards; (b) people are treated differently according to their membership in a class or group; (c) people are treated differently according to their relationship to the individual. This includes the classic case of family relationships which is omitted by Lipset.

2. *Achievement vs. ascription.* This concerns whether people are treated according to their actual or potential performance, or their other qualities, such as those derived from birth.

3. *Specificity vs. diffuseness.* This concerns whether the scope of the relationship is limited or broad.

4. *Neutrality vs. affectivity.* This concerns whether the reaction to people involves the inhibition of any immediate impulse gratification and emotional expression. This variable is omitted by Lipset.

To illustrate several of the preceding variables, consider the relationship of a salesclerk and a customer and compare this with a family relationship between parents and children or between husband and wife. The customer and clerk normally assume that the price is the same as to any other customer – that is universalism – and that their relationship is limited to the immediate transaction – that is specificity. In contrast, parents usually do not treat their children like all others, and their relationship extends over a broad range of matters. This example should appear very simple – it would only become interesting if the customer tries to make a date with the clerk and so turn the relationship into one that is affective, particularistic, and diffuse.

Lipset, while omitting the fourth pair, adds an additional one which he calls *equalitarian vs. elitist* (p. 211):

In an equalitarian society, the differences between low status and high status people are not stressed in social relationships and do not convey to the high status person a general claim to social deference. In contrast, in an elitist society, those who hold high positions in any structure, whether it be in business, in intellectual circles, or in government, are thought to deserve, and are actually given, general respect and deference.

Comments

Following up what was said earlier, we will generally use the terms *Gemeinschaft* and *Gesellschaft* to refer to types of relationships. *Gemeinschaft* relationships and *Gesellschaft* relationships are short-hand terms for relationships that are relatively particularistic, diffuse, ascriptive, etc., as opposed to universalistic, specific, achieved, etc. A *Gemeinschaft* or *Gesellschaft* nation is one where relationships are generally of one type or the other. It would be possible to find examples of the other usage where, for example, anthropologists might refer to an entire community as *a Gemeinschaft*, with some implication that all members share positive feelings and a sense of solidarity with each other. But it is assumed here that negative relationships can also be *Gemeinschaft* ones.

In this connection, it is a weakness of the Toennies/Parsons approach that they appear to be concerned only with relationships *within* some "in-group." Such an analysis may be fairly adequate for some of the relatively isolated cultures studied by anthropologists. But it seems clear that this does not apply to any of the large nations considered here. In such cases, *universalism–particularism* does not concern only whether different members of the ingroup are treated the same. It also concerns whether all members of the ingroup are treated differently from "outsiders." To the extent that treatment *is* the same, the separation between the ingroup and outsiders becomes less clear-cut. Indeed, this is precisely what will be argued here: that universalism tends to make the separation between ingroup and outsiders less clear.

The pattern variables are intended to be applicable to all societies and so provide a basis for comparative analysis. However, they only become usable after someone has designated which alternatives apply to a given case. Lipset meets this problem for the United States by assigning the *Gesellschaft* alternative for every variable. In other cases, he distinguishes between different features or institutions of a society. Thus, he says that the French became universalistic earlier in the political system than in the economy, while for Germany it was the other way around.

A major disadvantage of Lipset's treatment for present purposes is that he omits any reference to the classical *Gemeinschaft* examples of the family and "private" relationships generally. He deals virtually only with three features of society: the economy, the polity, and the social class system.

Parsons seems to have wanted to get away from a simple dichotomy with only two possibilities. His way of trying to do this was to treat the several variables as not only logically distinct but as independent of each other. Thus, with four pattern variables all of the 16 logically possible combinations would be of comparable importance. This assumption seems extremely implausible. The different pattern variables seem related to each other both conceptually and empirically – just as one would expect given their origins. Thus, all the *Gesellschaft* alternatives are characteristic of contractual relationships. Indeed, Parsons repeatedly notes that there seem to be such relationships between the several variables. But he persists in writing out tables that include all 16 of the logically possible combinations.

Putting the problem somewhat differently, Parsons does assume that each of the *separate* pattern variables is a strict dichotomy. This means that he can only allow for an intermediate or mixed case by assigning it the *Gemeinschaft* alternative for one variable and the *Gesellschaft* alternative for another.[1] This

---

[1] These assignments seem to be fairly arbitrary. Thus Parsons (1951) considers the cases of traditional China and of conservative Germany as from 1870 to 1918. Let us assume that both

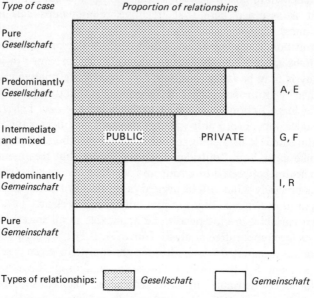

Figure 6.1 Typology for Relationships

Note: The letters at the right represent hypothesized classifications for the six "standard" nationalities considered: A = Americans; E = English; G = Germans; F = French; I = Italians; R = Russians.

assumption that each variable is a dichotomy seems to be another mistake. We have already seen that it is useful to allow for more than two alternatives. Thus, "Honor thy father and mother" is more particularistic than "Honor all those of high status" which, however, is more particularistic than "Treat everyone the same."

Now consider what happens when the pattern variables are used jointly. In order to escape a simple dichotomy, we need not follow Parsons and assume that the variables are independent of each other. Instead we can assume that the variables tend to share a common factor, but recognize various degrees along this dimension – and so allow for intermediate or mixed cases. For example, in Lipset's cases where he distinguishes between different features or institutions, the society as a whole would represent a mixed or intermediate

of these are intermediate or mixed cases. Parsons says that China represented universalism and ascription while Germany represented particularism and achievement. He proceeds to fill in additional features for these two combinations that fit the features of these two examples. However, it does not seem convincing that the differences between the two examples follow from the assigned pattern variables. Instead it is noticeable that the two combinations – which ought to be opposites in terms of the pattern variables assigned – are said to be similar in many respects, such as authoritarianism. Such similarity is just what one could expect if both cases were intermediate or mixed – each containing features of both universalism and particularism, and of both achievement and ascription.

case. Alternatively, if we allow for intermediate values on some or all of the variables, their combination will also be intermediate.

In principle, it would be elegant to move directly from a dichotomy to a continuum analogous to those used in the natural sciences. Here the continuum would represent the proportion of relationships that were *Gemeinschaft*-like or *Gesellschaft*-like. However, to keep the presentation here simpler, it will only move part way toward a continuum. Suppose that we instead recognize five possibilities. These are represented in Figure 6.1. At the logical extreme one could have cases that were pure *Gemeinschaft* or pure *Gesellschaft*. Alternatively one could have cases that were predominantly *Gemeinschaft* or predominantly *Gesellschaft*. Finally one could have cases that are intermediate or mixed.

Cases of pure *Gemeinschaft* or pure *Gesellschaft* may be useful conceptually as ideal types. Perhaps a pure *Gemeinschaft* may be approached empirically in the cultures studied by anthropologists. But these pure cases are not to be found among the large nations of interest here. Hence we are left with three cases. The predominantly *Gesellschaft* case is approached by the Americans and the English. The predominantly *Gemeinschaft* case is approached by the Italians and – quite differently – by the Russians. Intermediate or mixed cases are approached by the Germans and the French.

The intermediate or mixed cases tend to make a sharp distinction between relations that are "public" and "private" – public relationships follow the *Gesellschaft* alternatives and private relationships follow the *Gemeinschaft* alternatives. Note that "public" relationships may include both those in formal settings such as an office, but also those that take place out on the street.

In contrast to the mixed cases, for the other two cases the distinction between public and private is not as clear-cut. In the predominantly *Gemeinschaft* cases public relationships tend to be invaded by the *Gemeinschaft* alternatives. In the predominantly *Gesellschaft* cases private relationships tend to be invaded by the *Gesellschaft* alternatives.

(Thus, Americans should give little emphasis to private relationships. There is evidence that this point may even apply to American social scientists. At least this may have been true in the early 1960s, when Lipset's book makes no recognition of a sphere of private relationships. Similarly, at that time Almond and Verba (1963) published a well-known book on *The civic culture*. They provide a variety of evidence for much greater participation in public activities in the United States and Britain than in Germany, Italy, and Mexico. They celebrate such participation as supportive of political democracy. But they do not consider the possibility that such public participation might have as a "price" a lower degree of private relationships.)

II. Dahrendorf's analysis

Dahrendorf's (1969) analysis serves as a useful supplement to the preceding. He makes a clear distinction between public and private spheres, and considers that an emphasis on the "public virtues" is necessary (if not sufficient) for liberal democracy, but recognizes the price in the loss of the "private virtues."[1] It might seem strange to include as "comparative" ideas from Dahrendorf's (1969) *Society and democracy in Germany*, since his direct concern is with the problem of a single country – i.e., why did liberal democracy historically fail to develop in Germany? However, there is always an implicit comparison, and often an explicit one with England (and to a lesser extent, the United States). Moreover, Dahrendorf recognizes that characteristics similar to the German ones may also apply to other nations.[2]

Dahrendorf describes the English system as emphasizing rules of procedure that permit substantive conflict, and contrasts this with a German tendency to seek substantive solutions that are integrative for all parties to a conflict. He then illustrates this argument through a variety of German institutions: courtroom procedure, the academic pursuit of truth, the economy, the state.

Dahrendorf contrasts the "public virtues" of the English with the German "private virtues": the public virtues

may be described in terms of the values of sport, particularly of team sport. He who is virtuous in this sense is "a good sport"; he is "fair." He thus adheres to those rules whose rationale is to promote and at the same time domesticate the competitive effort of sports. In this process the individual with his worries and dreams, flights of nostalgia and of desperation, retreats. Getting along with others becomes more important than those concerns; and this can be accomplished only if one does not burden one's relation to others with one's own inner person. Frictionless relations are also unburdened relations. Perhaps the single maxim that best characterizes public virtues is "Keep smiling": make things easy for the others, even if this is hard for you! Do not burden others with matters that make it difficult to get along; keep what is private to yourself! There is a strong element of the contractual in public virtues; they copy, so to speak, the articles of the social contract for all spheres of life. Since the personal sphere is left out, men are evaluated for their visible ability to get on with others. All society is role play, but the public virtues turn role play into a moral maxim.

A society of public virtues could be described negatively as "dishonest, unnatural, and, above all, hypocritical. It is my intention to describe here with

[1] The differences we have been considering seem to represent two different attitudes among sociologists. Many sociologists, in particular classical German sociologists of the nineteenth century including Weber, express – at least implicitly – regret over a change from *Gemeinschaft* to *Gesellschaft*. In contrast, some American sociologists consider this change both inevitable and desirable, and regret any remaining *Gemeinschaft* tendencies (e.g., particularism on the part of American ethnic groups).

[2] "Here we are decidedly no longer concerned with the peculiarities of German society; with significant variations in substance, the same dominance of private virtues might be asserted for French, Russian, Italian, and Mexican society, and many others as well" (p. 290).

what I call public virtues precisely the attitudes that Germans like to decry in Englishmen as hypocritical, that is, the smiling role behavior in accordance with structured interests in every condition."

In contrast are the private virtues:

...Private values provide the individual with standards for his own perfection, which is conceived as being devoid of society. Patterns of intercourse between men that are virtuous in a private sense correspond to this notion: they are immediate, not domesticated by general rules, intent on honesty and profoundness rather than ease and lack of friction.

The maxim for private virtues might be something like "Be Truthful." "...the personality of man proves itself by not requiring others at all. But where men meet, truthfulness involves burdensome relations: How are you? Ah, well, I have a toothache, and moreover, I had a fight with my wife..." (Dahrendorf, 1969, pp. 286–7).

Dahrendorf goes on to trace the effect of these differences in institutions, especially the relative importance of the family and the schools in the socialization of children.

Comments

We note that Dahrendorf's first point about the relative importance of rules of procedure, which was concerned primarily with institutions, reappears in more psychological terms as rules for "fair play."

We note that Dahrendorf's "private virtues" are not defined primarily in interpersonal terms, but for the individual's "self-sufficient standards for his own perfection." Putting it differently, it is the "mixed" cases (e.g., the Germans and the French) who have traditionally put the greatest emphasis on the development of one's own unique potential. (We will call this "individuality" as a contrast with various Anglo-American forms of "individualism.") Dahrendorf goes on to cite a study by Hofstatter where Germans associated "loneliness" with "big," "strong," "healthy," "courageous," "deep"; and Americans with "small," "weak," "sick," "cowardly," "empty," "sad," "shallow," "obscure," "bad," "ugly."

While the social implications are secondary for the "private virtues," they are primary for the "public virtues."

Thus we may summarize Dahrendorf's points under three headings. (1) The relative emphasis on procedural rules for fair play. (2) Attitudes toward others, where public virtues emphasize general affability, and private virtues honesty and profoundness. (3) Attitudes toward oneself; with private virtues the individual has self-sufficient "standards for his own perfection" (what we will call "individuality"); public virtues involve a retreat from this.

III. The Protestant ethic and the legacy of religion

For a comparative approach to contemporary nationalities, we have found Max Weber's formulation about the Protestant ethic very useful. This may seem strange, since Weber was directly concerned with a single set of characteristics especially as they appeared in the seventeenth century. But Weber's approach is always implicitly comparative, and he outlines how these characteristics could remain relevant into the present century. By proposing a specific set of psychological characteristics, Weber makes it possible not only to look for these (or their residues) in the relevant nationalities (e.g., the English and the Americans) but to compare the contrasting alternatives among other nationalities. Thus one may say that traditional Russian and Italian national character represent, in different ways, opposites of the Protestant ethic.

By an "ethic" is meant the implications of a religion for conduct in everyday life. Weber proposed that Protestantism, and in particular Calvinism and some related sects, implied certain psychological characteristics (the "Protestant ethic") which overlapped with the characteristics conducive to modern industrial capitalism (the "spirit of capitalism"), and so influenced its origin.

It would be a logical possibility to distinguish between the psychological characteristics needed for the relatively few individuals who as entrepreneurs were critical for the historical origin of capitalism, and for the larger number of people who work under capitalism. Weber does not much develop this distinction. His primary concern is implicitly with the entrepreneurs, but he mentions that similar characteristics in the workers were also conducive to the development of capitalism.

Similarly, one could consider separately the characteristics needed for the origin of capitalism, and those needed for success under capitalism once it had developed. As cases to compare with Protestantism, Weber later wrote studies of Judaism and the religions of China and India. When placed within an existing capitalism – e.g., the Chinese in southeast Asia, the Indians in Africa – these groups all have shown striking success. However, Weber's point is that modern industrial capitalism did not *originate* among these cultures. This point is less relevant here.

We will consider, first, four aspects of the Protestant ethic emphasized by Weber, and then additional aspects which are not emphasized by Weber.

1. *The work ethic.* Hard work is obviously a factor relevant to economic development. Luther already introduced the view that every occupation should be considered a "calling," with the implication that there is positive ethical value in hard work within one's occupation. We shall call this value

on work as an end in itself "the work ethic."[1] It contrasts with the Catholic view that labor, and especially manual labor, is a necessary punishment (George and George, 1968). One could argue that this characteristic is the most relevant one for workers under capitalism.

2. *Achievement motivation.* The remaining characteristics Weber considered to be distinctive of Calvinism and related sects (e.g., Pietists, Methodists, Baptists). Thus the "Protestant ethic" really applies to these forms of Protestantism (and is therefore sometimes called the "Puritan" ethic) and not to others (e.g., Lutherans, Anglicans). Although we have separated out the "work ethic" as possibly applying to Lutherans as well, even here Weber would emphasize the greater emphasis on work under Calvinism. In Calvinist Protestantism the individual was driven to demonstrate proof of salvation through performance in the everyday world. An obvious form was the achievement of economic success.

Hard work, valued as an end in itself in the work ethic, thus is also a means to the end of achievement. Both support what Weber called "worldly" activity in everyday economic life.

McClelland's (1961) *The achieving society*, a major attempt to adapt Weber's analysis, treats "achievement motivation" as the key psychological variable, which he tries to measure with a variety of ingenious methods.

3. *Impulse-control and asceticism.* People have impulses that tend to be expressed unless they are controlled. Expression of these impulses will tend to divert not only money but also time and attention away from economic activity. (Weber specifically includes control over anger, anxiety, eating.)

High degrees of impulse-control are supported by "asceticism" – where impulse-expression is treated as morally wrong. Less extreme degrees of impulse-control can be based on a belief in moderation, as in classical Greek philosophy, or on *ad hoc* rules that regulate the expression of particular impulses.

Weber argued that peculiar to Calvinist Protestantism was "worldly asceticism" – a combination of asceticism and the "worldly" activity that we have represented as the work ethic and achievement. The combination contrasts with a dualistic Catholic emphasis on an ideal of asceticism directed toward another, transcendental world, undertaken only by a saintly minority, but, for the majority of ordinary people, acceptance of enjoyment of life in this world. Similar dualisms tend to apply to non-Calvinist Protestant denominations such as Lutheranism and Anglicanism.

---

[1] This terminology may be unsuccessful, since "work ethic" is widely used for any case where positive value is placed on work, regardless of whether this is as a means to other ends, or an end in itself.

4. *"Rationality."* The remaining key concept for Weber tends to heighten the degree of the others, and combines to form his trinity of "rational worldly asceticism." "Rationality" is a central concept for Weber, which he uses in a number of different senses. The most relevant of these will be considered later in this chapter. In the present context, the relevant one involves the systematic choice of means relative to some end. Weber argued that for Calvinism the end – proof of individual salvation – was based on one's life as a whole, and so required the methodical and continuous application of worldly asceticism, rather than a balance sheet between separate merits and sins, as in other religions. Thus the relevant meaning of "rational" involves systematic achievement in the occupational world, and systematic asceticism in the control of impulses toward the enjoyment of life. We shall review several other meanings of "rational" below, and see that they are generally not distinctive of the Protestant ethic.

The combination of systematic work and systematic limitation of consumption, to conclude Weber's argument, will inevitably lead to the accumulation of capital, although this is not itself a goal of the Protestant ethic, but an "unforeseen and even unwished for result" (p. 90).

However, the goal of economic self-interest soon tends to become substituted for the religious goal of salvation. Strictly speaking, the "Protestant ethic" should be used only when these characteristics are directed at the religious end; the same characteristics, when directed at the end of economic self-interest, become part of "the spirit of capitalism." However, like nearly everyone else, we will generally use the "Protestant ethic" more loosely to refer to the relevant characteristics whether or not they are directed at religious ends.

Additional characteristics

In addition to the characteristics of the Protestant ethic emphasized in Weber's essay, additional features deserve mention, although they are not emphasized by him. Weber focuses on certain characteristics that are crucial for the origin of modern capitalism and that are shared by the "Protestant ethic" and the "spirit of capitalism"; it is consistent with his approach that each should have additional features.

5. *"Universal otherhood."* Benjamin Nelson (1969) reviews the Judeo-Christian history of rules for loans with interest (usury), suggesting that this history is also representative of more general attitudes toward interpersonal relations. Among the many interpretations he considers, one can distinguish three main varieties. (a) In the old testament rules in Deuteronomy, taking interest was forbidden from "brother" co-religionists, but permitted from outgroup

foreigners. (b) In the medieval Catholic church, which aspired to universal brotherhood, loans for interest were forbidden altogether. (c) Reinterpretations by Luther, and more decisively by Calvin, allowed for taking interest even from co-religionists. In this interpretation what was universally applied was no longer the original rule for "brothers," but that for foreigners – "all men are 'brothers' in being equally 'others'."

Nelson suggests a parallel dilution for the ideals of friendship and brotherhood – indeed, a clear expression of ideal friendship was to serve as surety for a friend's loan, as by Antonio in *The merchant of Venice*.

Nelson considers why Weber did not make more use of these points. Certainly permitting loans for interest would be highly facilitative for capitalist development. By itself it does not have the same broad relevance to conduct in everyday life as the characteristics Weber did emphasize in the Protestant ethic. As regards more general attitudes toward others, Weber does touch on this in *The protestant ethic*, and more extensively in his other later writings, where he treats the change from "particularism" toward "universalism" (see above, p. 75) as a major feature of modern society. Outside of a small community, to treat everyone alike (universalism) necessarily means that no one is treated with the high degree of rights and duties implied by "brotherhood."

6. *Practicality/empiricism*. Although a concern for usefulness is only suggested briefly by Weber as characteristic of Calvinism, it may properly be included. For example, Merton (1938/1970) pursued Weber's suggestion in a study of scientists in seventeenth-century England (largely Puritan). He demonstrates how much their scientific work derived from their concern with practical problems: e.g., pumping water out of coal mines, the use of pendulums to establish longitude for ships, and artillery fire (the gas laws, ballistic trajectory, recoil and impact). "Even that 'purest' of disciplines, mathematics, held little interest for Newton save as it was designed for application to physical problems" (p. 182). Though Puritans favored both reason and empiricism, priority was given to the latter since scholasticism, which used rigorous syllogistic reasoning, was held to have come to false conclusions because of starting with false premises (p. 69). Logic is reduced to a subsidiary role: "the rational consideration of empirical data" (p. 71). Similar relations between Calvinism and science have been shown for other countries than England (Hooykaas, 1972). Of course, science is only a particularly dramatic illustration of the concern for practicality and empiricism. Within philosophy this concern could be related both to British empiricism with its tremendous emphasis on sensation and perception, and to the various forms of American pragmatism. More generally, this concern supports an emphasis on technique – a belief that, for almost any purpose, there is some method that will be relatively successful – at the expense of a theoretical emphasis. This concern

with technique appears most obviously as "technology" within industry, most dramatically in the Industrial Revolution, where the major advances especially within the textile industry did not involve major theoretical originality. But the same concern with technique can appear more generally ("How to build or repair your own home," "How to win friends and influence people").

7. *Individualism*. Another aspect of Protestantism that is not stressed by Weber is individual responsibility. Yet this could be considered as *the* most central feature of Protestantism, starting with Luther's idea of "every man a priest." Peyrefitte (1976) suggests that Weber concentrated on the specific problem of capital formation, and the elements of Protestantism leading to it. Peyrefitte wants a broader contrast between an "economic" mentality and an "anti-economic" one, with the critical factor from Protestantism being individual responsibility leading to achievement. McClelland's (1961) analysis of the Calvinist ethic also emphasizes the relation between individual responsibility in religion and in achievement. Some of the strongest evidence in his book involves a cross-cultural relation between achievement motivation and individual responsibility for contact with the Divine.

We need to distinguish at least three conceptions related to individualism. (a) Individual responsibility for achievement is a positive prescription. The pursuit of individual self-interest can be taken to have further implications for the acceptance of competition and a negative proscription against interference from others: (b) Individual freedom from interference. To make a clear distinction from these two forms of "individualism," it might help to refer to the third as "individuality:" (c) Individuality in developing one's own personality.

The Protestant ethic might properly include the first of these, but it supports the second only in part, and may easily contradict the third. We will see that the development of individuality is more a feature of non-Calvinist and Catholic nations.

As regards "freedom from interference," it is true that Calvinists did tend to reject any *outside* authority. However, Weber (1946) – in a supplement to his main essay on the Protestant ethic – emphasizes the exercise of social control within Calvinist sects. The members of the sect had to have certain qualities to be admitted to the community circle, and had to prove these repeatedly in order to hold their own within it. "The Puritan sects put the most powerful individual interest of social self-esteem in the service of their breeding of traits... The premiums were placed upon 'proving' oneself before God in the sense of attaining salvation – and proving oneself before man in the sense of holding one's own within the Puritan sects" (Weber, 1946, pp. 320–1). This is the antithesis of the Catholic church which assumes universal membership rather than being selective, and administers relief from guilt about specific acts rather than requiring repeated proof of more general character traits.

Thus the Protestant ethic, while fostering individual achievement, may tend to suppress "individuality" in favor of social conformity. Relevant here is Lipset's point (1961, p. 162 fn.) that Weber's conception of the Protestant ethic should not be confused with Riesman's (1950) conception of the "inner-directed" (as contrasted with the "other-directed") character type. In Riesman's conception of inner-directedness we need to distinguish two aspects: first, relative independence from major social influence, after a period of internalization during childhood (as contrasted with continued responsiveness to social influence by the "other-directed"); and secondly, the content of the characteristics of the "inner-directed" which for Riesman generally corresponds to the Protestant ethic as defined above.

Riesman defines "inner-directed" in terms of the first aspect, and tends to slip in the second. Weber defines the Protestant ethic in terms of the second aspect, and includes continued social influence as an important feature of the Calvinist sects. A combination of the Protestant ethic and social conformity is thus consistent with Weber, though not allowed for by Riesman.

Moralism. A further characteristic that might be added to the Protestant ethic would be a tendency to invoke moral values in a wide variety of situations. Such a tendency, which could be considered a form of the systematic "rationality" stressed by Weber, might be called "moralism." It is a source of accusations of "hypocrisy" towards the English (and Americans) by Europeans – e.g., when the former attribute aspects of their foreign policy to moral principles rather than to national self-interest.

Comments

Weber's proposals have been controversial on several grounds. Most prominently Weber has been criticized for emphasizing religious ideas as the cause of economic changes, in opposition to the "economic determinism" of Marxists and others, where economic factors are primary and ideas (including religious ones) are side-effects. In more balanced interpretations of both positions, the differences are considerably less. In his later writings, Weber agrees that the Protestant ethic is only one factor in the rise of capitalism, accepts a major importance for economic factors, and affirms that in other situations the sequence could also work the other way round – e.g., with the development of capitalism leading to the modification of religious beliefs. On the other hand, Marxism while emphasizing the primacy of economic factors for ideas, includes the possibility of ideas "reflecting" back on the economic system.

In general, we do not need to enter here into this and most of the other controversies connected with Weber's proposals. Weber's objective was to account for the beginnings of modern capitalism – ours is to consider the personality characteristics of different nationalities. The crucial value of Weber is to suggest some specific characteristics that may remain relevant to national differences. For our purposes, it is not crucial whether the relation originally arose from religious or economic developments, especially since we are interested in the application of this relation to the contemporary period. To illustrate the preceding points, we need to consider how one would extrapolate to the contemporary period from Weber's analysis of the seventeenth century. Weber himself implies a three-part sequence in this development.

1. By the seventeenth century, Protestant religious doctrines had become translated into a code of conduct for everyday life: the Protestant ethic – involving the characteristics of rational, worldly asceticism as means to a religious end (proof of salvation). These characteristics led to the beginning of modern capitalism.

2. The resulting wealth itself tended to undermine the religious roots of the Protestant ethic; by the eighteenth century the combination of rational, worldly asceticism remains, but the religious end tends to be replaced by the utilitarian one of economic self-interest – the "spirit of capitalism." Religious revival movements such as Wesley's attempt to reestablish the religious ends. Weber (p. 175) cites Wesley, the founder of Methodism, as to the paradox of such efforts: religion (in the form of the Protestant ethic) must necessarily produce both industry and frugality, and these cannot but produce riches. Riches in turn will tend to undermine the religious spirit.

3. The large-scale development of modern industrialism (in the nineteenth century) tends to impose these characteristics on everyone as an "iron cage." If we examine the situation at this point in causal terms, it is the economic system that is determining the characteristics of the individual. At this stage, then, Weber's account is the same as one that could be given by economic determinists, however they might disagree about stage (1).

Weber's proposals about the origins of capitalism are interesting enough so that we have summarized them in detail. However what is crucial for our purposes is only the relation between industrial development and individual characteristics for the contemporary period. Since the preceding sequence has brought us into the present century, it might seem that one could simply agree on which nationalities were more influenced by Puritanism or by the early development of industrialism (e.g., the English and the Americans), and make predictions. Unfortunately, such predictions are complicated by the possibility that a further stage of industrialism, which tends to reverse the Protestant ethic, has increased in importance since Weber wrote.

4. Consumption-oriented societies: the very material success of modern

capitalism may not only undermine the Protestant ethic, but eventually the spirit of capitalism as well. Hard work and asceticism when based on utilitarian grounds will tend to weaken in motivating force as material affluence is achieved. This process can be reinforced by the system of installment buying, whereby consumption is no longer deferred until after saving, and by the effort of mass advertising to encourage consumption. This effect may only gradually spread through society, and meanwhile is counteracted by upward mobility on the part of those who had not yet attained affluence. But eventually it may reach the majority of society.

Writing at the beginning of this century, Weber (1904–5/1930, p. 283) describes the United States as the field of the highest development of the pursuit of wealth, where the work ethic is no longer based either on spiritual values or on economic compulsion, but persists without any justification "as a kind of sport." This is not likely to be a lasting situation. Some evidence suggests a change already by the 1920s in the United States – e.g., a classic study of popular biographies (Lowenthal, 1961) showed a change at this time from heroes of production to heroes of consumption. Similar tendencies have been suggested for western Europe, especially since World War II.

In the consumption-oriented society, the Protestant ethic is replaced by other characteristics: for example, systematic asceticism is replaced by a hedonistic, present-time orientation – "self-indulgence"; individual responsibility for achievement is replaced by continued responsiveness to the changing preferences of others – "other-directedness."[1]

Such changes would complicate any predictions from Weber's analysis. Particularly if these changes are likely to occur first in the societies that were industrially advanced, such changes will tend to reverse the predictions that would otherwise be made. However, we must allow for the possibility of inertia or temporal lag for personality changes induced by economic ones. Some such cultural "lag" can be expected simply because adult personality characteristics are not easily changed, and we should expect the new characteristics to appear first in a younger generation. With the possible exception of the United States, the changes to the affluent society can plausibly be thought to have reached the majority only after 1950. Hence it still seems reasonable to make predictions for 1970 on the basis of Weber's analysis, recognizing that these may be in the process of change.

In addition, since our empirical data concerns *judgments about* national characteristics, we need to allow for an additional "perceptual lag" between changes in national characteristics and their recognition. We can predict that this lag is likely to be less for ingroup judgments and greater for judgments by other nationalities, who will be slower to recognize any changes.

[1] Snowman (1977), in a comparative study of Britain and America, lists four "new values": technique infatuation, participatoriness, transitoriness, and self-indulgence.

Relation to personality traits. In general it is fairly easy to represent Weber's formulation as traits of individuals, and so to some of the trait-adjectives used in our empirical study. One problem is that the Protestant ethic tends to emphasize "impersonal virtues" (e.g., *hard-working, honest*) at the expense of "interpersonal virtues" (e.g., *warm, easy-going*). As we have seen, both of these tended to be unrepresented in the selection of trait-adjectives. To this extent, some aspects of the Protestant ethic are under-represented in our scales.

However, many aspects of the Protestant ethic are well represented: e.g., impulse-control is represented by the first seven sets of scales called "Tight impulse-control vs. Loose impulse-expression"; practicality by the scale *practical* vs. *impractical*; the work ethic by the extra scale, *hard-working* vs. *lazy*.

Meanings of "rational." Before leaving the discussion of Weber, it will be useful to clarify some of the meanings of the word "rational." Weber and others treated "rationality" as the distinctive attribute of modern western culture, and tended to call "rational" a variety of trends that led in this direction. Weber (1930, pp. 76–8) was, however, clear that one particular meaning of rational was relevant to the Protestant ethic. We distinguish four meanings here that are relevant for present purposes – these distinctions are not identical with those most emphasized by Weber himself.

1. Systematic choice according to some general goal or principle: this is the meaning relevant to Weber's essay, in the form of systematic choice of means relative to some end (profit, in the case of modern capitalism). It might also be extended to social behavior that follows some general principle (e.g., "be considerate" or "be friendly"). The English and the Americans tend to this variety.

2. Systematic organization and application of rules: this is exemplified by bureaucratic administration, especially the legal system which, Weber points out, is more systematized in Latin countries than Anglo-American ones. It might also be extended to less official rules for social behavior. In such an extension, the rules will tend to be more specific as compared to the first meaning. Thus, Wylie (Wylie and Bégué, 1970) relates that as an American student in France, he said "hello" when passing his landlady in the street, and was later taken to task that he should have (a) stopped, (b) taken off his hat, (c) shaken hands, (d) told her where he was going. Evidently, systems of rules – where any applications of general principles have been made in advance – involve less individual choice and are congruent with a more hierarchical society.

3. Rationalism vs. empiricism: ideally, these types of systematization and others (e.g., modern science) should reflect both logic and experience. Nevertheless, it is useful to compare the relative emphasis on logic vs. truth,

on reasoning vs. experience. This comes close to a traditional distinction in philosophy between "rationalism" and "empiricism." The former is more associated with "continental" philosophy; the latter with Anglo-American practicality (and, as we have seen, with Puritanism).

4. Reason vs. Romanticism: one would also like to describe the "ends" (or premises) themselves as more or less "rational." Weber seems to suggest a procedural criterion (i.e., "formal" rather than "substantive"), using "rational" when there is deliberate choice, and "irrational" when choice is "affectual" or traditional. This usage again comes close to a historical one: the "classical" emphasis on reason in the eighteenth-century Enlightenment vs. the emphasis on emotions and tradition in the "Romanticism" of the nineteenth century. Weber points out that the former is most prominent in Latin countries. In contrast, Germany was heavily influenced by nineteenth-century Romanticism.

In sum, it is only the first meaning of "rational" that is relevant to the Protestant ethic. The other three meanings would all be more relevant to a tradition such as the French.

Comparative perspective: the legacy of religion. The "Protestant ethic" is not itself a comparative scheme. But, as noted earlier, Weber always took a comparative point of view, at least implicitly. Nations without an important Calvinist tradition should be less likely to show "rational worldly asceticism" and the other characteristics considered earlier. We must ask: what do such nations have instead? We have already noted several such comparative alternatives in passing.

In applying the Protestant ethic today, we are considering a historical legacy from religious traditions in nations that are now largely secular. One may generalize this to other nations, where we should expect comparable legacies from other religious traditions – e.g., Catholic, Lutheran, Russian Orthodox. We will not attempt here to give systematic formulations to these alternatives comparable to that for Calvinism. However, these alternatives are relevant in considering specific nationalities later on.

IV. Other approaches

Two other approaches will be mentioned more briefly.

Socio-economic roles

In their important book *Ethnocentrism*, Levine and Campbell (1972) propose that personality characteristics are ascribed to different socio-economic roles with regard to urbanism, occupation, and political–technological dominance. Thus, groups doing manual labor are seen as strong, stupid, pleasure-loving, improvident; groups occupied as businessmen and traders are seen as grasping, haughty, cunning, exclusive, and domineering. Further, these attributions may be extended to ethnic groups where these specialize differentially in different socio-economic roles. For example, much of the content of judgments about American Negroes and Jews is "predictable simply from the facts that the Negroes are predominantly manual workers of immediately rural origins and that the Jews are urban people in nonmanual occupations" (p. 158).

These proposals are quite compelling. Unfortunately they have only limited application to our problem of large European nations where each nationality generally fills all socio-economic roles. However, they would apply to any exceptions such as the heavy use during the 1950s and 1960s in northern and western Europe of laborers from southern and eastern Europe. In some cases these proposals might also be applied to differences between nations – for example, if southern Italy has remained relatively agricultural as compared to England.

These proposals could easily be related to social class differences in personality characteristics. The possibility of occupational and social class differences in personality generally has a more favorable reception from social scientists than that for national differences. Aside from the possibility suggested by Levine and Campbell that ethnic differences may result from occupational differences, it would be valuable to look at the joint operation of both variables: occupation or class, and nationality. For example, it might be that traditional national differences apply largely only to the middle class.[1] Thus some versions of the English working class (e.g. the comic-strip figure of Andy Capp) imply an impulse-expressiveness that is very different from the traditional self-controlled English national character. However interesting, such an investigation of class differences is not the present one, for which Levine and Campbell's proposals have only a limited direct relevance.

North–south differences

Levine and Campbell (1972, p. 162) also provide a convenient source[2] for a summary of the proposals of Ehrenfels regarding a recurrent pattern of north–south differences. In this pattern (1) northerners are seen as impulse-controlled (*thrifty/stingy*, *serious*) and southerners as impulse-expressive (*generous/wasteful*, *light-hearted*); (2) northerners are seen as having what we have called "impersonal virtues" (*hard-working, reliable*) that southerners may

---

[1] This possibility could be turned into one version of the argument against national characteristics based on variability within national groups, discussed in Chapter 1.
[2] Unfortunately, Ehrenfels' own presentations in English tend to be in periodicals published in India, and so not easily available to many readers. There are also presentations by Ehrenfels in other languages – e.g., Ehrenfels (1967).

lack (*lazy*); southerners as having "interpersonal virtues" (*obliging, amiable*) that northerners may lack (*hard-headed*); (3) northerners are seen as economically and militarily powerful and southerners as weak; (4) southerners are seen as more intelligent and sophisticated than northerners.

Ehrenfels developed his proposal originally for India, and generally has non-European examples in mind.[1] He is able to point to many historical cases where a more sophisticated culture is invaded by a group from the north (or from the south in the rarer cases in the southern hemisphere). If we try to extend it to modern Europe, we note that points (1) and (2) are consistent with Weber's formulation of the Protestant ethic, while point (3) follows from the development of industrialization. However, point (4) is more debatable – it is not clear that the more industrialized northern Europeans would now recognize in themselves a lack of sophistication and intelligence. (Compare Germans coming to Italy at the end of the Roman empire, and in the last 100 years.)

To resolve this problem, it seems useful to distinguish two historical cases. (a) Through much of history, more "civilized" regions (typically to the south) were more urbane and often became relatively impulse-expressive ("decadent"?), and might be conquered by groups (typically from the north) that were less urbane, more impulse-controlled, and stronger militarily. (Whether they were typically also stronger economically seems less clear.) (b) After the development of gun-powder, the military situation becomes reversed, and more "civilized" regions do the conquering. Later the center of industrialism (and the Protestant ethic) shifts to northern Europe which becomes impulse-controlled and hard-working, economically and militarily more powerful, and – at least in some respects – relatively sophisticated.

Ehrenfels considers possible explanations for the north–south differences, but (particularly in view of his non-European emphasis and our own European one) it is probably safer to treat his proposal simply as an empirical generalization especially concerning points (1) and (2). Ehrenfels emphasizes regional differences *within* countries rather than comparable differences *between* countries. "Thus, by reputation, the southern Irish are more 'southern' in personality than the northern French, the southern Germans and French more 'southern' than the northern Italians and Spanish" (Levine and Campbell, 1972, p. 162). However, we will consider that Ehrenfels' proposals might apply as well to differences *between* nations. Indeed, it is implicit in the above quotation that one would generally expect the Irish to be more "northern" than the French; Germans and French to be more "northern"

---

[1] Ehrenfels' proposals are actually cast in the form of reciprocal judgments by northerners and southerners about each other, and we have already used this as an example in Chapter 3 (see Table 3.2). Our version then hypothesized that between judges there was evaluative disagreement and descriptive agreement. In Ehrenfels' version the evaluative disagreement is only partial and less systematic. In the present treatment, we concentrate on what is descriptively common to judgments by both groups.

than the Italians and Spanish. The quoted examples are meant to be cases where the regional differences within nations outweigh the (implied) differences between nations. Thus it seems legitimate to apply Ehrenfels' proposals to differences between nations as well as between regions within a nation.

These generalizations seem to have considerable plausibility, but it is not clear how they could be explained. An explanation for Europe might be attempted along Weberian lines. One could then start with the fact that the Protestant–Catholic demarcation in Europe is a north–south one. This might explain some of the differences between nations and some within nations (e.g., the Germans, the Irish, the Dutch) but not others. One would then have to assume further that these religious differences and the corresponding economic and cultural ones set up a more general north–south gradient both between and within nations. We will not attempt a final explanation, but will simply leave these proposals as plausible empirical generalizations.

Relations between the approaches

The last section suggested some relation between the proposals of Weber and Ehrenfels. This leads into the general point that the various approaches we have considered are separate but nevertheless have important relations with each other. We will summarize some of these.

The analysis using the "pattern variables" considered the relative predominance of *Gesellschaft* and *Gemeinschaft* relationships. Dahrendorf's description of the "public" and the "private" virtues can be seen as fleshing out these abstract dimensions with some of the corresponding attitudes. Thus, Dahrendorf stresses in the "public virtues" the "contractual element" which is related to the *Gesellschaft* variables.

A contractual element is of course also part of modern capitalism. Weber's proposals about the Protestant ethic are generally consistent with the *Gesellschaft* relationships. Indeed, to the extent that Weber's historical account is correct, it would explain *why* nationalities such as the Americans and the English are assigned the *Gesellschaft* alternatives for the pattern variables. The pattern variable scheme by itself does not explain any such assignments.

There is also a clear relationship between Weber's formulation and Dahrendorf's proposals. The linkage becomes particularly clear if one can extend Weber, as we have here, to encompass Nelson's emphasis on "universal otherhood" which corresponds well with Dahrendorf's "public virtues."

In sum, while the four approaches considered in this chapter each add something separate, there are clear linkages between them. On the one hand, one has *Gesellschaft* relationships, emphasis on the procedural rules of the game and the public virtues, the Protestant ethic, and most of the "northern" characteristics of Ehrenfels. On the other hand, one has contrasts for all of these.

7 The English[1]

> Both elements, that of an unspoiled naive joy of life, and of a strictly regulated, reserved self-control, and conventional ethical conduct are even today combined to form the English national character.
>
> Weber, 1930, p. 173

For Weber the classic example of the Protestant ethic was England in the seventeenth century, together with revivals such as Wesley's in the next century. He did not consider that the English had previously been particularly inclined toward such characteristics. This view is strongly supported by other authors: Glyn (1970) mentions extremes of impulse-expressiveness in the consumption of food and drink in pre-Puritan England, Gorer (1955) the expression of aggression.

Weber held that these traditional characteristics tended to persist alongside the Puritan ones. Politically, the Puritans were only temporarily dominant, and the non-Puritan characteristics became more prominent in the Restoration period after 1660. However, the Protestant ethic returned strongly in the next century with the revival movement represented by Wesley, and may have reached its most widespread influence in the nineteenth-century Victorian period.

In any case, since the Puritan characteristics are the more distinctive ones, they are the more likely to be emphasized as English characteristics, especially in judgments by others. These implications need to be qualified to the extent that the English may be considered likely candidates (after the Americans) to have moved into a consumption-oriented stage of industrialism, tending to reverse the Puritan characteristics. Such a change would also be less likely to be recognized in judgments by others. Accordingly, at least for judgments by others, one might apply to the English the comparative approaches considered earlier: the Protestant ethic, the "pattern variables," and Dahrendorf's proposals. In addition, Snowman (1977) presents a recent comparison between the British and the Americans. We will begin with the last two sources, which are the most directly concerned with the contemporary

---

[1] In considering the "English," we avoid the question of similarities and differences with the other "British" peoples. However, many other authors considered below have written about the "British."

English; Snowman explicitly so, while in Dahrendorf's discussion of Germany there is always an implicit comparison with England.

Six English characteristics

Dahrendorf's (1969) analysis suggests three characteristics: the importance of rules of procedure for "fair play," the "public virtues" of getting along with others, and a lack of the "private virtues" involved in close interpersonal relationships. For Snowman (1977), "self-restraint" is the central, and almost all-encompassing British characteristic. (We recall that Weber also used "asceticism" in a broad sense, to include not only avoidance of sensory pleasures, but also of interpersonal emotions such as anger and warmth.) Snowman includes under "self-restraint" all of the following: the inhibition of emotions, especially in situations of crisis; acceptance of, and deference toward, a ruling elite, together with respect for their privacy and exclusiveness; the control of aggression, under which he includes discipline for children, studied laziness, aloofness or shyness, fairness and sportsmanship, and the use of euphemisms. It will be convenient here to reorganize the varieties of self-restraint into four types: the avoidance of obvious self-assertiveness, the inhibition of aggression, asceticism regarding sensory pleasures, and reserve and aloofness. This last can combine with Dahrendorf's lack of "private virtues," yielding six characteristics altogether.

An interesting book by Glyn (1970) considers a broad range of themes from British culture. It is tempting to try to reorganize these around some limited set of characteristics. With a little imagination, it is possible to relate most of the themes represented in Glyn's chapters to the six characteristics just listed.

1. *The rules of the game.* Dahrendorf argued that the emphasis on rules of procedure provided a context in which substantive conflict could take place. Related themes from Glyn include the importance of sports, with emphasis not on winning but on fair play and cooperation – "not letting down the side" (Ch. 16), and more general attitudes emphasizing rules of procedure and fairness (Ch. 15).

2. *The "public virtues."* Dahrendorf actually introduced the "public virtues" in relation to team sports, emphasizing getting along with others. At least some aspects of the English emphasis on humor (Glyn, Ch. 14) seem to be another example. The general emphasis on humor should perhaps be considered primarily below as an example of Snowman's "self-restraint" in the avoidance of (more serious) emotions, most especially in crisis situations ("if humor is desirable in normal social life, it is regarded as completely essential at all moments of crisis" – Glyn, p. 197). However, the use of humor

(preferably about the weather) in casual public interactions could properly be considered an example of the "public virtues," as it is also for Americans. (However, there must be some crucial difference between English and American humor – perhaps American humor is typically more obvious or more self-assertive. In the Katz and Braly type studies – Karlins *et al.*, 1969 – Americans describe the English as "humorless"! – this for "the greatest British national asset" – Glyn, p. 196.)

Also related to the public virtues is the English readiness to participate with others in voluntary associations – committees and clubs (Glyn, Ch. 18). Snowman (1977) cites evidence from Almond and Verba (1963) that the British show somewhat less tendency than the Americans to this kind of participation, which de Tocqueville felt to be at the root of American democracy. However, the wider comparison provided by Almond and Verba's additional three nationalities makes it clear that the English and Americans are basically similar and high in such participation.

3. *The avoidance of obvious self-assertion.* This characteristic is related to, but need not be identical with, the inhibition of hostility. It is quite compatible with a quiet self-confidence, which may be seen by foreigners as arrogance. It can easily take the form of actual self-depreciation. An obvious example from Glyn's themes (p. 194) again involves humor which for the English is most preferably directed at oneself.

More puzzling is the interpretation of Glyn's themes of a historical preference for heroic losers (Ch. 3) or, as necessary (if the British empire is to be explained), for winning against the odds (Ch. 4). The emphasis on the "rules of the game," discussed earlier, means that self-respect depends more on "playing the game" properly than on winning. But why there should be an actual preference for losers remains a puzzle. In victory there is the temptation to show some self-satisfaction and so become a bad winner: "All Britishmen are deeply suspicious of victory and the victorious" (Glyn, p. 31). Perhaps this danger is so great as to support an actual preference for identification with the loser.

Some of the "euphemisms" cited by Snowman (1977, p. 95) are most easily interpreted as (apparent) self-depreciation: a well-brought-up Englishman will "tend to be effusive with his apologies, his 'I'd be awfully grateful ifs' and his 'Thank you very much indeeds.'"

4. *The inhibition of hostility.* Weber included anger among the impulses subject to Puritan asceticism. Gorer (1955) makes the inhibition of aggression his first assumption about the English (and argues at length that this inhibition extended to the working class only after the creation of a national police force in 1856). Snowman (1977, p. 95) gives examples of the euphemisms used: when disagreeing with someone, the English "would often begin by saying

something like 'I may be wrong, but...' or 'There is just one thing in all that you have been saying that worries me a little...'."

Glyn (1970, p. 185) argues that the British are not insensitive but hypersensitive to the point of touchiness. This is similar to Gorer's claim that the English are quite aggressive at some latent level. But in any case the expression of manifest hostility is avoided. In Glyn's terms, the touchiness is carefully concealed from the outsider. There is no overt complaint, so no apology is possible. In cases of annoyance at a pub or hotel, the customers simply take their business elsewhere. In the case of a Italian hotel owner, Glyn comments (p. 188) "He must have been surprised that we did not return another year." This example of the British inhibition of hostility is made the more compelling by the author's unlikely assumption that the non-English hotel owner would spend his time searching for such subtle, entirely indirect indications of hostility.

5. *Asceticism.* Here we use asceticism in the narrower sense of avoidance of sensory pleasures. Weber suggested that Puritan asceticism was always combined in the English character with a more hedonistic non-Puritan tradition. Some appearances suggest a major shift toward hedonistic self-indulgence in recent times. However, in our comparative context, there is evidence that considerable asceticism persisted into the contemporary period. We will concentrate on two sensory pleasures: food and sex.

With regard to food, Glyn (Ch. 6) contrasts the feasts of the pre-Puritan past – "Shall we ever see them again, or is it fish fingers forever?" (p. 74) – with the meagre present, representing the Puritan tradition that food is a necessary evil, so that money spent on food is money wasted, and only plain food is not suspect. Hunger (and cold) are thought to be good for children's character (Ch. 10).

Gorer (1955, p. 22) included as one of his three central assumptions about the English "strong moral principles," especially regarding sex. Much of the data he presents on sex, love, and marriage gives a strong impression of considerable inhibition. Two examples: (a) when asked at what age they started being really interested in the opposite sex, the age nearest the median was 16 (p. 78)! (This age showed a systematic decline with time, and has doubtless continued to do so.) (b) To the question "Not counting marriage, have you ever had a real love affair?", over half of those answering said "No" (p. 86). Among the remainder, Gorer notes the frequent appearance of foreigners as partners.

Glyn (Ch. 12) tries heroically to modify the impression that the British are largely disinterested in sex, making it clear that this does not apply to the non-Puritan tradition. The British often think about sex, although they rarely speak about it, since it is "not part of the British way of life." Sex is subject to its own "rules of the game" which favor orthodox positions, standard times, formal attire, an unromantic approach, and being a "good loser."

6. *"Reserve."* The characteristic of "universal otherhood" that we have added to the Protestant ethic implies that everyone is to be treated alike as a stranger. The combination of the "public virtues" and "self-restraint" implies for the English a smiling affability together with considerable aloofness and formality (this last in contrast to American informality).

A large number of the themes from Glyn (1970) can be related to this characteristic, some more directly and others less so.

a. Coolness and formality in the relation of parents to children (Ch. 10), who ideally are sent off early to the Spartan discipline of a boarding school. "To suit a Britishman, contact between parents and their children must be as reserved and formal as it can be made" (p. 142).

b. Similarly, other family relationships (Ch. 11) show the same "calculated undemonstrativeness" (p. 145). "In the ideal British family, non-communication among its various members should be as total as human ingenuity can make it" (p. 143).

c. Presumably in compensation, there are sentimental attachments to animals (Ch. 9). The Royal Society for the Prevention of Cruelty to Animals was founded more than 60 years before the National Society for the Prevention of Cruelty to Children. These preferences seem to be the opposite of those for Italians (p. 123), while the French hold that Puritanism and kindness to animals make Protestant countries incapable of developing a great cuisine (de Gramont, 1969, p. 369).

d. Extreme privacy (Glyn, Ch. 13) illustrated by the following anecdote (p. 184): "Two officers happened to meet after a long separation. One asked the other what he was doing these days, and he received the reply, 'Minding my own business, I hope.' Most Britishmen would not answer quite so bluntly..." The concern for privacy is expressed particularly within the hedged-in home.[1] "But if there is little contact between members of a British family, there is even less between one family and another" (p. 176).

e. Gardening is an overwhelmingly popular leisure activity (Ch. 19) that serves to reduce interaction between husband and wife, and as another substitute for close family relations.

f. A readiness to live abroad for extended periods – departing and returning quite casually – suggests a lack of strong interpersonal ties. There is a less dramatic American parallel here in the readiness to move geographically within a large country.

The pervasiveness of aloofness in Glyn's account – whose general tone is

---

[1] Note that a concern for "privacy" is compatible with a lack of the "private virtues" of close interpersonal relationships.

not unsympathetic to the British – deserves some comment: his description may refer particularly to the upper classes, although he does not say so;[1] his account does not preclude the possibility of close friendships outside the family between those of the same sex, although he does not affirm this; some of the aloofness may represent "shyness" and therefore apply particularly to strangers, but this is contradicted by his description of relations with children and other family members.

Gorer (1955) did propose that "shyness" was a central English characteristic and presented data from a large survey. Over half the answers said that as young people they had been "exceptionally shy" (p. 77). Other relevant material (Gorer, Ch. 4) concerns neighbors rather than friends as such. Gorer summarizes the relationship as one of "distant cordiality," and the general impression is one of "isolation and loneliness." Even if this impression is only half true, it would still represent an extreme and heart-rending situation.

Comment

The preceding brief consideration of six characteristics has nevertheless touched on most of the themes from Glyn's (1970) 25 chapters. A few of Glyn's themes have not been dealt with – e.g., drinking tea and in the pub. On the other hand, it is noteworthy that Glyn does not devote a chapter to social class – central to many analyses of the English – and treats it largely in peripheral contexts – e.g., differences regarding tea vs. coffee, and dinner–high tea–supper vs. lunch–dinner.

In the analysis of Lipset (1963), on the other hand, deference related to class differences has a central place. He says that "Britain has come to accept the values of achievement in its economic and educational system, and to some extent in its political system..." (p. 215) and in general the economy and the polity are characterized by achievement and universalism (p. 217). At the same time, Britain retains a social class system involving diffuse deference to those with higher status, so that elitist tendencies extend to the economy and polity as well. (It would seem that Lipset's "elitism" and "universalism" are in some conflict for which some resolution is needed. In the sporting metaphor, everyone may follow the same "rules of the game," but the "gentlemen" and the (non-gentlemen) "players" were usually not playing in the same game.)

According to Lipset, in contrast to the "insulative" nature of the traditional German and French aristocracy, it has historically been possible to *achieve* entry into the "incorporative" British elite, to which some deference is then *ascribed*. Lipset argues that the British type of elitist democracy (as compared with the populist tendencies in the more equalitarian American one) is more

[1] Snowman (1977, p. 117) cites an account by a working-class student at Oxford who decides that what he is missing is interpersonal warmth.

likely to support the "rules of the game," with tolerance of opposition and of non-conformity, and respect for due process of the law (p. 268).

The Protestant ethic

It would be an interesting effort – which will not be attempted seriously here – to trace the roots of English characteristics into the Puritan and non-Puritan traditions. It is clear that the last four of the six characteristics considered earlier could, as forms of "self-restraint," be related to Puritan asceticism. But it is not clear that the Puritan tradition did not also contribute to the other two emphases on the "rules of the game" and the "public virtues." Thus, as regards "fair play," while Puritan asceticism opposed sports as such,[1] it also included strong equalitarian tendencies and opposed privilege. In general, one could assume that characteristics associated with the aristocracy would represent the non-Puritan tradition. For example, it is the aristocracy, secure in their ascribed status positions, who provide the most striking example of eccentricity that would be unlikely among Americans.

In his comparative study of Britain and America, Snowman (1977) treats the "Puritan ethic" as primarily American, to which, however, the British were susceptible to some aspects. The main reason is that he treats the "Puritan ethic" as primarily the "work ethic," with only secondary attention to other aspects such as thrift, extra-marital chastity, and charity. In any case, if we follow Weber's conception where equal emphasis is given to systematic "worldly" work and achievement, and to systematic "asceticism," it is consistent with Snowman's comparison of the British and Americans to say that the British emphasize more the latter and the Americans the former. This difference is also deserving of explanation.

We will now consider more systematically the relation of the English to the different aspects of the Protestant ethic.

Asceticism. In Weber's broad usage, asceticism is equivalent to the "self-restraint" that Snowman (1977) makes the central British characteristic, and which we have subdivided here into four (of six) main English characteristics. Although there may have been a decline in some of these, we have already seen that they have persisted into the contemporary period.

Work and achievement. Snowman (1977, p. 108) argues that the work ethic – the grafting of a strong moral sanction onto the performance of hard work – did not become widespread in Britain until the Industrial Revolution, whereas in America "it was a major social value pre-dating industrialization

---

[1] Weber (1930, pp. 166–8) pointed to the attempt of James I and Charles I to impose *The book of sports* "expressly as a means of counteracting Puritanism." This met with the "fanatical opposition of Puritans" as involving the "impulsive enjoyment of life."

by two centuries." Moreover, it is widely thought that the ethic of work and achievement has declined for the English since the Victorian era and especially since 1945; with the coming of the "welfare state," Weber's "iron cage" of working for economic necessity has been bent, and England moved toward a consumption-oriented society. According to Glyn (p. 250), work is no longer valued as an end-in-itself (as it might be by the Germans or the Swiss), but only as a means to earning a living or to accomplish something.

The non-Puritan aristocratic tradition never favored the work ethic as such. On the contrary, it was important to avoid (appearing to) work for money and especially with one's hands (Snowman, 1977, pp. 109, 110–12). However, in contrast to other aristocracies, idleness was to be avoided in favor of doing something useful, preferably for those less fortunate than oneself or for the common good, but at least for one's self-respect (Glyn, 1970, pp. 252–4; Snowman, 1977, p. 114). (Since Glyn holds that unpaid activity for oneself and voluntary activity are considered forms of work, one could argue that the work ethic is simply present in a different form.) This shades off into the important English cult of the "amateur," which includes distrust of the expert in favor of common sense and versatility (Glyn, 1970, pp. 211–12, 228–9; Snowman, 1977, pp. 110–11).

Individualism. We have included individualism in the Protestant ethic under the two related themes of individual responsibility for achievement and individual freedom from interference by others. Both of these have been important themes of English culture but perhaps in less extreme forms than for Americans. According to Snowman's (1977) comparison, the first is modified by the British being more group-oriented and less individualistic: competition is more likely on behalf of one's group against another (p. 113), and there is less optimism about social mobility, a result of the immobilizing effects of one's membership in a social class (p. 131).

Individual liberty remains an important English value, which (in contrast to the Americans and the French) clearly takes precedence over equality (Snowman, 1977, pp. 115–28).

Practicality/empiricism. This characteristic has been a multi-faceted part of English culture. Perhaps the best-known aspects are in the legal and political spheres, with the absence of a legal code (in favor of common law based on concrete cases) and of any written constitution. Historically, the English emphasis on science and technology was the source of the Industrial Revolution. In philosophy, the British tradition of empiricism, emphasizing sense experience rather than rational thought, continues into the present. Although practicality and empiricism are thus clearly identifiable in the English cultural tradition, for some reason they have not been emphasized by writers on the national characteristics of individuals.

"Universal otherhood." This characteristic involves a tendency to treat everyone equally as like strangers. We may distinguish the general tendency not to separate sharply between "public" and "private" relationships, which – we will argue – is shared with Americans, and the specific form which this tendency takes, which is different for the English and the Americans. We have already discussed the latter under the English characteristic of "reserve." We will here comment briefly on the general tendency to treat everyone alike as expressed in the English language.

The tendency not to make a sharp distinction between public and private relationships is nicely paralleled by the disappearance in the English language of the distinction between "you" and "thou/thee" comparable to distinctions that remain in other European languages. According to Jespersen's (1968, p. 223) account, the Quakers objected to the distinction as

obscuring the equality of all human beings; they therefore *thou'd* (or rather *thee'd*) everybody. But the same democratic leveling that they wanted to effect in this way was achieved a century and a half later in society at large...when the pronoun *you* was gradually extended to the lower classes and thus lost more and more of its previous character of deference.

This period coincides with the growth of industrial capitalism with its tendencies toward universalistic relationships. As will be argued below, a comparable (although different) lack of sharp distinction between public and private relationships is to be found among Americans. This case seems to provide an example of the much criticized Sapir–Whorf hypotheses, at least in the weak form that predicts parallels between language and life (as opposed to the strong form that implies that the linguistic factors are the causally determining ones).

To summarize: nearly all of the characteristics of the Protestant ethic can be found in English traditions, but there is reason to think that many of them are now on the decline.

Comparison with empirical results

We will present results for all groups of judges, but will generally comment only on the consensus and the ingroup judgments. Table 7.1 presents summary results for judgments about the English on the two major descriptive dimensions. The consensus judgments are that the English are high on impulse-control and low on assertiveness. (Since the latter result generally involves low positive rather than negative relationships, it could justifiably be called only "non-assertive" rather than "unassertive." But in comparison with the other large nationalities included as standard targets, the English are judged the least assertive.) Both of these consensus results have close parallels

Table 7.1. *Judgments about the English: summary*

Judges	Descriptive factors	
	Tight–Loose	Assertive–Unassertive
Consensus	0.69	0.18
English	0.37	0.16
Germans	0.80	−0.07
French	0.72	0.12
Italians	0.84	0.39
Austrians	0.71	0.20
Finnish	0.72	0.28
Greeks	0.85	0.30

in our earlier list of English characteristics: the several characteristics related to self-restraint, and the avoidance of obvious self-assertiveness.

The ingroup judgments by the English judges agree with the consensus regarding the low assertiveness, but differ from the consensus in recognizing only a moderate degree of impulse-control. Detailed results for the scales are given in Table 7.2.

Impulse-control. The consensus judgments show a descriptive component of notable size in the direction of Tight impulse-control on *all* of the first seven sets of scales, as well as the other scales (8a and 9a) with a strong relation to this dimension, and even those scales (13a and 14a) where the relation is weaker. Thus the consensus gives large ratings on all of the "Tight" virtues for the English as *thrifty, self-controlled, serious, skeptical, firm, persistent, selective, cautious,* and *calm.* These results are strongly in accord with Snowman's use of "self-restraint" as the central British characteristic.

In contrast, the ingroup judgments by the English judges for *no* pair of scales indicate the same degree of impulse-control as the consensus. For the ingroup, the descriptive component is in this direction to a "notable" degree (at least 0.5) only on set 2 (*self-controlled/inhibited*), and shows an actual reversal of direction on sets 1, 3, and 4. On these latter cases, the ingroup judgments (in contrast to the consensus) rate the English as *generous* (*extravagant*) rather than *thrifty* (*stingy*), and as *gay,* and *trusting.*

How might one explain these differences between the ingroup judgments and the consensus judgments indicating consistent impulse-control? Several of the judgment principles proposed in Chapter 3 might be relevant.

Following the discussion there (p. 40 above), the existence of actual reversals by the ingroup of the direction of consensus judgment leads us to focus on the principles of descriptive consistency and of perceived change. As between these two principles, the principle of "descriptive consistency" is favored if the ingroup choice represents a relatively long-run exception. There are several candidates as such long-run English characteristics among the ingroup choices that differ from the consensus – e.g., *flexible* rather than *inflexible*, *broad-minded* rather than *choosy*. According to the principle of descriptive consistency, in outgroup judgments these characteristics are more likely to be made consistent with the overall dimension of impulse-control.

In contrast, the principle of "perceived change" is favored if the ingroup choices represent relatively "new" national characteristics. Possible candidates among the ingroup choices might include *gay* and *generous/extravagant*. According to the principle of perceived change, changes will be perceived sooner by the ingroup than by outgroups. One would prefer to have other evidence for the relevant change (or at least apparent change). In the present case, one could argue that there *was* evidence for change toward impulse-expressiveness in the England of the 1960s with the "swinging London" of the Beatles and the miniskirt.

Assertiveness. The English are judged less assertive than any of the other five standard targets – this appears most clearly on scale 10a where, in consensus judgments, the English are judged *peaceful*, while all the other standard targets are judged *aggressive*. These results fit the proposals earlier that the English avoid obvious assertiveness, and tend to inhibit aggression. In addition to the unassertive virtues, the English generally receive favorable ratings for the assertive virtues as well (e.g., as *bold*, *active*, *forceful*) and so pile up favorable evaluative components on these sets. On set 11, the ingroup judgments follow a similar pattern, but the consensus judgments are clearly in the assertive direction – as *self-confident/conceited* – judgments that are given to nearly all targets. On set 9, the difference tends to be the other way around; the ingroup judgments indicate that the English are more *active* and less *calm* than the consensus.

Other scales. On set 12 there is disagreement, which is unusual between outgroup judges, about the direction of the descriptive component. The English are judged more *cooperative* and *conforming* by the French and Italian judges, and more *independent* and *uncooperative* by the Austrians and Greeks. This set may represent a conflict dilemma between the individualism included in the Protestant ethic, and the stress on cooperation (cf. "not letting down the side").

Relevant to the "public virtues," the English are judged *tactful* – far more so than any of the other standard targets.

The judgment of the English as *practical* is consistent with a traditional English characteristic.

On the primarily evaluative scales, the consensus judgments of the English as *admirable* and *likeable* are slightly more favorable than for an average target.

Table 7.2. *Judgments about the English*

Scales	Consensus	Judges						
		Eng.	Germ.	Fr.	Ital.	Aust.	Finn.	Greek
1a. Thrifty (+)-Extravagant (-)	0.9	-0.1	1.3	0.8	1.0	0.8	1.6	0.7
b. Stingy (-)-Generous (+)	-0.4	0.6	-0.4	0.0	-1.2	-0.5	-0.7	-0.2
Evaluative component	+0.3	+0.2	+0.5	+0.4	-0.1	+0.1	+0.4	+0.3
Descriptive component	0.6A	0.3B	0.9A	0.4A	1.1A	0.6A	1.1A	0.4A
2a. Self-controlled (+)-Impulsive (-)	1.8	1.0	2.2	1.6	2.2	1.7	2.1	1.4
b. Inhibited (-)-Spontaneous (+)	-0.2	-0.3	0.0	-0.1	-0.4	0.1	-0.4	-0.7
Evaluative component	+0.8	+0.4	+1.1	+0.8	+0.9	+0.9	+0.9	+0.4
Descriptive component	1.0A	0.6A	1.1A	0.8A	1.3A	0.8A	1.3A	1.1A
3a. Serious (+)-Frivolous (-)	1.0	0.8	1.1	0.4	1.3	1.4	1.2	1.7
b. Grim (-)-Gay (+)	0.0	0.9	0.6	0.2	-0.8	-0.5	0.2	-0.4
Evaluative component	+0.5	+0.8	+0.6	+0.3	+0.3	+0.5	+0.7	+0.6
Descriptive component	0.5A	0.1B	0.6B	0.1A	1.0A	1.0A	0.5A	1.0A
4a. Skeptical (+)-Gullible (-)	1.1	0.6	1.4	0.9	1.8	1.2	0.7	1.4
b. Distrustful (-)-Trusting (+)	-0.2	0.9	-0.5	0.0	-1.4	-0.5	0.2	-0.2
Evaluative component	+0.4	+0.7	+0.4	+0.5	+0.2	+0.3	+0.4	+0.6
Descriptive component	0.7A	0.1B	0.9A	0.5A	1.6A	0.8A	0.3A	0.8A
5a. Firm (+)-Lax (-)	1.0	1.0	0.9	0.3	1.3	1.1	1.3	1.3
b. Severe (-)-Lenient (+)	-0.2	0.3	0.2	-0.2	-1.2	-0.5	0.3	-1.1
Evaluative component	+0.4	+0.7	+0.6	0.0	0.0	+0.3	+0.8	+0.1
Descriptive component	0.6A	0.4A	0.3A	0.2A	1.2A	0.8A	0.5A	1.2A
6a. Persistent (+)-Vacillating (-)	1.4	1.2	1.5	0.9	1.8	1.5	1.3	1.4
b. Inflexible (-)-Flexible (+)	-0.5	0.7	-0.7	-0.4	-1.2	-1.3	-0.3	-1.2
Evaluative component	+0.4	+0.9	+0.4	+0.3	+0.3	+0.1	+0.5	+0.1
Descriptive component	1.0A	0.3A	1.1A	0.7A	1.5A	1.4A	0.8A	1.3A
7a. Selective (+)-Undiscriminating (-)	1.4	1.2	1.4	0.8	1.5	1.7	1.7	1.3
b. Choosy (-)-Broad-minded (+)	-0.1	0.4	1.0	-0.5	-1.1	0.8	-1.4	0.0
Evaluative component	+0.6	+0.8	+1.2	+0.2	-0.2	+1.2	+0.1	+0.6
Descriptive component	0.8A	0.4A	0.2A	0.7A	1.3A	0.5A	1.6A	0.7A
8a. Cautious (+)-Rash (-)	1.4	1.2	1.9	0.8	2.1	1.1	1.3	1.5
b. Timid (-)-Bold (+)	0.4	0.6	0.2	0.3	0.1	0.8	0.6	1.3

Evaluative component	+0.9	+0.9	+1.0	+0.5	+1.1	+1.0	+0.9	+1.4
Descriptive component	0.5A	0.3A	0.9A	0.3A	1.0A	0.1A	0.3A	0.1A
9a. Calm (+)–Agitated (−)	1.6	0.8	1.8	1.4	1.9	1.8	1.6	0.9
b. Inactive (−)–Active (+)	0.8	1.2	−0.3	0.7	1.9	−0.4	1.4	0.8
Evaluative component	+1.1	+1.0	+0.8	+1.1	+1.9	+0.7	+1.5	+0.8
Descriptive component	0.4A	0.2B	1.0A	0.4A	0.0	1.1A	0.1A	0.1A
10a. Peaceful (+)–Aggressive (−)	1.2	0.8	1.5	1.6	0.8	0.6	1.7	0.9
b. Passive (−)–Forceful (+)	0.6	0.2	0.3	0.4	0.9	0.2	1.5	0.6
Evaluative component	+0.9	+0.5	+0.9	+1.0	+0.8	+0.4	+1.6	+0.7
Descriptive component	0.3A	0.3A	0.6A	0.6A	0.1B	0.2A	0.1A	0.1A
11a. Modest (+)–Conceited (−)	−0.4	0.6	0.0	−0.5	−1.1	−1.0	−0.7	0.4
b. Unassured (−)–Self-confident (+)	1.4	0.6	1.6	1.2	1.8	1.7	1.6	1.3
Evaluative component	+0.5	+0.6	+0.8	+0.4	+0.4	+0.3	+0.5	+0.9
Descriptive component	0.9B	0.0	0.8B	0.9B	1.4B	1.4B	1.1B	0.5B
12a. Cooperative (+)–Uncooperative (−)	0.4	1.4	0.0	0.4	0.7	−0.9	0.9	−0.3
b. Conforming (−)–Independent (+)	0.1	0.0	−0.1	−0.4	−0.4	0.1	1.4	0.5
Evaluative component	+0.3	+0.7	+1.5	+0.7	+0.2	−0.4	+1.2	+0.1
Descriptive component	0.2A	0.7A	0.5A	0.4A	0.5A	0.5B	0.2B	0.4B
13a. Tactful (+)–Tactless (−)	1.6	0.9	2.0	1.2	1.9	1.7	1.9	1.6
b. Devious (−)–Frank (+)	0.7	1.0	1.1	0.1	0.2	0.7	1.0	0.4
Evaluative component	+1.1	+0.9	+1.5	+0.7	+1.0	+1.2	+1.5	+1.0
Descriptive component	0.5A	0.0	0.5A	0.6A	0.8A	0.5A	0.4A	0.6A
14a. Practical (+)–Impractical (−)	1.2	1.2	1.1	0.6	1.8	1.4	1.1	1.4
b. Opportunistic (−)–Idealistic (+)	0.1	0.4	0.3	0.0	0.1	0.7	−0.6	0.3
Evaluative component	+0.7	+0.8	+0.7	+0.3	+1.0	+1.0	+0.2	+0.9
Descriptive component	0.5A	0.4A	0.4A	0.3A	0.8A	0.4A	0.9A	0.5A
15a. Admirable (+)–Deplorable (−)	0.6	1.1	0.4	0.6	0.7	0.3	0.7	0.5[a]
b. Not likeable (−)–Likeable (+)	0.9	1.4	1.3	1.1	−0.1	0.5	1.3	—
Evaluative component	+0.8	+1.2	+0.9	+0.8	+0.3	+0.4	+1.0	—
Descriptive component	0.1B	0.2B	0.5B	0.3B	0.4A	0.1B	0.3B	—
16. Hard-working (+)–Lazy (−)	0.9	0.7	0.8	0.9	0.6	0.7	1.5	0.3
17. Intelligent (+)–Stupid (−)	1.3	1.7	1.0	1.1	1.4	1.2	1.5	0.8

[a] In set 15, the Greek judges used the single scale, *desirable–undesirable*.

In contrast to the historic view of England as "perfidious Albion," only the Italian judges do not rate the English as "likeable." As regards the consensus judgments of the English as *intelligent* and *hard-working*, the former puts them in the highest rated category (together with the Germans and the Russians) but the latter puts them in a middle category, below these same two nationalities, and together with the Americans. This last result is consistent with the suggestion that the English are no longer on the highest level for the traditional work ethic.

Conclusion

Although our comments have tended to emphasize differences between the ingroup judgments and the consensus, there is, nevertheless, overall agreement between them: the average correlation between ingroup judgments and the other five standard judges is 0.33 (as against an average correlation between the latter of 0.75).

The consensus judgments are clearly in general agreement with accounts of English national character. The departures from the consensus by the ingroup judgments may be attributed to lower descriptive consistency in the ingroup judgments, and to greater recognition of apparent change toward greater impulse-expression.

8 The Germans

The "unsurmounted past" of the National Socialist period from 1933 to 1945 was not without effect on accounts of German national characteristics. The theory of the "authoritarian personality" and that of German national character became virtually identical.

At worst, some of these accounts came close to implying a categorical view of German national character, in some respects not too different from the racist theories which reached their extreme in the National Socialist period. Indeed, Roger Brown (1965) suggests a comparison between the authoritarian personality and the types of the German psychologist Jaentsch, a comparison that could easily be put into one of our cross-classifications, perhaps closest to set 6: *persistent* ($+$)/*inflexible* ($-$) vs. *flexible* ($+$)/*vacillating* ($-$).

Comparison of two typologies (after Brown, 1965)

	Germans	vs.	Contrast
Jaentsch	J-type (good) *stable*		Anti-type (bad) *unstable*
Authoritarian personality	Authoritarian (bad) *rigid*		Democratic (good) *flexible*

Obviously, it is incumbent on our approach to separate evaluative and descriptive aspects of German national characteristics.

Actually, if one considers accounts of German national characteristics over a longer historical period these provide some of the best evidence against a racially inherited, and so basically unchanging, view of national characteristics. Consider Madame de Stael (1859), who made observations about the Germans while exiled by Napoleon I, at a time when the power relations between France and Germany were the reverse of those in more recent times. Some of her descriptions contrast sharply with the more recent versions of the Germans as overbearing, energetic, militaristic conformists. She describes the Germans as not "haughty" (p. 37), "slow and inert" (p. 35), "lacking military spirit" (p. 39), and showing "independence of spirit" (p. 39) (in contrast to the responsiveness to others of the French). Many accounts of German characteristics contrast the "two Germanies" – the peaceful, scholarly

Germany of "poets and thinkers" and the aggressive "furor teutonicus" of the two world wars. This appears strikingly in Emil Ludwig (1943), who treats all of German history as an alternation between the two Germanies, between periods of cultural achievement and political weakness alternating with periods of political strength and cultural decline. In the last century, there tends to be a switch from the former to the latter picture that coincides with the increased political and military role of united Germany from 1871 to 1945.

Hellpach's characteristics

We must certainly include a consideration of the views of Willy Hellpach (1954) a long-time observer of German characteristics, who was also a candidate for German President in 1925 and received a million and a half votes. Hellpach suggest six "partial constants" of German national character:

1. *The urge to work.*
2. *Thoroughness.*
3. *Love of order* – "Ordnungsliebe" – this usually suggests primarily the ordering of things, but Hellpach uses it mainly for the acceptance of the social order.
4. *Rejection of civility*, including coarseness and bad manners.
5. *Willfulness.* Hellpach explicates it as a "volatile stubbornness."
6. *Romanticism.*

Hellpach's characteristics will not be considered separately, but will be related to the relevant parts of the discussion below.

Lipset's analysis of value patterns

In Lipset's account (1963, pp. 232–9), Germany is the obverse of France, in that the working class had earlier access to the economy than to the polity. Until 1918 at least, ascriptive and particularistic values were maintained in the non-economic areas of life, while the economic order encouraged achievement and universalism but not equalitarianism. Many conservative groups never accepted the Weimar republic and its universalistic norms. The support for Nazism has been linked to the German emphasis on ascription and elitism. Since 1945 major changes appear to have developed that weaken ascriptive and particularistic values. Nevertheless, ascriptive, elitist values are far from dead: men are reacted to in terms of status positions, and elite groups claim a diffuse respect.

Implications from Weber

Germany, divided by the most ferocious struggle between Protestants and Catholics, was in the end unified under Lutheran Prussia and the unified country was in majority Protestant. In West Germany since World War II the majority has been somewhat the other way around, but we might nevertheless expect some overall influence from Lutheran and north German traditions. In any case, their relative distinctiveness implies that the Lutheran and north German traditions will be more emphasized by observers.

Weber ascribes to Luther what we have called the "work ethic" – work in one's "calling" has value in itself – but not the other features of the Puritan ethic. It was in Calvinist Protestantism, according to Weber, that systematic work (and systematic asceticism) were means to an end (proof of salvation for the Protestant ethic, later replaced by economic achievement in the "spirit of capitalism"). This would seem to open up the logical possibility of distinguishing between work as an end in itself (as a possible Lutheran and German characteristic) and work as a means to achievement (as a Puritan characteristic). It was in an effort to allow for this possibility that in presenting the Protestant ethic we distinguished within Weber's "worldly" activity between work as an end (which we called the "work ethic") and achievement motivation. But Weber does not himself develop this possibility, and indeed provides an anecdote (Weber, 1930, p. 283) implying that around 1900 the work ethic existed in more extreme form among Americans than Germans. However the situation may then have been, the work ethic (Hellpach's "urge to work") seems a prominent German characteristic perhaps most distinctively among the working class, and spectacularly so in the period immediately after World War II in relation to the West German "economic miracle" of the 1950s.

Otherwise, Weber's singleminded concern with Calvinism means that he mentions the Germans only incidentally as contrasting cases that lack systematic asceticism. Nevertheless, some of Weber's general concepts seem useful for an account of German characteristics. More specifically, where the Protestant ethic involves a combination of "rationality" and "worldly asceticism," one can consider "rationality" separately as a central German characteristic.

Some German characteristics

1. *Systematization.* A central characteristic is a tendency to "rationality":[1] the systematization of ideas and actions, and the relationship between the two.

---

[1] This characteristic was suggested in a discussion by several Austrian colleagues, asked to comment on the crucial difference between Germans and Austrians, in view of the obvious similarities.

Hellpach's "thoroughness" clearly belongs here. In larger systems, some principle tends to be traced back to its ultimate origins and forward to its final application. But even relatively minor matters tend to be related back at least one step to a more general rule – e.g., "X is done on this occasion because X is generally done." One is reminded of the "principle of sufficient reason" of the German philosopher Leibniz: there is always a sufficient reason why something should be or should not be. As one illustration, in a comparison of German and American adolescents, McClelland *et al.* (1958) point to significantly greater agreement by their German subjects with the statement: "A child should never be asked to do anything unless he is told why he is asked to do it."

This systematization tends to be applied to all spheres of life and not especially to the economic one. Thus, while "efficiency" is attributed to both Germans and Americans (Karlins *et al.*, 1969), the American examples that come to mind are economic ones, while the German examples are as likely to involve the armed forces, or even the state bureaucracy.

It is instructive to compare this German tendency with the French, who are also said to show tendencies toward "rational" systematization. The German version seems to differ from the French in at least two respects. First, at least in the last century, the Germans were more likely to carry out their ideas in action. (Significantly, this is less true of accounts before 1871, where the Germans were held to separate ideas from actions.) Secondly, the premises or ends to which the systematization is applied are often for the Germans not the rational ones of the Enlightenment, but those of nineteenth-century Romanticism, emphasizing tradition and emotions (Hellpach's "Romanticism").[1] This can lead to the apparent paradox of a systematic "rationality" being applied to "irrational" premises. This is one way of describing National Socialism.

2. *Supra-individual goals*. As already suggested, the ends to which systematization is applied are not typically (as in capitalism) those of individual economic gain. These ends – as also the related political ones of individualistic liberal democracy – tend to be seen by Germans as selfish. Instead, there is a tendency to prefer supra-individual goals. McClelland *et al.* (1958) emphasize this point in their German/American comparison, and argue that German "obedience,"

---

[1] In terms of the four meanings of "rational" considered in Chapter 6, what is proposed here is that (a) the Germans and French share "rational" tendencies for systematic rules (e.g., bureaucracy, a legal code) and systematization of ideas (e.g., rationalism in philosophy), but the Germans extend the use of rules more broadly into all spheres of life, and in particular to the relation of ideas to action; (b) the Germans and French may differ concerning ends or premises that follow "Romanticism" or "reason."

Much more could be added (e.g., Craig, 1982) for a more complete account of the relative failure of the Enlightenment, and the influence of Romanticism – for example the special roles of "Nature" (Mosse, 1964) and of music.

rather than being a separate personality trait, itself reflects a commitment to an idealistic obligation to society as a whole. This idealism need not take a political form, although it may be converted into this.

3. *Rules of the social order.* In public life, these supra-individual goals, and the rules following from them, are thought to apply to everyone. According to Dahrendorf (1969), Germans traditionally tried to avoid conflict in society on substantive issues (necessary for liberal democracy) but to seek authoritative solutions in some synthesis representing a single goal for society as a whole.

Where the Anglo-American model emphasizes procedural rules and general substantive principles, the Germans tend to have more specific substantive rules. The public rules are considered what Weber calls a "legitimate order" (cf. Hellpach's "love of order") – these rules have ethical legitimacy, and one has a duty not only for carrying them out oneself, but supervising that others do so as well. (Germans will often spontaneously offer as justification for these rules a version of Kant's "categorical imperative": if everyone broke the rule the social order would break down.) Two examples of responsibility for supervising others: (a) at least until recently strange adults would take responsibility for correcting the behavior of children in public (unlikely, for example, for Americans); (b) it has happened in both Germany and Austria that in parking a car in a limited space, a passer-by has closely supervised and commented upon the possibility of touching the bumper of the adjacent cars. In America such concern would be likely only from an owner of one of these cars.

This didactic affirmation of the rules of the "legitimate order" is consistent with a degree of friction in social interaction. In Dahrendorf's terminology, such interaction does not demand the "public virtues" (of the English and Americans): behavior that is affable, frictionless (and impersonal). The Germans see this as "dishonest, unnatural, and above all, hypocritical" (Dahrendorf, 1969, p. 301). On the other hand, the Germans tend to lack the rules of formal politeness of the French and Italians. The resulting surface abrasiveness of the German public life is Hellpach's "rejection of civility."[1]

4. *The "private virtues."* The "public" sphere is sharply contrasted with a "private" one. In the private sphere, relations with intimates (symbolized linguistically by those addressed as "Du" rather than "Sie") are highly personal, and may involve almost unlimited rights and obligations. According to Dahrendorf, traditionally the important virtues were the "private virtues" favoring interaction that is "immediate, not domesticated by general rules, intent on honesty and profoundness rather than ease and lack of friction" (Dahrendorf, 1969, p. 300). These private virtues contrast with Anglo-

---

[1] Hellpach (1954), focusing on the French/Italian contrast, calls this "rejection of forms."

American tendencies to make no such sharp distinction and to apply the "public virtues" universally. The private virtues apply not only to the expression of negative emotions but also to positive ones. Thus, Weber (p. 127) holds that "the typical German quality often called good nature (*Gemütlichkeit*) or naturalness contrasts strongly...with the effects of that thorough destruction of the *status naturalis* in the Anglo-American atmosphere, which Germans are accustomed to judge unfavorably as narrowness, unfreeness, and inner constraint."

A similar contrast is central to Kurt Lewin's (1936) classic comparison of Germans with Americans. Germans show more "social distance" or less accessibility to "peripheral" parts of the personality open to the public, but greater accessibility to "central" parts of the personality in private relationships.

These same principles extend to the person's relation to himself. Indeed, in Dahrendorf's presentation the "private virtues" begin with oneself: "Private values provide the individual with standards for his own perfection, which is conceived as being devoid of society"[1] (p. 286). This development of one's own personality is what we have called (in Chapter 6) "individuality" (to distinguish it from two versions of "individualism" that relate to the Protestant ethic: individual responsibility for achievement and individual freedom from interference). The emphasis is on accessibility to emotions, and on ideas rather than action. Such tendencies have been related to "subjectivity" and "individualism" in nineteenth-century German philosophy (Ginsberg, 1945).

In relation to politics, the greater ethical value of the private virtues may be interpreted, at least in retrospect, as a compensation for the relative impotency in the public sphere of fragmented pre-unification Germany. After 1871 the same principle can allow for a relegation of politics to "Realpolitik" where ethical values are of minor importance (Mann, 1945, p. 13). Inner freedom and individuality are more important than, and consistent with, what may outwardly appear as conformity.

Impulse-expression

It is clear that there is no general principle, like asceticism, that would condemn sensory pleasures and the expression of emotions. Sensory pleasures, such as food, drink, and sex, are thought to be natural.[2] We have already seen that the expression of negative emotions is ethically approved in at least

---

[1] As mentioned earlier, Dahrendorf goes on to cite Hofstatter's study where "loneliness" was rated positively by Germans, and negatively by Americans.

[2] Bailey (1972, p. 128) goes so far as to propose an explanation for the often-noted observation that German profanity is usually fecal rather than sexual: sex is not wicked at all, whereas dirt, and particularly human excreta, are disapproved by the cult of cleanliness.

two contexts: first, the affirmation of the social rules in the public sphere, and secondly, in private relationships.

Instead of principles, there may be specific rules regarding the circumstances for impulse-expression. Weber (1930, p. 240) pointed to the ad hoc quality of Lutheran ethics for personal conduct. But in general, German rules are not particularly concerned with private morals.

In contrast, the Anglo-American model may lack specific rules, but traditionally included general principles for the inhibition of negative emotions and asceticism at least at a residual level. This can lead to an apparent paradox: an American may see Germans as "up-tight" because of a large number of specific rules (in contrast to American "spontaneous informality") while a German may be struck by a residual asceticism that restricts the American's enjoyment of ordinary pleasures such as food, drink, and sex.

It will be noted that we, like many of the writers we have cited, have repeatedly considered German characteristics by comparison with the English and the Americans. But in many respects it is the latter that are distinctive, and the Germans are basically similar to other nationalities – the Russians, the French, and the Italians and indeed most societies in the world.[1] Some features wherein the Germans differ from the latter – the work ethic, high technology – must encourage the Anglo-American comparisons. In a more general context, we must not expect that the absence of asceticism among Germans will necessarily be reflected in judgments of Germans as impulse-expressive. Moreover, in our own analysis, the expression of aggressive impulses – which, as we have seen, may be favorably sanctioned for Germans – does not appear on the dimension we have called "impulse-expressiveness" but on a second dimension we have called "assertiveness." Thus, an important form of German impulse-expression will not be reflected on the former dimension.

Some data

Some data from Almond and Verba's (1963) *The civic culture* can be used to support what has been said about the contrast between the public and private virtues. In their study, Americans and Britons in contrast to Germans (as well as Italians and Mexicans) more often tended to choose "outgoing" (e.g., group) leisure-time activities (p. 263); to say that they would organize with others to try to influence local government (p. 191); and to say that it would not matter if their child married a supporter of the party they opposed (p. 289).

---

[1] Compare Dahrendorf (1969, p. 290) "...with significant variations in substance, the same dominance of private virtues might be asserted for French, Russian, Italian and Mexican society, and many others as well."

Characteristics from the authoritarian personality

It may be surprising that it has been possible to go through the preceding account without invoking the theory of the "authoritarian personality" (Adorno *et al.*, 1950), or the many related formulations, as by Fromm (1941) and Erikson (1950). What should be taken from these sources to add to our account? We will deal with two points.[1]

The need for structure. We may start with the proposal of Fromm (1941) that humans have a need for some systematic account of the world and of their place in it. The medieval solution to this problem was disrupted by the Reformation, increasing individual freedom but arousing anxiety to find an alternative solution to this need, and thus "escape from freedom." If it is implied that this tendency is particularly strong among Germans – for whatever reason – this is consistent with our first point above regarding a German tendency to seek systematization.

In traditional treatments of German national character the reason would be referred to the geographical situation of Germany in the center of Europe and lacking natural frontiers. In authoritarian personality theory the reason implied would be an overresolution of the Oedipus conflict,[2] resulting in a complete repression of any negative ambivalence toward the overthreatening father. This "intolerance of ambivalence" generalizes as a general cognitive style of "intolerance of ambiguity," involving categorical thinking.

Hierarchical relations. According to the theory, the overresolution of the Oedipus complex is also generalized in other respects. There is a generalized tendency to glorify superordinates, and conversely (by displacement of the repressed hostility originally felt toward the father) to be harsh with subordinates. In the theory these tendencies are called "authoritarian submission" and "authoritarian aggression." Whatever the merits of the theory, it is at least widely accepted that Germans tend to accept clear hierarchical relations. This can take the extreme form of being "crawling before the superordinate; overbearing to the subordinate" – more pleasantly expressed in the metaphor of the "bicyclist" (Morsbach, 1977) who bows forward, but is at the same time treading on something underneath.

[1] Of the other characteristics of the authoritarian syndrome, some are related to qualities already discussed (e.g., Romanticism), while others may be correct descriptions of tendencies in National Socialism but not of Germans generally (e.g., Anti-intraception).

[2] This formulation of the theory is never stated explicitly in *The authoritarian personality*, but is suggested more clearly in Sanford (1956).

Table 8.1. *Judgments about the Germans: summary*

Judges	Descriptive factors	
	Tight–Loose	Assertive–Unassertive
Consensus	0.56	0.58
Germans	0.79	0.10
English	0.58	0.75
French	0.53	0.55
Italians	0.66	0.67
Austrians	0.31	0.80
Finnish (W. Germans)	0.47	0.62
Finnish (E. Germans)	0.77	0.26
Greeks	0.64	0.63

Comparison with judgment results

We will present results for all groups of judges, but will generally comment only on the consensus and the ingroup judgments. Table 8.1 presents summary results for judgments about the Germans on the two major descriptive dimensions. The consensus judgments are that the Germans show comparably high degrees of "Tight" impulse-control and of assertiveness. The ingroup judgments of the German judges agree with the consensus regarding the former, but disagree about the latter, judging Germans as low on assertiveness. Detailed results for the separate scales are given in Table 8.2.

Impulse-control. The judgment of the Germans as impulse-controlled is presented by descriptive components in that direction on *all* of the first seven sets of scales for both the consensus and the ingroup judgments by the German judges. Should such judgments be considered consistent or inconsistent with the preceding accounts of German national character? The answer is not simple, and will be discussed under five points. We will include a comparison with the English, for whom consensus judgments are generally quite similar.

a. Accounts of German national character do not imply that Germans are *generally* impulse-controlled (in the same way as do accounts of the English). Thus we must consider *what* impulses are involved.

b. In particular, asceticism about sensory pleasures is not said to be a German characteristic. However, if we look at the scales actually used we see that their implications are generally *not* about asceticism in the narrower sense. The closest approach is probably set 2 (*self-controlled/inhibited*) which has the most general implications and so might most easily include reference to asceticism. And it is precisely on this set that the consensus descriptive

Table 8.2. Judgments about the Germans

Scales	Consensus	Germ.	Eng.	Fr.	Judges Ital.	Aust.	Finn.[a]	Finn.[b]	Greek
1a. Thrifty (+)-Extravagant (−)	1.1	1.5	0.6	1.5	0.9	0.3	1.9	1.6	1.5
b. Stingy (−)-Generous (+)	−0.3	−0.8	−0.1	1.0	−1.0	0.0	−1.0	−0.9	−1.2
Evaluative component	+0.4	+0.3	+0.2	+1.3	0.0	+0.2	+0.4	+0.3	+0.1
Descriptive component	0.7A	1.2A	0.4A	0.2A	1.0A	0.2A	1.5A	1.2A	1.4A
2a. Self-controlled (+)-Impulsive (−)	0.6	0.0	0.5	0.7	1.3	0.1	1.2	1.2	1.3
b. Inhibited (−)-Spontaneous (+)	0.0	−1.0	−0.2	0.2	−0.2	0.6	0.4	−0.7	0.0
Evaluative component	+0.3	−0.5	+0.1	+0.5	+0.6	+0.3	+0.8	+0.2	+0.6
Descriptive component	0.3A	0.5A	0.3A	0.3A	0.7A	0.2B	0.4A	0.9A	0.6A
3a. Serious (+)-Frivolous (−)	1.3	1.4	1.5	1.4	2.3	0.4	0.8	1.5	1.9
b. Grim (−)-Gay (+)	0.0	−0.4	−0.1	0.7	−1.5	0.5	0.7	−0.1	−0.7
Evaluative component	+0.7	+0.5	+0.7	+1.1	+0.4	+0.4	+0.8	+0.7	+0.6
Descriptive component	0.7A	0.9A	0.8A	0.3A	1.9A	0.0	0.1A	0.8A	1.3A
4a. Skeptical (+)-Gullible (−)	0.8	0.0	1.0	0.1	2.1	0.7	0.9	0.5	1.0
b. Distrustful (−)-Trusting (+)	−0.4	−0.3	−0.3	0.1	−1.7	−0.2	0.1	−0.5	−0.7
Evaluative component	+0.2	−0.1	+0.4	+0.1	+0.2	+0.2	+0.5	0.0	+0.1
Descriptive component	0.6A	0.2A	0.7A	0.0	1.9A	0.4A	0.4A	0.5A	0.8A
5a. Firm (+)-Lax (−)	1.8	0.9	2.1	2.1	2.7	1.5	1.7	1.3	2.0
b. Severe (−)-Lenient (+)	−1.0	+0.5	−1.4	−1.2	−2.5	−0.9	0.2	0.2	−1.8
Evaluative component	+0.4	+0.2	+0.3	+0.5	+0.1	+0.3	+0.9	+0.8	+0.1
Descriptive component	1.4A	0.7A	1.7A	1.7A	2.6A	1.2A	0.7A	0.5A	1.9A
6a. Persistent (+)-Vacillating (−)	1.5	0.6	1.5	1.6	2.4	1.4	1.2	0.6	2.0
b. Inflexible (−)-Flexible (+)	−1.0	−0.5	−0.5	−1.0	−2.7	−0.5	−0.5	−0.3	−1.4
Evaluative component	−0.2	0.0	+0.5	+0.3	−0.2	+0.5	+0.3	+0.1	+0.3
Descriptive component	1.2A	0.6A	1.0A	1.3A	2.6A	1.0A	0.8A	0.5A	1.7A
7a. Selective (+)-Undiscriminating (−)	1.1	−0.2	1.1	0.9	2.4	1.0	1.5	0.8	1.1
b. Choosy (−)-Broad-minded (+)	−0.9	−0.8	−0.6	0.0	−1.5	−0.5	−1.7	−1.4	−0.7
Evaluative component	+0.1	−0.5	+0.2	+0.5	+0.5	+0.2	−0.1	−0.3	+0.2
Descriptive component	1.0A	0.3A	0.8A	0.5A	2.0A	0.8A	1.6A	1.1A	0.9A
8a. Cautious (+)-Rash (−)	0.9	1.1	1.2	0.3	1.5	0.9	0.3	0.8	1.6
b. Timid (−)-Bold (+)	1.0	0.2	1.6	0.7	1.3	1.0	1.3	0.3	1.6
Evaluative component	+1.0	+0.6	+1.4	+0.5	+1.4	+1.0	+0.8	+0.6	+1.6
Descriptive component	0.1B	0.5A	0.2B	0.2B	0.1A	0.0	0.5B	0.3A	0.0

9a. Calm (+)–Agitated (−)	0.4	0.7	0.2	0.7	0.4	0.1	0.6	0.8	−0.5
b. Inactive (−)–Active (+)	1.4	−0.4	1.5	1.9	2.5	0.6	2.4	1.7	2.2
Evaluative component	+0.9	+0.2	+0.8	+1.3	+1.4	+0.3	+1.5	+1.2	+0.8
Descriptive component	0.5B	0.5A	0.7B	0.6B	1.1B	0.3B	0.9B	0.4B	1.3B
10a. Peaceful (+)–Aggressive (−)	−0.6	0.0	−0.6	0.1	−2.0	−0.7	−0.1	0.4	−2.1
b. Passive (−)–Forceful (+)	1.6	0.3	1.4	1.8	2.6	1.4	2.0	1.6	1.1
Evaluative component	+0.5	+0.1	+0.4	+1.0	+0.3	+0.4	+1.0	+1.0	−0.5
Descriptive component	1.1B	0.2B	0.1B	0.8B	2.3B	1.1B	1.0B	0.6B	1.6B
11a. Modest (+)–Conceited (−)	−0.9	−0.5	−0.5	0.0	−1.7	−2.0	−0.5	0.5	0.3
b. Unassured (−)–Self-confident (+)	1.4	0.6	1.7	1.0	2.0	1.6	1.6	0.3	1.8
Evaluative component	+0.3	0.0	+0.6	+0.5	+0.1	−0.2	+0.5	+0.4	+1.0
Descriptive component	1.1B	0.6B	1.1B	0.5B	1.9B	1.8B	1.1B	0.1A	0.8B
12a. Cooperative (+)–Uncooperative (−)	0.5	0.1	0.6	1.0	0.7	−0.3	1.1	1.0	0.8
b. Conforming (−)–Independent (+)	−0.1	−1.3	0.5	−1.1	0.1	−0.3	1.4	−0.3	0.2
Evaluative component	+0.2	−0.6	+0.5	0.0	+0.4	−0.3	+1.2	+0.4	+0.5
Descriptive component	0.3A	0.7A	0.0	1.0A	0.3A	0.0	0.1B	0.6A	0.3A
13a. Tactful (+)–Tactless (−)	0.4	−0.1	0.4	0.7	1.1	−0.7	1.2	0.5	0.7
b. Devious (−)–Frank (+)	0.5	0.5	0.7	1.2	0.2	0.3	0.5	0.7	0.0
Evaluative component	+0.5	0.2	+0.5	+0.9	+0.7	−0.2	+0.8	+0.6	+0.3
Descriptive component	0.1B	0.3B	0.2B	0.2B	0.5A	0.5B	0.3A	0.1B	0.4A
14a. Practical (+)–Impractical (−)	1.3	0.5	1.6	1.1	2.2	1.3	1.3	1.1	2.0
b. Opportunistic (−)–Idealistic (+)	0.1	−0.1	0.2	0.3	1.2	0.4	−1.2	−0.6	−0.1
Evaluative component	+0.7	+0.2	+0.9	+0.7	+1.7	+0.9	0.0	+0.3	+1.0
Descriptive component	0.6A	0.3A	0.7A	0.4A	0.5A	0.5A	1.3A	0.8A	1.0A
15a. Admirable (+)–Deplorable (−)	0.3	−0.4	0.5	0.7	0.3	0.1	0.8	0.2	−0.4c
b. Not likeable (−)–Likeable (+)	0.2	0.3	0.3	1.4	−1.0	−0.7	1.1	0.7	—
Evaluative component	+0.3	0.0	+0.4	+1.1	−0.3	−0.3	+1.0	+0.5	—
Descriptive component	0.0	0.4B	0.1A	0.3B	0.7A	0.4A	0.1B	0.3B	—
16. Hard-working (+)–Lazy (−)	2.0	1.5	1.9	2.1	2.6	2.1	2.0	1.7	2.6
17. Intelligent (+)–Stupid (−)	1.3	0.9	1.7	1.2	2.1	0.8	1.5	1.0	1.4

[a] Finns judging WEST GERMANS.
[b] Finns judging EAST GERMANS.
[c] In set 15, the Greek judges used the single scale, *desirable–undesirable*.

component shows the weakest degree of impulse-control for Germans and a notably lower degree of impulse-control compared to the English.

c. Many of the scales have implications about social relationships, where the German rules about the social order could support an impression of "Tight" impulse-control. The clearest example is set 5 (*firm/severe*), which has some implication of a superordinate–subordinate relationship, where the German rules could allow for harshness toward subordinates. And it is precisely on this set that the consensus judgments about Germans show the strongest degree of Tight control and a notably higher degree compared to the English.

To summarize the last two points: the judgments about Germans as impulse-controlled are not inconsistent with the Germans being un-ascetic. The judgments of Germans as distinctively (a) low or (b) high on impulse-control are on scales that are (a) more related or (b) unrelated to asceticism.

d. For some characteristics the judgments of impulse-control must be compared with accounts of national character which suggest that these are at least conflict dilemmas for Germans. Candidates are sets 4 and 6, where the consensus judges the Germans *skeptical/distrustful*, and *persistent/inflexible*. With regard to the first, it can be argued[1] that the conflict of loyalty vs. betrayal is a central one in German traditions. This suggests that the first of Erikson's conflict dilemmas, trust vs. mistrust, may be a critical one for Germans (as it seems to be – in a different form – for Russians). However, a dilemma implies that one of the conflicting tendencies – here mistrust – should not be permanently dominant. Indeed in accounts of national character, the Germans do not approach the deep mistrust of the Italians and the French. It may be that this is a case of historical change, perhaps temporary – that after an excess of gullibility in the Hitler era, the Germans of the postwar period became relatively *skeptical* and *distrustful*. This hypothesis is consistent with evidence cited by Almond and Verba (1963, p. 268) where 93% of Germans expressed generalized mistrust in 1948, and 59% in 1959.

The consensus of the Germans as *persistent* and *inflexible* compares with Hellpach's discussion of "volatile stubbornness," which implies that *persistent* vs. *vacillating* may be another German conflict dilemma. However, in this case it is easier to argue that the persistent tendencies are more generally manifest and more distinctive.

We conclude that the possible inconsistency (between judgments of Germans as impulse-controlled and accounts of national character) can be largely accounted for.

e. Finally, we have thus far not dealt with the important impulses involving assertiveness and aggression, since in our empirical results these are related to a different descriptive dimension. On the expression of these impulses, the consensus judges the Germans high and the English low.

---

[1] Bailey (1972) is a recent example.

Self-assertiveness. In the consensus judgments, the Germans are not only high on the general dimension of assertiveness (surpassed only by the Americans), but are notably assertive on most of the relevant scales, as *bold, active, forceful,* and *aggressive; self-confident* and *conceited.*

The ingroup judgments are weaker in every case, approaching the vanishing point in all but the last two cases, and show an actual reversal for ingroup judgments of *inactive* where all outgroups judge Germans strongly *active.*

How might one explain this discrepancy between the consensus and the ingroup? If one tries to apply the general judgment principles developed in Chapter 3, they turn out to be unsatisfactory in the present case.[1]

There remain two other possible explanations. It may be that the ingroup judgments reflect the tendency to extend the "character of the nation" to the national characteristics of individuals – a tendency that seemed particularly likely for characteristics related to assertiveness (p. 45 above). Thus, the relative political weakness of post-1945 Germany may have extended in ingroup judgments to Germans as individuals – who may in fact have actually felt less assertive. Such an extension would not apply to outgroup judges, where the consensus judges Germans *more* forceful than any other standard target.

Another possibility is to apply the principle of "behavior vs. conscious experience," which in this case might follow the Jones–Nisbett principle: the outgroups attribute the manifest active behavior as a German characteristic, while the Germans experience themselves as basically inactive but compelled into activity by the demands of the external situation.

In any case the ingroup judgments of low assertiveness appear to be an exception to the rule, suggested by most of our judgment principles, that ingroup judgments are, if anything, likely to be *more* accurate than outgroup judgments.

Other characteristics. On set 12, the consensus is that Germans are *cooperative* and slightly *conforming.* The ingroup judges (together with the French judges) accentuate the *conforming.*

---

[1] This conclusion may be explicated further here. The presence of an actual reversal for *inactive* vs. *active,* leads us to focus on the principles of descriptive consistency and of perceived change. (a) The principle of descriptive consistency could explain the present consensus/ingroup differences, in particular the reversal for *active* vs. *inactive,* if inactivity was recognized as a special long-run German characteristic by the ingroup but not by outgroup judges. But such recognition *was* made *earlier* by outgroup judges: Madame de Stael (1859) described the Germans as "slow and inert": while "stolid" is an adjective (now itself obsolescent) traditionally applied to Germans – for example in the Katz and Braly type studies (Karlins *et al.*, 1969). (b) The principle of perceived change could explain the present results if there has been (at least apparent) change recently toward inactivity, a change so far recognized only by the ingroup. But it is hard to see evidence for this; historical evidence would be consistent with a change in the opposite direction, toward greater activity (and greater assertiveness generally), sometime after 1871.

On set 13 the ingroup judges Germans as *frank* and slightly *tactless*. This is consistent with the stress on candor, representing the "private virtues" ("be truthful") and the lack of "public virtues." But the second judgment (as *tactless*) is shared only by the Austrian judges. (Indeed this set is the subject of many classic contracts between Prussians and Austrians – e.g., Hoffmansthal, 1924). It is puzzling that the other outgroup judges rate the Germans as *tactful*.

On set 14, the strong consensus judgment of the Germans as *practical* is consistent with German technological achievement.

On the primarily evaluative scales, the Germans are the only one of the six standard targets rated more *admirable* than *likeable*.

The rating of the Germans as *hard-working* is much higher, and as *intelligent* slightly higher than for any other standard target. The former finding is consistent with our earlier discussion regarding the "work ethic."

The Finnish judges rated "West Germans" and "East Germans" as separate targets. In general, they rated the East Germans as more impulse-controlled (e.g., *inhibited, serious, grim*) and unassertive (e.g., *peaceful, modest*, and less *self-confident*). Indeed, the Finnish judges' ratings of the East Germans most closely resembles the ingroup judgments by (West) German judges. Two explanations suggest themselves for the differences for the Finnish judges: the differences could reflect the differences in political and economic systems since 1945; the differences could reflect the fact that "East Germans" are from north Germany (and generally "Prussian" in an extended sense of that word). Certainly Prussians would traditionally have been considered more impulse-controlled than Germans in general.

Comparison with other studies

The Katz and Braly type studies (Karlins *et al.*, 1969) include some themes not represented in our own scales. In three studies (from 1933, 1951, and 1967) *scientifically-minded, industrious*, and *methodical* remain frequent choices throughout. After 1933 there is an increase in *aggressive, arrogant*, and *extremely nationalistic*. A more temporary effect occurs for adjectives that decline in 1951 but reappear or increase in 1967: *efficient, progressive*, and *practical*.

Conclusion

Although our comments have emphasized the differences between the ingroup judgments and the consensus, there is overall agreement between them: the average correlation between ingroup judgments and the other five standard judges is 0.59, as against an average correlation between the latter of 0.71.

The overall judgment – by both the consensus and the ingroup – of the Germans as impulse-controlled suggests a possible inconsistency with accounts of German national character, but this can be largely accounted for. The consensus judgment of high assertiveness for Germans is more easily explained than the ingroup judgment of the Germans as low on assertiveness.

9 The French

With Seignobos [who holds that French character became
established during the seventeenth century] we are far from the
notion of an "eternal France" born in some vague period before
the Roman Conquest. What makes his conception more useful to us
is that he bases it on definable social classes:
  It is a peasant, artisan, bourgeois type of character, prudent,
  distrustful, thrifty, much inclined to vanity, very sociable but not
  very hospitable, endowed with a quick, clear, and precise mind,
  more disposed to mockery than to enthusiasm, talking easily and
  enjoying it, skilled in psychological observation, more thoughtful
  than ready speech and frequent gesture might lead a foreigner to
  suppose, accustomed to a regular existence, attached to the habits
  of daily life, abler in individual work than in collective
  undertakings, capable of being good soldiers if forced to it, but
  having no taste for war – in short, very different from the usual
  idea that foreigners hold of French character.

Virtanen, 1967, p. 84

Since the concept of a national character arises out of the comparison
of nations one with another, the best self-portrait is likely to be less
valid than the pictures painted by foreign observers.

Virtanen, 1967, p. 84

It is appropriate to begin consideration of French characteristics with the
recent and extensive treatment by Peyrefitte (1976) on "The French illness."
Peyrefitte's account has the advantages that it parallels the emphasis here on
the factors stressed by Weber; it includes direct reference to several other
writers (e.g., Crozier, Pitts); and it complements several additional analyses
not directly mentioned by Peyrefitte.

Peyrefitte supports, and indeed wants to broaden, the analysis by Weber,
who – Peyrefitte feels – concentrated on the specific problem of capital
formation and the elements of Protestantism leading to it. Peyrefitte wants
a broader contrast between an "economic" mentality and an "anti-economic"
one, with the critical factors from Protestantism being individual responsibility
leading to achievement and to a society of trust.

From the seventeenth century, Peyrefitte sees a divergence between the
underdevelopment of the Latin countries, and other countries that remained

124

Catholic, and the growth of Protestant countries – with comparable differences *within* religiously divided countries. The growth represented a continuation of tendencies that had begun during the Renaissance, and at least as strongly in the Latin countries. Hence, like Luethy (1964), for Peyrefitte the critical factor is not the Reformation itself (which permitted a continuation of these tendencies) but the Counter-reformation (which stifled them). Previously, Christianity had involved two conflicting elements: an emphasis on individual salvation, derived from Jesus, and a hierarchical organization inherited from the Roman empire. These now tended to diverge, with the Reformation emphasizing the first and the Counter-reformation the second. From defensiveness, the Catholic states tended to copy the centralization of the church. Results include: a lack of participation by the individual, immobilism in resisting change leading eventually to polarized opposition and periodic convulsive changes.

France generally follows this Latin model but to a modified degree. The modification Peyrefitte traces primarily to the strength of the French state relative to the church. Able to resist religious control from Rome, the Gallican church could apply the Counter-reformation selectively. Some consequences of the Reformation entered later via the "Enlightenment." The state – especially from the reign of Louis XIV – became the sacred authority, and centralized control by the state has continued to increase through all the later developments.

Pitts (1963) starts with two tendencies in Catholicism similar to Peyrefitte's for Christianity: individual freedom of choice, and the collectivist organization of the church. The French developed the latter more towards perfection of doctrine than organizational discipline: all behavior should have some deductive relation to ideas that incarnate spirituality. Pitts calls this the "doctrinaire-hierarchical" aspect of French culture.

The individualistic aspect also remains within French culture, taking the form of "prowess," where the individual distinguishes himself by action or aesthetic sensibility as a man of honor or taste – now often in the form of consumption and life style. Pitts calls this the "aesthetic-individualistic" aspect of French culture. As taken over from the aristocracy, this includes what Peyrefitte would call "anti-economic" attitudes devaluing production dependent on the random customer.

Two traditional institutions in which these values were expressed are the bourgeois family and the "delinquent community." Pitts describes the French bourgeois family as "a great creation of the human mind," "taking its place in the pantheon of organizations next to the Catholic church, the Roman army, the American corporation, the German general staff, and the British Commonwealth" (p. 254). Acceptance of the legitimate authority of the father is combined with an effort to develop "preferential relationships" with individual members of the family, often in the extended family outside the nuclear family. (This effort – to gain particularistic preference within an apparently universalistic system – may continue outside the family: "France is a nation which operates on multiple circuits of favoritism…wherever there is a queue, there is someone being let in the back way" (de Gramont, 1969, p. 44).)

The prototype of the "delinquent community" is the peer group among school children. Not recognized officially, as in England or America, and not rejecting the legitimacy of the teacher's demand for intellectual performance, the peer group nevertheless develops a "negative solidarity" in providing an atmosphere for expressing individualistic and rebellious tendencies against authority. This is the prototype of other solidary groups beyond the extended family – characterized by jealous equalitarianism among members, and a conspiracy of silence against authority.

Crozier (1964), in an analysis of French organizations that includes a comparative point of view, argues that equalitarianism and resistance to authority (values shared with Americans) have several consequences for French organizations – e.g., an insistence on equality within groups, and a "negative solidarity" directed against outside influence (like Pitts' "delinquent communities"); despite acceptance in principle of the need for authority, there is avoidance of direct face-to-face authority relationships (as in supervision and bargaining), resulting in a lack of communication, or "isolation between strata" within the hierarchy. Two results are mentioned. (1) Authority tends to be converted into impersonal rules. For example, the principle of seniority avoids the authority of superordinates in deciding on promotion. (2) Decisions are referred higher up the centralized hierarchy. For example, labor-management negotiations tend not to take place locally, but are referred to state intervention at the national level.

Lipset (1963) stresses the values of the French Revolution – equalitarianism, as well as universalism and achievement. These values have, at least formally, dominated the political structure (and the government bureaucracy itself), but they did not achieve consensus against the ascriptive–particularistic values of the aristocracy and much of the bourgeoisie, nor some of their key institutional supports, particularly the church. These latter values have persisted in the economy more than for any other industrial nation. Tension arises from the conflict between these values in the economic sector, which facilitates politics along class lines, and the legitimacy of the values of the Revolution, which leads the less privileged sharply to resent their position. The French problem is the obverse of the German one, where the lower classes achieved rights sooner in the economy than in the political system.

The discussion thus far has emphasized mainly characteristics of the social system, and so, for present purposes, still needs further translation into individual characteristics. Such an emphasis on society seems to be especially typical for discussions of the French, a fact that may itself be significant.

Perhaps as a consequence, we have so far touched only tangentially on the quality of Cartesian rationalism, a characteristic that is made the central one in many treatments of the French, such as that of de Madariaga (1928). Peyrefitte suggests that such tendencies (including an abstract curriculum) are characteristic of Latin countries generally, and certainly there is a similar Italian tradition. What is distinctive about the French may simply be the degree of emphasis on the rational. Of the varieties of the "rational" discussed earlier (Chapter 6), the French lack only the version that Weber considered crucial for capitalism – systematic choice of means relative to (long-run) economic ends – but otherwise represent all varieties: (1) systematic choice tends to be based on (more immediate) general self-interest; (2) systematic rules are exemplified not only in the legal codes and the centralized bureaucracy, but also in the less official code of politeness; (3) the relative emphasis is on reasoning over experience (e.g., rationalism vs. empiricism in philosophy); (4) the ends (or premises) themselves emphasize reason rather than Romanticism.

Only a few of the many possible illustrations will be given. As an example from science de Gramont (1969, p. 315) cites the discovery of the planet Neptune by the astronomer Leverrier. "Instead of exploring the heavens with a telescope, he calculated that the hitherto unexplained perturbations in the orbit of the planet Uranus had to be caused by another planet which had escaped the observations of astronomers." He instructed the Berlin observatory where to look for it, but Leverrier himself refused to look into the telescope at the planet he had discovered.

Some of the examples bring out the mutually reinforcing effect of an emphasis on theory combined with a centralized bureaucracy.

A general who devises a perfect battle plan with incomplete information about enemy capacity, and goes on to elegant defeat, is Cartesian. An engineer from the ministry of Ponts et Chaussées who designs a bridge for a town in the Drôme which he has never visited, on the basis of topographical maps, is Cartesian. When he is told that the bridge has been washed away by floods, he merely says: "That is impossible."

(de Gramont, 1969, pp. 318–19.)

Peyrefitte begins his book with an account of a visit to Schweitzer's hospital at Lambaréné in French equatorial Africa. Schweitzer first complains at the French constructing a hospital conceived in Paris and ill-adapted to local conditions. The French have their ideas already preformed. Schweitzer's assistants are generally from Protestant countries:

They face up to reality...while the Latins prefer theory...Consider, even the writer Gilbert Cesbron, who dedicated a book to me [*It is midnight, Doctor Schweitzer*]. He certainly has great talent, but do you believe that he would visit Lambaréné before writing? No. He must have read some newspaper articles. In the first line, my interne says to me: "It is midnight, Doctor Schweitzer, it is time for you to go to bed." And I answer him: "At this hour, the sun is rising in Alsace, the church bell is ringing."

If Cesbron had come to visit here, he would have noticed that he didn't need to change his watch, Alsace and Gabon are situated in the same time zone; so when it is midnight at Lambaréné, it is midnight at Gunsbach.

(Peyrefitte, 1976, pp. 5–6.)

More complex forms of Cartesian rationalism may apply largely to an intellectual elite, so we need to emphasize those that could have wider implications for French life: (1) a tendency to classification and codification; a prominent example is the Napoleonic legal code which attempts to include all possibilities in advance in contrast to the Anglo-American common law system; (2) belief in the power of ideas and in an intellectual caste that is appointed to guard them (de Gramont, 1969, p. 332); (3) an emphasis on orderly (sequential) thought; (4) emphasis on theoretical principles over experience; (5) an emphasis on foresight before action and on control by the intellect.

Impulse-expression. For two important sets of characteristics – impulse-control and social mistrust – we encounter the paradox that they are stressed by analysts of the French (and the Italians), but these qualities are not prominent to surface observation by outsiders. Consideration of impulse-control follows appropriately from that aspect of rationalism that involves emphasis on foresight before action, and control by the intellect.

In the Anglo-American model, there remains a residual asceticism from the Protestant ethic involving internalization of inhibitions against impulse-expression. In the absence of such internalized inhibitions, the Latin model tries to follow the classical Greek goal of moderation by deliberate selection of the circumstance for impulse expression. Virtanen (1967, p. 86) cites Madariaga's comparison of the English and French words for "control": "The Frenchman supervises rather than represses his sensual impulses." In general many of the distinctive French developments – cuisine, wine, fashion, the "art of love" – involve the opposite of Puritan asceticism. "The paradox of a totally uninhibited but totally disciplined attitude toward sex" (de Gramont, 1969, p. 414) nicely illustrates the combination of a lack of internalized inhibitions together with deliberate rational control.

Along these lines, one might account for the apparent paradox that while writers on the French (and Italians) stress the prescriptions for self-control, outside observers generally judge them impulse-expressive.

Consider the principle of "behavior vs. conscious experience" proposed in Chapter 6: outgroup judgments are more dependent on the manifest behavior of the ingroup, while the ingroup may have access to their own conscious experience. In the present case, outgroup judges might be more influenced by the considerable impulse-expressive behavior of the French, but the ingroup is conscious of the effort at deliberate impulse-control. In contrast, a group with more internalized inhibitions might be less conscious of temptations and of an effort to control them, but actually display less manifest impulse-expression.

To push this paradox further toward a more specific example, consider an informal public setting such as a street scene in a French or Italian city. Such settings are generally judged as extraordinarily lively not only by northern Europeans such as the English or Germans (who may *generally* act more formally), but also by Americans (who would generally be considered more informal). Closer examination suggests a point seldom mentioned explicitly: the most important single factor is the open expression – expressed in a variety of ways – of sexual attraction by the males toward the females. This expression applies not only to young females but extends to older women, as would be less likely for Americans. The presumption is that sexual attraction is to be expressed, unless there is some reason not to. In contrast, the Anglo-American presumption is that sexual attraction is not to be expressed (or even experienced) unless there are positive indicators. The Latin presumption involves both more impulse-expression and more deliberate control.

Social mistrust. A comparable paradox pertains to social mistrust. Instead of the optimism of Rousseau, the centralization of the Latin model goes with a pessimistic idea of human nature – an idea of Catholic origin – that people cannot be trusted to decide for themselves (Goguel, 1954). For Peyrefitte this becomes part of a general climate of distrust of others (perhaps of all others outside the family).

In the Anglo-American model, there is internalization of the "public virtues" of generalized friendliness. In the Latin model, social interaction is based on more immediate utilitarian grounds. Thus avoidance of aggression is based less on an internalized ethical norm than on the possibility of retaliation. However, these very grounds oppose the open expression of the distrust or of the utilitarian grounds themselves, which are concealed under a code of polite behavior. The French recognize that these forms are only "the imitations of esteem" and are necessary to avoid social friction.[1] These rules prevent underlying mistrust from being as apparent to outside observers. These rules for the French permit both an unsmiling demeanor in public, and a lively sociability if interaction takes place.

Thus we propose that the paradox about social mistrust, and that of impulse-expression, are both instances of the principle that outside observers are more influenced by behavior, while ingroup members can be more aware of their inner feelings and intentions.

[1] Wylie and Bégué, 1970, pp. 112–13. They say that Americans regard these polite forms as hypocritical, preferring spontaneity. On the other hand (p. 413) the French regard the Americans' "spontaneous" friendliness as superficial and so hypocritical.

Privacy and individuality. The French make sharp distinctions between formal and informal situations, and between public and private spheres. The latter relationships are limited to family and friends. In accordance with Seignobos' description, quoted at the beginning of the chapter, that the French are "sociable but not hospitable," the French are disposed to protect the privacy of home and hearth. In addition, even within the family, recognition is given to a sphere of privacy for the individual (e.g., a child's own room), and a right to personal solitude.

This is consistent with a strong value that is placed on the development of a unique personality and style of life that we have called "individuality."[1] This real "self" of the individual is sharply distinguished from any official role. Wylie and Bégué (1976, p. 132) cite Montaigne's insistence that his real self (Montaigne) was quite distinct from his role as mayor of Bordeaux.

The above features are consistent with what Dahrendorf calls the "private virtues." They tend to represent strong contrasts for the French with Americans, for whom the distinctions between public and private relationships are relatively weak, privacy is treated as relatively unimportant, the demand for individual responsibility in achievement is consistent with conformity in personality and style of life, and the person's occupational role is often central for his self-identity.

Conflict dilemmas. With all of the foregoing as background, it is possible to consider the interesting proposals of Leites (1969). Leites derives his proposals from statements used as illustrations in a French dictionary (Robert), statements by others from Montaigne to Valéry, and from his own observations of French politics in the 1950s.

Leites' proposals are generally in the form of conflict dilemmas like those of Erik Erikson. While Leites sometimes implies that the French show more inclination for one of the conflicting tendencies, in other cases one could only say that both tendencies are important. For a more definite interpretation, we would need once again to introduce a comparative viewpoint: for example, while Leites suggests that carrying through decisions is a conflict dilemma for the French, for other nationalities (e.g., Germans and Americans) this might be less problematical.

Many of the dilemmas proposed by Leites could be cast in the form of some (Cartesian) adult standard that is urged against the natural tendency of the child. However, adults may indulge themselves in this same tendency, which may be stronger than the standard for them. (For example, as against the Cartesian standards of lucidity and precision, Leites emphasizes the tendencies to ambiguity, allusion, and euphemism.) From a Freudian point of view, there

---

[1] Compare the proposals of Pitts, mentioned above, regarding the "aesthetic-individualistic" aspect of French culture.

Table 9.1. *Judgments about the French: summary*

| | Descriptive factors | |
Judges	Tight–Loose	Assertive–Unassertive
Consensus	−0.60	0.52
French	−0.23	0.77
English	−0.63	0.61
Germans	−0.60	0.60
Italians	−0.85	0.11
Austrians	−0.58	0.58
Finns	−0.68	0.45
Greeks	−0.16	0.55

seems to be a striking degree of awareness of the conflicting tendencies (instead of repressing the child-like one). We will mention only a sampling of Leites' proposals: the French value recognition of the complexity of the world, the making of distinctions, disentangling things. Many conditions must be realized for happiness, and action generally presents more dangers (especially from other persons) than opportunities. Hence, there is value in avoiding commitment to a decision, retaining freedom of choice and allowing for flexibility and "suppleness." The dangers of change can lead to immobilism, with action in the end only to avoid a worse outcome. On the other hand, there is more optimism that the situation may improve through waiting, again favoring last-minute action and improvisation.

Regarding impulse-control, the standards stress self-control, reflection, and moderation, the avoidance of waste and the use of small resources by finding the correct trick or gimmick. Aggression is controlled to avoid retaliation. Honesty and frankness may hurt and are dangerous. Appearances are often a façade for a generally less favorable reality.

It is not surprising that other writers than Leites often suggest conflict dilemmas for the French. Peyrefitte's set of reactions to the French situation include both submission and rebellion. Pitts' two sets of values ("doctrinaire-hierarchical" and "aesthetic-individualistic") may reflect a similar conflict. Virtanen (1967, p. 86) suggests dilemmas between "logicality and impulsiveness" and between "idealism and realism."

Comparison with empirical results

We will report results for all groups of judges, but will generally comment only on the consensus and ingroup judgments. Table 9.1 presents a summary of judgments about the French relative to the two major descriptive dimensions. The consensus judgments for the French indicate "Loose" impulse-

Table 9.2. Judgments about the French

Scales	Consensus	Judges						
		Fr.	Eng.	Germ.	Ital.	Aust.	Finn.	Greek
1a. Thrifty (+)–Extravagant (−)	−0.8	−0.5	−0.6	−1.3	−0.7	−1.1	−0.9	−0.3
b. Stingy (−)–Generous (+)	0.7	−0.4	0.5	1.4	1.1	0.9	0.6	−0.2
Evaluative component	−0.1	−0.4	−0.1	+0.1	+0.2	−0.1	−0.2	0.0
Descriptive component:	0.8B	0.0	0.6B	1.3B	0.9B	1.0B	0.7B	0.2A
2a. Self-controlled (+)–Impulsive (−)	−1.0	−1.0	−1.4	−0.6	−1.0	−1.4	−0.6	0.1
b. Inhibited (−)–Spontaneous (+)	1.4	0.8	0.9	1.5	1.5	1.8	2.1	1.2
Evaluative component	+0.2	−0.1	−0.2	+0.4	+0.2	+0.2	+0.8	+0.7
Descriptive component	1.2B	0.9B	1.2B	1.0B	1.3B	1.6B	1.3B	0.6B
3a. Serious (+)–Frivolous (−)	−0.8	−0.7	−0.5	−0.6	−1.0	−0.3	−1.7	−0.2
b. Grim (−)–Gay (+)	1.7	1.6	1.5	1.8	2.0	1.4	2.1	1.2
Evaluative component	+0.4	+0.4	+0.5	+0.6	+0.5	+0.5	+0.2	+0.5
Descriptive component	1.3B	1.2B	1.0B	1.2B	1.5B	0.8B	1.9B	0.7B
4a. Skeptical (+)–Gullible (−)	0.1	0.6	−0.2	0.7	0.0	0.0	−0.6	1.0
b. Distrustful (−)–Trusting (+)	0.1	−0.8	0.2	0.3	1.1	0.0	−0.1	−1.0
Evaluative component	+0.1	−0.1	0.0	+0.5	+0.5	0.0	−0.4	+0.5
Descriptive component	0.0	0.7A	0.2B	0.2A	0.5B	0.0	0.2B	1.0A
5a. Firm (+)–Lax (−)	−0.2	−0.8	0.3	0.1	−0.6	0.0	−0.3	0.3
b. Severe (−)–Lenient (+)	0.3	−0.6	−0.1	0.2	1.1	0.3	1.1	0.7
Evaluative component	+0.1	−0.7	+0.1	+0.1	+0.2	+0.2	+0.4	+0.5
Descriptive component	0.3B	0.1B	0.2A	0.1B	0.9B	0.2B	0.7B	0.2B
6a. Persistent (+)–Vacillating (−)	−0.2	−0.1	0.7	−0.2	−0.9	−0.6	−0.2	0.3
b. Inflexible (−)–Flexible (+)	0.7	−1.0	0.4	1.5	1.4	1.1	0.8	0.5
Evaluative component	+0.2	−0.6	+0.6	+0.6	+0.2	+0.2	+0.3	+0.4
Descriptive component	0.5B	0.5A	0.2A	0.8B	1.1B	0.9B	0.5B	0.1B
7a. Selective (+)–Undiscriminating (−)	0.6	0.9	0.1	1.2	−0.7	1.2	0.9	0.9
b. Choosy (−)–Broad-minded (+)	0.6	−0.7	0.4	0.0	1.3	0.6	0.9	0.6
Evaluative component	+0.6	+0.1	+0.3	+1.0	+0.3	+0.9	+0.9	+0.8
Descriptive component	0.0	0.8A	0.2A	0.2A	1.0B	0.3A	0.0	0.2A
8a. Cautious (+)–Rash (−)	−0.2	0.3	−0.6	0.1	−0.5	−0.4	−0.4	0.6
b. Timid (−)–Bold (+)	0.6	0.9	0.6	0.7	0.2	0.1	1.0	0.6
Evaluative component	+0.2	+0.6	0.0	+0.4	−0.2	−0.1	+0.3	+0.6
Descriptive component	0.4B	0.3B	0.6B	0.3B	0.3B	0.3B	0.7B	0.0

9a. Calm (+)–Agitated (−)	−0.8	−1.3	−0.9	−0.6	−0.2	−1.2	−1.0	0.2
b. Inactive (−)–Active (+)	1.3	0.5	0.6	2.0	1.1	2.3	1.1	1.1
Evaluative component	+0.2	−0.4	−0.1	+0.7	+0.5	+0.6	+0.1	+0.6
Descriptive component	1.1B	0.9B	0.8B	1.3B	0.6B	1.7B	1.1B	0.4B
10a. Peaceful (+)–Aggressive (−)	−0.3	−1.3	0.0	−0.3	0.7	−0.4	−0.2	0.1
b. Passive (−)–Forceful (+)	0.5	0.3	0.4	1.0	0.3	0.6	0.4	0.5
Evaluative component	+0.1	−0.5	+0.2	+0.3	+0.5	+0.1	+0.1	+0.3
Descriptive component	0.4B	0.8B	0.2B	0.7B	0.2A	0.5B	0.3B	0.2B
11a. Modest (+)–Conceited (−)	−1.2	−1.6	−0.6	−1.0	−1.1	−1.4	−1.6	−0.3
b. Unassured (−)–Self-confident (+)	1.3	0.9	1.4	1.7	0.4	1.7	1.4	0.9
Evaluative component	0.0	−0.3	+0.4	+0.3	−0.3	+0.1	−0.1	+0.3
Descriptive component	1.2B	1.2B	1.0B	1.4B	0.8B	1.5B	1.5B	0.6B
12a. Cooperative (+)–Uncooperative (−)	0.2	−0.6	0.2	0.0	1.4	−0.6	0.8	0.5
b. Conforming (−)–+Independent (+)	0.7	0.9	0.4	0.6	0.9	0.8	0.9	0.7
Evaluative component	+0.5	+0.1	+0.3	+0.3	+1.1	+0.1	+0.8	+0.6
Descriptive component	0.3B	0.7B	0.1B	0.3B	0.3A	0.7B	0.1B	0.1B
13a. Tactful (+)–Tactless (−)	0.7	−0.8	0.1	1.4	0.9	1.2	1.5	1.0
b. Devious (−)–Frank (+)	0.2	0.1	0.2	0.9	0.9	−0.2	−0.6	−0.2
Evaluative component	+0.5	−0.3	+0.2	+1.2	+0.9	+0.5	+0.5	+0.4
Descriptive component	0.3A	0.4B	0.1B	0.3A	0.0	0.7A	1.0A	0.6A
14a. Practical (+)–Impractical (−)	0.2	0.7	0.0	0.5	0.4	−0.1	−0.3	1.0
b. Opportunistic (−)–Idealistic (+)	0.5	0.1	0.5	0.7	0.7	0.1	0.8	0.8
Evaluative component	+0.3	+0.4	+0.3	+0.6	+0.6	0.0	+0.3	+0.9
Descriptive component	0.1B	0.3A	0.3B	0.1B	0.1B	0.1B	0.5B	0.1A
15a. Admirable (+)–Deplorable (−).	0.6	−0.3	0.6	0.6	1.0	0.8	0.6	0.6
b. Not likeable (−)–Likeable (+)	1.2	1.1	0.9	1.7	1.2	1.0	1.3	1.3
Evaluative component	+0.9	+0.4	+0.7	+1.1	+1.1	+0.9	+1.0	1.0[a]
Descriptive component	0.3B	0.7B	0.1B	0.5B	0.1B	0.1B	0.4B	—
16. Hard-working (+)–Lazy (−)	−0.2	−0.4	0.0	0.1	−0.2	−0.6	0.0	1.1
17. Intelligent (+)–Stupid (−)	0.8	0.8	0.4	0.9	1.1	0.8	1.0	1.5

[a] In set 15, the Greek judges used the single scale, *desirable–undesirable*.

expressiveness and assertiveness.[1] In the ingroup judgments by the French judges, the impulse-expressiveness appears much more weakly, the assertiveness somewhat more strongly. More detailed results for the separate scales are given in Table 9.2.

Impulse-expressiveness. The consensus and ingroup judgments agree that the French are notably impulse-expressive on sets 2 and 3: *spontaneous* (+) and *impulsive* (−); *gay* (+) and *frivolous* (−). On other sets there is disagreement, with the consensus judgments generally more in the direction of impulse-expressiveness: the consensus judgment of the French as impulse-expressive is not shared on set 1 by the ingroup (who judge the French *stingy* rather than *generous*), and is reversed on set 6 (where the ingroup judges the French *inflexible* rather than *flexible*). Alternatively, the consensus does not share on sets 4 and 7 the ingroup judgment that the French are impulse-controlled − i.e., *skeptical* and *distrustful*; *choosy* rather than *broad-minded*.

It is notable that these ingroup choices include some classically French traits: avarice as the "national vice" (de Gramont, 1969, Chapter 10), Cartesian skepticism, and mistrust. How might one explain these ingroup–outgroup differences? Among the judgment principles of Chapter 3, two suggest themselves. One principle is that "descriptive consistency" should be greater for outgroup judgments, which generalize the overall judgment of impulse-expressiveness to characteristics where the ingroup judgments show a more differentiated view. A second principle − "behavior vs. conscious experience" − was already suggested above: outgroup judgments may tend to reflect the impulse-expressiveness of actual behavior, while ingroup judgments reflect the consciousness of the effort at deliberate self-control.

Other results. The consensus and the ingroup judges generally agree in ascribing traits related to assertiveness,[2] the ingroup notably more so for *aggressive*. The ingroup judgments include the negative traits *uncooperative* (individualism is "the most celebrated French trait" − (de Gramont, 1969, p. 43)), and *tactless* as against the consensus' *tactful*. As before, a possible interpretation is that the outgroup judges are more influenced by overt behavior which in these cases could reflect the code of politeness.

We note that one consequence of the ingroup judges' including various negative characteristics omitted by the outgroup judges is that the overall evaluative component was more negative for the ingroup than for any of the outgroups. This pattern continues on the "extra" scales: the consensus and the ingroup agree that the French are *likeable* ("*sympathique*") but where the consensus judgment is *admirable*, the ingroup judgment is for slightly

---

[1] The Italian judges are an exception for the latter.
[2] The Italian judges differ from the others most decisively on two scales (10a and 12a), judging the French as *peaceful* (rather than *aggressive*) and as highly *cooperative*.

deplorable. The consensus and the ingroup agree that the French are *intelligent* and slightly *lazy* (rather than *hard-working*).

Conclusion

We have emphasized the difference between the ingroup judgments and the other judges included in the consensus. However, there is overall agreement between them: the average correlation between ingroup judgments and the other five standard judges is 0.51 (as against an average correlation between the latter of 0.75).

Given the paradoxes included in the accounts of French national character, these seem generally to show greater agreement than disagreement with our empirical judgments – more with the ingroup judgments than the outgroup ones.

10　The Italians

> In the heart of every man, wherever he is born, whatever his
> education and tastes, there is one small corner which is Italian, that
> part which finds regimentation irksome, the dangers of war
> frightening, strict morality stifling, that part that loves frivolous
> and entertaining art, admires larger-than-life-size solitary heroes,
> and dreams of an impossible liberation from the strictures of a tidy
> existence.
>
> > Barzini, 1968, p. 367

"I know of no sure way to ascertain the Italian national character...There
are no authors to rely on. Descriptions of Italian habits and customs by Italian
writers are very rare and seldom explicit...": thus writes Barzini (1968, p.
15), in one of the few exceptions. How should one then proceed?

As a first approximation (and as a contrast to the Protestant ethic), one
might start here by considering similarities between the Italians and the
French, treating them as different modifications of a shared "Latin" model.
As regards the difference between the French and Italian versions, it is not
difficult to state the major difference in historical terms: the French
modification of a Latin model is related to the early importance of a centralized
state relative to the church, the Italian version to the relative absence and
lateness of this. This historical difference may relate to psychological
differences, which are more difficult to state.

On the whole, the Italian version would seem to come closer to the general
Latin model, and within Italy the south Italian version closer than the north
Italians. Again as a first approximation, the north Italian version can be
considered as a modification in the direction of some of the characteristics
of northern Europeans.

It will be seen that the Italian version emphasizes "*Gemeinschaft* relationships" (e.g., "particularistic" relationships for the family and its allies as
opposed to "universalistic" ones). At the same time there is a lack of the
"community feeling" often associated with "a *Gemeinschaft*" – or, alternatively, such feeling is limited to the family and its allies. Toward others in the
community there is instead an attitude of social distrust – a feature of many
peasant societies.

Although Lipset (1963) does not write about Italy, it ought to be possible
to extend Lipset's "variables" (which are intended to apply universally) to

Italians. Lipset suggested that the Germans became universalistic more in the economic than in the political system, and the French the other way around. In these terms, one might propose that the Italians tended to remain particularistic throughout. Thus, one could propose as a summary that the Italians, especially the southern Italians, have remained a refuge for the *Gemeinschaft* relationships that were once shared by everyone.

Some Italian characteristics

In the absence of other sources, an attempt to state some more specific Italian characteristics necessarily depends heavily on extracting them from Barzini's (1968) account. However, a more logical sequence is possible if we begin with a principle that is included by Barzini, but is made more central and stated with more brutal explicitness by another source.

1. *Self-interest.* In a study of a village in southern Italy, Banfield (1958) suggests the following as their underlying principle: *one should favor the short-run material self-interest of oneself and one's family,*[1] *and assume that others will do the same.*[2]

Banfield (1958, pp. 135–7) provides striking evidence for the importance of family interest by asking respondents in his village for preferences between pairs of value alternatives. The choices were all consistent with family interest: e.g., alternatives seen as family-serving were selected, alternatives seen as family-threatening were avoided.

Banfield's principle itself is only one side of the situation. The other side is the relative absence of other principles, that might elsewhere be presumed. It is this absence of more universalistic principles that leads Banfield to label his principle "amoral familism," which he recognizes could be misleading. The duty to sacrifice for others in the family would seem "moral" enough, although not the kind of more universalistic morality that Banfield is looking for. As Barzini (1968, p. 218) puts it:

Most Italians still obey a double standard. There is one code valid within the family circle, with relatives and honorary relatives, intimate friends and close associates, and there is another regulating life outside. Within, they assiduously demonstrate all the qualities which are not usually attributed to them by superficial observers: they are relatively reliable, honest, truthful, just, obedient, generous, disciplined, brave, and capable of self-sacrifice.

[1] In Banfield's village the "family" tended to be limited to the "nuclear" family of parents and children, but Banfield recognized that in much of Italy the family would be an "extended" one, including a wider range of relatives.
[2] Compare Barzini's (1968, p. 187) citation of Guicciardini's formula: "'Those men conduct their affairs well who keep in front of their eyes their own private interest and measure all their actions according to its necessities.'"

It is outside these "private" relationships that the absence of other principles becomes important. There seems to be an absence not only of the rules necessary for capitalism (which may derive from Protestantism), but also of the rules of any "legitimate order" that may derive from feudalism.

Consider capitalism: Banfield's principle might seem very similar to a statement of the principle of capitalism as the individual pursuit of economic self-interest – aside from the obvious difference that modern capitalism considers long-run profit rather than short-run self-interest. But the pursuit of economic self-interest in capitalism is possible only within certain (more universalistic) rules, for example, rules of contractual obligations, and so require a limited degree of social trust at least in the probable fulfilment of these rules.[1] Barzini (1968, p. 207) says that for most Italians who miss its moral character, the contemporary capitalistic world is still "almost incomprehensible."

Classical capitalism (and classical liberal democracy) does not as such involve any direct concern for the common good. More generally, we need to compare the pure pursuit of (family) self-interest – said to be characteristic for Italians – with the absence of two kinds of alternatives: certain rules within which the pursuit of self-interest takes place, with classical capitalism and liberal democracy as two examples, and direct concern for some common goals. In our own comparative terms, Dahrendorf treats the former as more characteristic for the English, and the latter for the Germans. For Italians both of these alternatives tend to be lacking. Barzini includes examples of both in the "remnants of the feudal code" on which "the modern world still functions" (but which are largely lacking for Italians): "Reverence for truth, fair play, respect for laws, rules, and regulations; respect for one's opponents; capacity to work in teams; willingness to apply to oneself and one's friends the same rules one applies to all others; loyalty to one's convictions and faith, loyalty to one's party, class, school, country..." (p. 207).

2. *Producing favorable appearances.* Barzini's (1968) own account starts at a different point. He describes as the "fundamental trait of the national character" (p. 111) the emphasis on producing favorable appearances, "striving for effects" (p. 94) – whether in architecture and the arts, or in social interaction. These appearances may or may not coincide with reality. In cases where coincidence is lacking, there may be what looks to others like duplicity. The concern with appearances may serve three purposes. (a) It can make life more acceptable and endurable. The Italian secret is "that life can be ennobled as a representation of life, that it can be made into a work of art" (p. 97). Polite lies and flattery – even when transparent deceptions – tend to make the other person feel a unique human being. (b) It can serve utilitarian

---

[1] As one example of the weakness of such rules in Italy, Banfield (1958, p. 93) says that a worker is likely to be paid afterward only at the employer's convenience.

purposes. (c) It can be used as a defense when life is particularly threatening (e.g., under foreign occupation).

3. *"Realism."* Italians are more aware than foreigners of the possible discrepancy between appearance and reality. Famous Italian adventurers like Casanova and Cagliostro had most success abroad and came to grief on returning to Italy. Foreigners fail to recognize the extent of the possible discrepancy between appearance and reality; Barzini implies that this is still true even for such an exceptional observer as Stendhal: there seems to be

a tense dramatic quality, a shameless directness, about Italians which is refreshing to foreigners accustomed to nordic self-control, to feigned or real frigidity. These people still seek, like Stendhal, "that combination of love, sensuality, and sincerity" which apparently still characterizes the race. Here "a man who plays a role is as rare...as a natural and simple man in Paris," and, one might add, anywhere in the northern hemisphere.

(Barzini, 1968, p. 65)

But Barzini makes it clear elsewhere that he considers this impression misleading.

The reality itself often involves poverty, ignorance, injustice, and fear. A common reaction is to try to set up a limited, but secure situation ("sistemazione").

[Italians] learned long ago to beware privately of their own show and to be sober and clear-eyed realists in all circumstances. They mind their own business. They behave with circumspection, caution, and even cynicism. They are incredulous: they do not want to be fooled by seductive appearances and honeyed words. They cannot afford to be carried away by emotions. They keep them under control. This does not mean that they are a cold people. When it is safe to do so, they enjoy genuine and unrestrained emotions as well as anybody...For all these reasons they tend to be concrete people, never allowing their imagination to stray too far, preoccupied with concrete problems, situations, men and things as they are. They cultivate tangible pleasures, the pleasures of the senses, and, when they can, those, just as substantial, which wealth and power afford. The imperative...is...not to be made a fool of.

(Barzini, 1968, pp. 188–9)

4. *Social distrust.* The possible discrepancy between appearance and reality is increased by a low estimate of what reality is. There is distrust of apparent disinterested or idealistic motives. Here Barzini's account converges with Banfield's principle. Social mistrust is supported by a combination of two earlier characteristics: according to the second part of Banfield's principle, one assumes that others are really pursuing the immediate self-interest of themselves and their family (and no other reliable rules); according to the principle of presenting favorable appearances, this reality is likely to be concealed.

There is not only a relative absence of other rules for social behavior, but official institutions are weak and unstable: "the law is flexible and unreliable, the state discredited and easily dominated by powerful persons or groups..." (Barzini, 1968, p. 205).

The situation is a mutually reinforcing one. The concern with (family) self-interest is understandable on the assumption of social mistrust toward others and the weakness of official institutions. But it also contributes to the mistrust and the weakness. As Barzini puts it: "The strength of the family is not only, therefore, the bulwark against disorder, but, at the same time, one of the principal causes" (p. 215).

The result approaches a Hobbesian situation, where it is assumed "that life is fundamentally a merciless game, that man should find his protection in the warp and woof of society; that curbs on man's instincts constitute the essence of civilized living. Without such protections man is alone in the world, as alone as a beast of prey or as the prey itself, waiting to be devoured" (pp. 204–5).

The pervasiveness of social mistrust is strongly documented in the extensive cross-national survey of Almond and Verba (1963). They summarize their results for Italians as providing a picture "of relatively unrelieved political alienation and of social isolation and distrust" (p. 402). Only a few of the most striking findings will be cited here. Only 7% of Italians (e.g., compared with 55% of Americans) agreed with the statement "Most people can be trusted." This mistrust extends to the interviewer, to whom 32% of Italians (e.g., compared with 2% of Americans) refused to report their vote in the last election. Political polarization is extreme: asked to pick statements describing supporters of an opposing party, Italians averaged 6% positive and 62% negative qualities (Americans averaged 67% positive and 20% negative qualities). Perhaps most revealing are responses to the question: how active should the ordinary man be in his local community? In the display below we compare the answer "be active" with a combination of two answers "only be upright in personal life" plus "do nothing in local community."

How active the ordinary man should be in his local community, by nation

	US	UK	Germany	Italy
Be active	51%	39%	22%	10%
Be upright in personal life, plus do nothing in local community	4%	7%	18%	26%

Source: Almond and Verba, 1963, p. 169.

5. *Particularistic relationships.* In this situation, how is one to survive or even succeed? In the absence of universalistic rules, one depends on particularistic relationships – first within the family, and then outside. Barzini recapitulates the rules for survival:

One must cultivate one's family, entertain as many useful friends and as few dangerous enemies as one can, and therefore perfect the art of being obliging and *simpatico* at all times and at all costs...On the negative side these are things one must avoid: one should never be too conspicuous, daring, confident, explicit, trusting, credulous; one should not officially embrace definite opinions, nor be out of step with the crowd. Above all, one should remember at all times that conflicts are not decided on the basis of the law, abstract considerations of justice or the relative merits of the contestants, but most frequently by a pure confrontation of power.

(Barzini, 1968, p. 252)

On the other side, one who has succeeded has an obligation to take care of the more dependent members of the family or larger grouping. Among the positive consequences of a concentration on particularistic relationships are a tolerance for the idiosyncrasies of others and a cultivation of one's own individuality. "The single man's private virtues" were honed "to an edge unsurpassed anywhere else... 'The plant man grows in Italy second to none'" (Barzini, 1968, p. 356).

Two paradoxes

Two themes – social mistrust and impulse-control – deserve special comment, although they have already been touched on in the preceding account. Both themes present a certain paradox, since they tend to be stressed by writers on the Italians (and the French), but they do not seem salient to observers of the surface of Italian life.

Social mistrust. This has already been discussed above. Why is it relatively unrecognized by outside observers (aside from the few who are truly initiated)? The answer is suggested by Barzini's emphasis on the presentation of favorable appearances. One's underlying social mistrust will not be included in this presentation; indeed it will generally seem advantageous to suggest the opposite. Italians are more likely to be aware of the possible discrepancy than foreign observers. The Italian version of this paradox seems to be more extreme than the French, who may both have somewhat less social mistrust and make it more apparent.

Impulse-control. Gambino (1974) writes primarily about Italian-Americans, but includes a relatively comprehensive account of the southern Italy from which they came. He repeatedly emphasizes the prescription for control over impulse-expression. But outgroup observers are more typically impressed by impulse-expression than impulse-control (granting that there may be large variations between regions, social classes and historical periods – Gambino, for example, stresses the reserved dignity of Sicilians).

The resolution of this paradox would seem to be similar to that we have suggested for the French. In the relative absence of internalized inhibitions (such as might derive from the asceticism of the Protestant ethic) impulse-control depends on deliberate supervision over impulse-expression, and social arrangements that provide external control. While Gambino emphasizes self-control, this is based less on internalization than on appreciation of the external controls.

Consider aggression: according to Banfield (1958, pp. 142–4) the "war of all against all" is limited, not by internalized values, but by the perceived likelihood that the law might be enforced, and the danger of reprisals.

Another illustration is provided by sex. Traditionally, in the absence of reliable birth control, the possibility of an illegitimate child was a severe threat to the family system. For this and other reasons, premarital sex for the woman was strongly proscribed. However, this proscription did not take the form of internalized inhibitions of an ascetic nature, but rather a system of external control preventing males and females from being alone together,[1] along with the threat of retaliation by the male relatives of the female against a sexual intruder. All parties retained a positive attitude toward sensuality and sex, and there was no guilt about sex, as such. But its expression was deliberately controlled. Gambino contrasts this with the situation of the early generations of Italian-American immigrants: "As the chaperone system was more difficult to enforce in the U.S., the older generation instilled a broad sense of sexual guilt in their children to preserve premarital chastity" (p. 179). Thus Puritan asceticism was taken up by Catholic immigrants.

Comparison with judgment results

The Italian judges. In general, in our judgment results the differences between groups of judges are relatively unimportant as compared with the differences between the nationalities judged as "targets" (see Appendix A). However, the Italian judges deserve some comment since they come closest to being an exception. (1) The mean judgments for Italian judges tend to be more extreme (polarized) than for other judges. (2) These more extreme judgments represent larger descriptive components (not evaluative ones). Consider the most obvious comparisons using the six standard judges and the six standard targets. Here the measure of descriptive variance (see Appendix A) averages twice as large (2.1) for Italian judges as for the five other groups of standard judges (who are all in a narrow range between 0.8 and 1.1). (3) In particular, the Italian judges tend to follow the dimension of impulse-control vs. impulse-expression consistently across all the first seven sets of scales – e.g.,

---

[1] Banfield (1958, p. 140) suggests that this arrangement has the "characteristics of a self-fulfilling prophecy." "In a society in which everyone believes that a man and woman will make love if they are not restrained from doing so by outward circumstances, a man who finds himself alone with a woman is virtually compelled to make love, for not to do so would imply a question about her charms or his virility."

Table 10.1. *Judgments about the Italians: summary*

Judges	Tight–Loose	Assertive–Unassertive
		Descriptive factors
Consensus	−0.67	0.41
Italians	−0.79	0.04
English	−0.71	0.55
Germans	−0.58	0.57
French	−0.55	0.67
Austrian	−0.65	0.50
Finnish	−0.74	0.14
Greek	−0.83	−0.07

judging the English and Germans consistently as impulse-controlled; the French and themselves as consistently impulse-expressive. (From another point of view, the Italian judges are thus a major support for the appearance in our analyses of the dimension itself.) One conclusion is that findings where Italian ingroup judgments are simply more extreme than consensus judgments – findings which would be unusual for other ingroups[1] – do not in themselves require any special interpretation.

Summary results. We will report results for all groups of judges, but will generally comment only on the consensus and ingroup judgments. Table 10.1 presents a summary of judgments about the Italians on the two major descriptive dimensions. The consensus judgment is that the Italians are impulse-expressive and assertive. The Italian ingroup judges agree about the impulse-expressiveness but disagree in judging Italians as low on assertiveness. More detailed results for the separate scales are given in Table 10.2.

Italian ingroup judgments. We have spoken earlier of a common "Latin model" partly shared by the Italians and the French. In part there is a high correlation between judgments about the Italians and the French, for each group of judges including the Italian judges (for whom the correlation is 0.88) and the French judges. However, their two versions of the Latin model vary in opposite directions, so that the correlation between the Italian and the French ingroup judgments is a tiny 0.16! Focusing on their comparison may provide a more subtle understanding of Italian ingroup judgments.

Without trying to explain all the special features of the Italian ingroup

---

[1] Indeed, in our earlier discussion of judgment principles in Chapter 3, the principle of "homogeneity" implies that ingroup judgments will *generally* tend to be *less* polarized than outgroup ones.

Table 10.2. Judgments about the Italians

Scales	Consensus	Ital.	Eng.	Judges Germ.	Fr.	Aust.	Finn.	Greek
1a. Thrifty (+)–Extravagant (–)	−0.8	−1.1	−0.9	−0.3	−0.8	−0.9	−0.9	−1.2
b. Stingy (−)–Generous (+)	0.7	1.6	0.7	1.0	0.3	0.3	0.5	1.1
Evaluative component	0.0	+0.3	−0.1	+0.3	−0.3	−0.3	−0.2	−0.1
Descriptive component	0.8B	1.4B	0.8B	0.7B	0.6B	0.6B	0.7B	1.1B
2a. Self-controlled (+)–Impulsive (−)	−1.7	−1.7	−1.5	−1.9	−1.8	−2.0	−1.5	−1.3
b. Inhibited (−)–Spontaneous (+)	1.5	1.0	1.2	1.1	1.6	1.6	2.3	1.5
Evaluative component	−0.1	−0.4	−0.2	−0.4	−0.1	−0.2	+0.4	+0.1
Descriptive component	1.6B	1.4B	1.4B	1.5B	1.7B	1.8B	1.9B	1.4B
3a. Serious (+)–Frivolous (−)	−1.2	−0.7	−1.2	−1.0	−1.0	−1.0	−1.9	−1.7
b. Grim (−)–Gay (+)	2.1	2.3	2.1	1.8	1.8	2.1	2.2	2.0
Evaluative component	+0.4	+0.8	+0.4	+0.4	+0.4	+0.5	+0.1	+0.2
Descriptive component	1.6B	1.5B	1.7B	1.4B	1.4B	1.6B	2.1B	1.8B
4a. Skeptical (+)–Gullible (−)	−0.5	−0.5	−0.3	−0.5	−0.5	−0.6	−0.8	−0.1
b. Distrustful (−)–Trusting (+)	0.0	1.3	−0.2	0.2	0.0	−0.4	−0.8	1.1
Evaluative component	−0.3	+0.4	−0.3	−0.1	−0.3	−0.5	−0.8	+0.5
Descriptive component	0.3B	0.9B	0.1B	0.4B	0.2B	0.1B	0.0	0.6B
5a. Firm (+)–Lax (−)	−0.6	−1.2	0.1	−0.2	−0.5	−0.8	−0.9	−0.9
b. Severe (−)–Lenient (+)	0.4	1.5	0.0	−0.3	0.1	−0.2	1.2	1.5
Evaluative component	−0.1	+0.2	0.0	−0.3	−0.2	−0.5	+0.1	+0.3
Descriptive component	0.5B	1.3B	0.0	0.1A	0.3B	0.3B	1.0B	1.2B
6a. Persistent (+)–Vacillating (−)	−0.7	−1.4	0.7	−0.7	−0.3	−1.2	−1.1	−0.9
b. Inflexible (−)–Flexible (+)	0.5	1.8	0.6	0.9	−1.2	1.2	−0.1	1.7
Evaluative component	−0.1	+0.2	+0.7	+0.1	−0.8	0.0	−0.6	+0.4
Descriptive component	0.6B	1.6B	0.0	0.8B	0.5A	1.2B	0.5B	1.3B
7a. Selective (+)–Undiscriminating (−)	−0.3	−1.3	−0.3	0.4	0.3	−0.4	−0.2	−0.2
b. Choosy (−)–Broad-minded (+)	0.3	0.3	0.8	−0.1	−0.4	−0.3	1.4	0.9
Evaluative component	0.0	−0.5	+0.2	+0.1	−0.1	−0.4	+0.6	+0.4
Descriptive component	0.3B	0.5B	0.5B	0.2A	0.4A	0.0	0.8B	0.5B
8a. Cautious (+)–Rash (−)	−0.6	−1.0	−0.7	−0.3	−0.4	−0.6	−0.6	−0.8
b. Timid (−)–Bold (+)	0.5	0.0	1.1	0.7	1.7	−0.8	0.3	−1.3
Evaluative component	−0.1	−0.5	+0.2	+0.2	+0.7	−0.7	−0.2	−1.1
Descriptive component	0.6B	0.5B	0.9B	0.5B	1.1B	0.1A	0.4B	0.3A

9a. Calm (+)–Agitated (–)	−1.6	−0.5	−1.4	−2.1	−1.8	−2.2	−1.6	0.1
b. Inactive (–)–Active (+)	1.0	0.8	0.6	2.5	0.6	2.3	−0.6	0.4
Evaluative component	−0.3	+0.2	−0.4	+0.2	−0.6	0.0	−1.1	+0.2
Descriptive component	1.3B	0.7B	1.0B	2.3B	1.2B	2.3B	0.5B	0.1B
10a. Peaceful (+)–Aggressive (–)	−0.6	0.4	−0.3	−1.1	−1.0	−0.8	−0.9	0.7
b. Passive (–)–Forceful (+)	0.2	0.3	0.4	1.2	0.2	0.2	−1.2	0.6
Evaluative component	−0.2	+0.4	0.0	0.0	−0.4	−0.3	−1.0	+0.6
Descriptive component	0.4B	0.1A	0.3B	1.2B	0.6B	0.5B	0.1A	0.1A
11a. Modest (+)–Conceited (–)	−0.8	−1.2	−0.4	−0.1	−0.8	−1.2	−1.4	−0.5
b. Unassured (–)–Self-confident (+)	0.8	−0.3	1.2	0.9	1.2	1.1	0.5	−0.4
Evaluative component	0.0	−0.7	+0.4	+0.4	+0.2	0.0	−0.4	−0.4
Descriptive component	0.8B	0.4B	0.8B	0.5B	1.0B	1.2B	0.9B	0.0
12a. Cooperative (+)–Uncooperative (–)	0.2	0.6	0.3	0.1	0.2	−0.5	0.4	0.4
b. Conforming (–)–Independent (+)	−0.3	−0.8	0.1	−0.8	0.4	−0.3	−0.2	0.5
Evaluative component	0.0	−0.1	+0.2	−0.3	+0.3	−0.4	+0.1	+0.5
Descriptive component	0.2A	0.7A	0.1A	0.4A	0.1B	0.1B	0.3A	0.0
13a. Tactful (+)–Tactless (–)	−0.1	0.0	−0.5	0.1	−0.8	−0.3	0.7	−0.3
b. Devious (–)–Frank (+)	−0.1	1.2	−0.2	0.2	−0.1	−0.7	−1.1	0.0
Evaluative component	−0.1	+0.1	−0.3	+0.2	−0.4	−0.5	−0.2	−0.2
Descriptive component	0.0	0.6B	0.2B	0.1B	0.3B	0.2A	0.9A	0.1B
14a. Practical (+)–Impractical (–)	−0.2	0.8	0.2	−0.2	0.1	−0.7	−1.4	0.6
b. Opportunistic (–)–Idealistic (+)	0.3	0.3	0.2	0.5	0.0	−0.4	0.9	0.1
Evaluative component	0.0	+0.6	+0.2	+0.2	+0.1	−0.5	−0.3	+0.3
Descriptive component	0.2B	0.3A	0.0	0.4B	0.1A	0.1B	1.2B	0.2A
15a. Admirable (+)–Deplorable (–)	0.3	1.4	0.0	0.2	0.1	0.0	−0.1	0.9[a]
b. Not likeable (–)–Likeable (+)	0.7	2.3	0.3	0.6	0.6	0.0	0.7	—
Evaluative component	+0.5	+1.8	+0.2	+0.4	+0.4	0.0	+0.3	—
Descriptive component	0.2B	0.5B	0.1B	0.2B	0.3B	0.0	0.4B	—
16. Hard-working (+)–Lazy (–)	−0.6	−0.5	−0.6	−0.1	0.1	−1.4	−1.1	−0.1
17. Intelligent (+)–Stupid (–)	0.4	1.6	−0.3	0.5	0.6	−0.1	−0.1	1.3

[a] In set 15, the Greek judges used the single scale, *desirable–undesirable*.

judgments, we can summarize many of them under two headings: the Italians judge themselves as relatively "influencable" and "ingenuous."

Influencability. Under "influencable" we mean to include first of all several characteristics generally related to the dimension of assertiveness. Here the ingroup judgment of Italians as unassertive (e.g. *peaceful, unassured*) disagrees with the consensus judgments about Italians (as *aggressive* and *self-confident*) – and with judgments about the French by both the ingroup and the consensus. In addition, there are other characteristics where the Italian ingroup judgments are not just slightly, but much more extreme than the consensus: of Italians as *vacillating* and *flexible, undiscriminating, cooperative,* and *conforming.*

Can one account for this greater emphasis in ingroup judgments on the Italians as "influencable"? Certainly, in a *general* way we are prepared by Barzini's account (which emphasizes the possible discrepancy between appearance and reality) for the possibility of a discrepancy between Italian ingroup judgments and those by outsiders. Moreover, Barzini's account would certainly include, for example, "self-confidence" as one of these possibilities where the self-confidence apparent to outsiders would contrast with ingroup consciousness of unassuredness. But it is not really clear why a discrepancy should appear in *these* cases, and not in others to which Barzini gives at least equal emphasis, such as impulse-control and, particularly, social distrust. This last case we consider next under "ingenuousness."

Ingenuousness. Under "ingenuous" we include the ingroup judgments of Italians as *gullible, trusting,* and *frank.* The consensus agrees with only the first of these judgments. (In comparison, the French in ingroup judgments are *skeptical* and *distrustful.*)

The Italian self-judgments seem sharply inconsistent with the preceding account where "social distrust" was included as a major Italian characteristic. For such a paradoxical finding, any interpretation is likely to seem paradoxical. One interpretation is suggested by Leites' (1969) proposals for the French, which we have suggested can be understood as conflict dilemmas about fulfilling some standard – a prescription, or proscription. For Italians, perhaps even more than for the French, one such proscription is to avoid being too trusting or credulous and so "being made a fool of" (Barzini, 1968; Gambino, 1974). The French define themselves as meeting this standard, and so as *skeptical* and *distrustful.* In contrast, the Italians – in the context of what may be a more untrustworthy social environment – judge themselves as not meeting this standard, and so as *gullible, trusting,* and *frank.* On this interpretation, although Italians may consider themselves ingenuous from an Italian perspective, from a comparative perspective they should be considered *skeptical, distrustful,* and not necessarily *frank.*

The preceding interpretation has too much of an ad hoc quality to be really satisfying. In any case, however, we are left with the fact that our Italian ingroup judgments show some striking features, which we have summarized as emphasizing influencability and ingenuousness.

Other results. A somewhat negative tone has pervaded our account of the Italians, not only the description of Italian characteristics (where the accounts tend to undermine what appear on the surface as pleasant Italian characteristics), but also in the empirical results, including the self-judgments. This last is relieved by the ingroup results on the extra scales where the Italians judge themselves highly *admirable*, *likeable*, and *intelligent*. The first two of these results on the primarily evaluative scales, where the combined evaluative component is $+1.8$, contrast with the weak evaluative component for the ingroup on the regular 28 scales, which averages only $+0.1$. This contrast is reminiscent of that found earlier for the Filipinos, where the ingroup judgments represented a relatively weak evaluative component ($+0.4$) on the regular scales but a robust $+1.6$ on the evaluative scale *desirable* vs. *undesirable*. It seems that groups judged impulse-expressive *may* admit that they lack some of the virtues of impulse-control (and so are *extravagant*, etc.), but do not treat this as important in their overall favorable self-evaluation on evaluative scales.

Conclusion

Although our comments have emphasized the differences between the ingroup judgments and the consensus, there is overall agreement between them: the average correlation between ingroup judgments and the other five standard judges is 0.55, as against an average correlation between the latter of 0.71.

What can one conclude about the correspondence between our empirical results and the preceding account of Italian characteristics? The conclusion is complicated by the emphasis for Italians on the discrepancy between appearance and reality. We can say that in general, the consensus judgments tend to correspond to the apparent Italian characteristics. About the ingroup judgments, we certainly cannot say that they generally correspond more to the "real" Italian characteristics described earlier. Most often, the ingroup judgments are similar to the consensus. Moreover (e.g., in the case of "ingenuousness"), the ingroup deviation from the consensus may show, in comparative terms, *less* correspondence with the reality (in this case, social distrust). On this last interpretation the Italians would represent an exception to the *general* implication of the judgment principles developed earlier that ingroup judgments were, if anything, likely to be *more* accurate than outgroup judgments.

11 The Russians

[Among the Russians first met in England] personal relationships and personal development had an importance, a development, a naturalness and "sincerity"... such as I had never imagined...

However, my dominant impression of the people, on first going into Russia, was of quite another character. A sea of rather gray-blond faces...almost all these Russian faces had one thing in common. They were peculiarly expressionless and detached; they seemed neither very self-aware nor aware of much outside themselves.

There was no challenge in people's eyes as they looked at each other in passing; in fact they looked at each other but little. They bumped into each other without apology and apparently without offence...

It was only much later that I came across a clue, in conversation with a woman who had worked at one time for Intourist, the state organization which handles foreign tourists..."We noticed," she said, "that English people and all foreigners smile very much...When we Russians meet a new person we do not smile unless, of course, we think we like the person at once. It is not necessary to smile unless we feel like it. So among the guides we had a saying – 'Remember, many smiles!'"

So that was the key to the dull expressions of the shuffling crowds. The offhandedness was...the Russian individual, weary, unused to city habits, drowning in a sea of strangers, who was unable to raise interest in a casual enquiry, and who had not yet acquired the pleasing if hollow urbanity of the city dweller in some other countries. He was being true to himself in his offhand or lifeless way...I now understood why there was among Russians so little tossing of greetings or playing ball with banal remarks to warm up good fellowship...Faces would light up when there was sufficient reason, and not merely for the small change of personal intercourse...   Miller, 1960, pp. 65, 66–7, 71–2

Traditional Russian national character

Russian characteristics are often related to the climate and the land (Crankshaw, 1948; Miller, 1960). The long winters (when the traditional peasant could only hole up from the cold) were surrounded by periods of mud, with only a brief growing season. This is said to have produced an alternating pattern of lethargy vs. intense activity. The contemporary counterpart might be in the slow pace of factory production at the beginning of each month, followed by a crescendo of activity trying to meet the monthly production quota by "storm."

The endless plain is said to lead to tendencies for immoderation, for going to extremes and for cosmic emotionality. Becoming more historical, the open plain is said to have encouraged peasants to wander off from their previous masters, leading to edicts to prevent this. This is said to relate to a dualism between independence to the point of anarchy counteracted by an acceptance of centralized authority. (Somewhat similar combinations have been suggested for the French and the Germans.)

This last relates to a third type of explanation which involves a dualism between the Tartar domination and the underlying Slavic characteristics (which include equalitarianism), and possibly between two types of resulting family structure.

Then there is the "swaddling hypothesis": the proposal by Gorer (Gorer and Rickman, 1949) that many traditional Russian characteristics can be related to the practice of keeping infants wrapped up tightly, being unwrapped only at intervals for feeding. As with Freud's hypothesis about the origin of society in *Totem and Tabu*, it is more useful to treat this hypothesis as a metaphorical story summarizing some psychological characteristics than as a literal truth about their origins. For Gorer, the characteristics related to swaddling include the following.

a. Intense anger (aroused by the constraint) which is also projected as a vaguely threatening environment, leading to diffuse fear and guilt, alternating with impotent exhaustion, loneliness and depression.
b. Lack of sharp distinctions between others in the environment and unconsciously between self and not-self (resulting from inhibition of exploration of the environment).
c. A preference for alternation between total and minimal gratification, and between kindness and cruelty (derived from the alternation of unconstricted feeding with angry, lonely constriction).

Modal Russian personality characteristics

As it happens, it is not necessary to continue to pursue the traditional accounts in an effort to extract a systematic formulation. Instead we can turn to a systematic formulation based on the study of individual Russians (with an American comparison group) using a variety of methods, as reported by Inkeles *et al.* (1958). This formulation can serve as a basis for comparisons, including a comparison with accounts of traditional Russian national character. It is paradoxical, since the Russians might have seemed the least accessible of the nationalities that we consider in detail, that this formulation comes closer to the ideal for our purposes than is available for other nationalities. Indeed, if comparable formulations existed for all our nationalities, we could considerably improve and shorten our presentation, by reducing the effort to extract some statement about national character from a variety of less suitable materials.

Accordingly, this formulation of Russian "modal personality characteristics" will be used as a focus here. The study has two obvious disadvantages. First, it was carried out with refugees from Russia, who might not be representative of the Russian population. An extensive series of counter-arguments were marshalled against this criticism (Bauer *et al.*, 1956, Chapter 1). Secondly, the study was carried out in 1950; accordingly there is a question of what changes may have occurred since that time. We will try to deal with both of these problems, by comparing the formulation with what reports are available from inside Russia subsequently.

We will summarize the formulation of Russian modal characteristics as given by Inkeles *et al.* (1958), and then compare this with traditional Russian national character, with the Protestant ethic and the "new Soviet man" advocated by the Soviet regime, and with more recent reports about contemporary Russian characteristics. Partly because of the American comparison group, it is generally possible to add to each of the Russian characteristics some "contrasts" that are not characteristic of Russians.

1. *Personal relationships.* A central characteristic was a need for *affiliation*: a need for intensive face-to-face relationships, and satisfaction from warm and personal contact with others. Russians were not tensely anxious about others' opinions of them, and lacked strong needs for *approval* and *autonomy* that were prominent for the American comparison group. They valued people for what they are, not for what they have done. Neither group showed strong needs for dominance, securing positions of superordination, or for controlling or manipulating others and enforcing authority over them.

The most prominent conflict dilemma for Russians was *trust* vs. *mistrust* – the need for close interpersonal relations in conflict with the danger of self-revelation.

Guilt and shame did not noticeably differ in relative importance between Russians and Americans, but were felt by Russians about moral or interpersonal behavior, as in matters involving personal honesty, sincerity, trust, or loyalty to a friend – and not, as by Americans, about failure to live up to "public norms" such as etiquette and failure in achievement.

2. *Expression of emotions and impulses.* The Russians showed a high degree of expressiveness and emotional aliveness. This included a greater freedom and spontaneity in criticism than was true for the Americans.

Regarding basic impulses – such as oral gratification, sex, aggression, and dependence – Russians tended to have *high awareness* of them, to *accept* them freely as something normal or "natural" rather than bad and offensive, and to *give in* to these impulses freely and *live them out.*

They had rather high and secure self-esteem and were not given to self-examination, but were unafraid to face up to their own motivations and those of others.

Defense mechanisms and self-control were weak. Instead, Russians appear to feel in need for help in impulse-control from the group or from authority.

3. *Dependence on authority and the group.* Though without a strong need for submission, the Russians showed a need for dependence on others for emotional support, on the group and authority to provide moral rules for impulse control, and on authority to provide the initiation, direction, and organization of performance that are not expected from the average individual.

There is a profound acceptance of group membership and relatedness, unthreatened by mutual dependence.

What is important about authority is that it be warm, nurturant, and considerate of the individual's problems and welfare, and not its preservation of rules of procedure as in the Anglo-American approach to law and government.

The Russians lacked the emphasis on individual achievement of Americans, and the American tendency to feel guilt and shame about ineptness, incompetence, or inability to meet production, sports, or similar performance standards.

4. *Contradictoriness.* The Russian tendency to show contradictory tendencies was called by Dicks (1952, p. 168) "the outstanding trait of the Russian personality." This does not mean the Russians necessarily have more underlying conflicts,[1] but that both of the conflicting tendencies appear at the manifest level, instead of one tendency being suppressed either by internalized inhibitions or by deliberate self-control. Two important conflicts (in addition to that of *trust* and *mistrust*, already considered) concern *activity* vs. *passivity*

---

[1] But perhaps different ones. Thus, Inkeles *et al.* (1958) suggest that Erikson's dilemma of *trust* vs. *mistrust* is central for Russians but not for Americans, while other dilemmas such as *intimacy* vs. *isolation* or *autonomy* vs. *belongingness* were major problems for Americans but not for Russians.

and *optimism* vs. *pessimism*. In relation to the American comparison group, which clearly favored *activity* and *optimism*, the Russians showed more tendencies to *passivity* and *pessimism*. As compared with the consistent striving of the Americans, the Russians showed less persistence and some alternation between bursts of activity and passive accommodation to the apparent hard facts of the situation. As against the American optimism, the Russians showed more tendencies to pessimism, depression, and despair.

The preceding four-point summary reorganizes the formulation by Inkeles *et al.* (1958), who themselves use eight categories, organized differently. This formulation will now be compared with several others.

1. *The formulation of Russian modal characteristics is similar to those of traditional Russian national character.* It seems clear that the preceding formulation is basically similar to formulations of traditional Russian national character. These formulations might relate historically the acceptance of dependence on the group to the traditional communal village (*mir*), and to Russian Orthodox church practices such as group confession, with the central event not individual communion but the pentecostal descent of the Holy Spirit on the whole congregation simultaneously (Gorer and Rickman, 1949, p. 134). Acceptance of authority is also consistent with the historical explanations.

The similarity between the two formulations is such that we may treat the formulation of Russian modal characteristics as a systematic explication of traditional Russian character, together with evidence that it had persisted into the Soviet period.

2. *Traditional Russian national character is dissimilar to the Protestant ethic and to the "new Soviet man."* We have used Weber's formulation of the "Protestant ethic" as a major basis for comparative analysis. As compared with the Protestant ethic, traditional Russian national character is very dissimilar and close to an antithesis. Probably more than Catholicism, the Russian Orthodox church was other-worldly and mystical. Any worldly environmentalistic tendencies – which can be found in Russian objective psychology as well as Marxism – had to take on the character of an ideological rebellion, rather than being implicit in the society as was behaviorism in America. Similarly, with the fusion of church and state (the Tsar was in absolute control of the church) any effort at political reform had to take on the form of a religious heresy.

In the Orthodox church, asceticism had a dualistic form, similar to that in Catholicism: asceticism was enjoined for a saintly minority, but impulse-expressiveness was expected from the majority.

Indeed, one could argue that traditional Russian character contrasted in almost every respect with the Protestant ethic as we have analyzed it: spasms of activity instead of systematic work and achievement; impulse-expression instead of impulse-control; intense personalness instead of the impersonalness of "universal otherhood"; group orientation instead of individualism.

Rebels against the Tsarist system tended to the ascetic tradition; since they were looking for changes in this world, they represented a combination of worldly asceticism similar to the Protestant ethic. After the Bolshevik revolution in 1917, and particularly with the initiation of large-scale industrialization in 1928, the leadership tried to foster the characteristics of the "new Soviet man" in the general population: disciplined, working steadily and consistently, puritanical in conduct and motivation. Dicks (1952) explicates further this ideal: "active, tireless energy, ruthless but humane consistency and efficiency, wholehearted commitment, resolution, optimism, perseverance...leadership, initiative, and improvisation" (p. 120). "Great stress is laid on the virtues of sobriety, punctuality, and discipline, avoidance of waste..." (p. 126).

Obviously, these characteristics bear a close resemblance to those of the Protestant ethic. In effect, the Soviet leadership is accepting the assumption that such personality characteristics are congruent with an industrial society. On the other hand, it follows that the traditional Russian national character is incongruent with this aim. "Indeed, the psychological characteristics of the regime's ideal were largely developed to combat, control, or overcome many of the typical characteristics of traditional Russian personality" (Bauer *et al.*, 1956, p. 162). In Dicks' (1952, p. 162) more psychoanalytic terminology, "oral" spontaneity is confronted by the "anal" demand for control and routine.

Two further consequences are likely. First, there will be a selection into more important positions of those with characteristics resembling the new Soviet man rather than traditional Russian national character. Secondly, in the long run there will tend to be a change from traditional Russian national character towards the new Soviet man, for a variety of reasons. One of the less obvious reasons is that parents will deliberately bring up their children so as to encourage changes that will be adaptive for the new conditions (Inkeles, 1955). The question remains as to the rate at which this change has taken place.

3. *More recent evidence suggests that contemporary Russians may have shifted part-way toward the "new Soviet man," but still are more similar to traditional Russian characteristics.* We now confront directly the problem that the formulation of Inkeles *et al.* (1958) was based on interviews in 1950 with refugees who left Russia earlier. We therefore consider reports from inside Russia extending into the more recent period.

Wright Miller's (1960) *Russians as people* is based on visits to Russia from 1934 to 1960. One may start with the contrast (excerpted at the beginning of this chapter) between the expressionlessness of the crowd in the Russian city and the lively responsiveness of personal interaction. He explains both as representing a tendency to express directly whatever emotions are felt – including the boredom and detachment felt in the city crowd (in contrast to the public smiling of the English and other foreigners). This obviously involves both the emotional expressiveness and the need for personal relationships included in the earlier formulation of modal characteristics.

The second central characteristic for Miller is a "strong, largely unconscious sense of community." Other characteristics described by Miller include: a readiness to abandon themselves to either melancholy or optimism and to occasional orgiastic outbursts; a lack of organization (including punctuality) in both private life and work when not under discipline; a disinterest in the nature of objects as opposed to people. Many of these characteristics involve concentration on some focus of attention with the neglect of other considerations. In general these characteristics resemble traditional Russian ones.

Hedrick Smith was correspondent for the *New York Times* in Moscow from 1971 to 1974. He describes a clear contrast between public and "official" relationships and those that are private and personal: " ... they adopt two very different codes of behavior for their two lives – in one, they are taciturn, hypocritical, careful, cagey, passive; in the other, they are voluble, honest, direct, open, passionate. In one, thoughts and feelings are held in check... in the other, emotions flow warmly, without moderation" (1976, p. 140).

This description indicates that the Russians have developed some ways of dealing with *Gesellschaft* situations. But one can hardly say that (like the Germans) they have adopted *Gesellschaft* rules as their own – their reaction is more (like the Italians) that of a peasant culture: distrustful toward outside officials – "taciturn, hypocritical, careful, cagey, passive." In any case, it is clear that private relationships are much more important.

Precisely because their public lives are so supervised... Russians invest their friendships with enormous importance. Many of them, in the cities at least, are only-children whose closest friends come to take the place of missing brothers and sisters. They will visit each other almost daily, like members of the family. Their social circles are usually narrower than those of Westerners, especially Americans, who put such great stock in popularity, but relations between Russians are usually more intense, more demanding, more enduring and often more rewarding.

(Smith, 1976, pp. 143–4.)

These relationships involve a central feature of Dahrendorf's "private virtues": the sharing of misfortune and suffering, "unhindered by the very American compulsion... to disguise the reality of sorrow, disappointment or pain. To Russians, suffering is a natural part of life, and so they find it in their friendships to intrude on each other with their problems and to exult in that sharing" (Smith, 1976, p. 144). "Friendships are not only compensation for the cold impersonality of public life but a vital source of personal identity...'[Friends] are the one part of our lives where we can make our own choice completely for ourselves'" (p. 146). When the two conflict, there is a clear preference for the particularistic values of friendship over more universalistic ones: "...Russians want a total commitment from a friend. They do not understand a journalist who regards it his job to maintain open contacts with all and professes ideals of independence and nonpartisanship. Russians are not after decency or fair play; they want allies, partisans" (pp. 147–8).

Smith offers some suggestions relevant to a comparative approach. Americans feel that the Russian openness is similar to their own immediate and informal, if only partial, openness: "...Americans feel that Russians are like them in temperament, more so than the complicated French or the restrained British and Germans" (p. 148). The Russians are like the Latin peoples in their love of strong emotions and undiluted heroics.

In conclusion, although some change may have taken place, the Russians in the 1970s still seem closer to the traditional Russian characteristics than to its antithesis in the "new Soviet man." It may be possible to detect some evidence of change between Miller's (1960) earlier account, and Smith's (1976) later one. The traditional Russian village a generation or so back may have approached a "pure *Gemeinschaft*" situation. On moving to the industrial centers, the migrant was faced with the demands of *Gesellschaft* rules. Logically, one could distinguish several steps in the transition to a "mixed" case: (a) at first the migrant may have difficulty in behaving according to *Gesellschaft* rules; (b) at a later stage, the individual may be able to behave according to *Gesellschaft* rules, but does not recognize them as legitimate; (c) at a further stage, the *Gesellschaft* rules for public situations might be recognized as legitimate, as in the German case. One might interpret Miller's (1960) description as closer to (a), and Smith's (1976) account as closer to (b). Smith clearly implies a definite "code of behavior" for public situations (although it is a wholly defensive one), while in Miller's account such a code is less clear. In both accounts, the Russians are still far from accepting the *Gesellschaft* rules as legitimate.

Comment

We have argued that the modal Russian personality characteristics were generally similar to formulations of traditional Russian national character, and generally dissimilar to the characteristics of the Protestant ethic and the "new Soviet man" favored by the Soviet regime. The evidence from inside Russia since 1950 suggests that Russians are still more similar to the former than the latter. The evidence is not inconsistent with the assumption of a long-run change toward characteristics like the new Soviet man which would be more congruent with the social system, but it suggests that the critical part of such a change has still to take place.

In the various eastern European countries since 1945, efforts were made to impose similar centralized industrial systems. Comparison between them thus permits illustration – sometimes dramatically – of differences in national characteristics. An example can be given from my own experience. In 1970 I took an automobile trip that included extended sections of both Soviet Russia and East Germany. In both countries foreign tourists were supposed to restrict themselves to certain permitted roads. But this policy was carried out quite differently in the two countries. In Russia there were generally no signs indicating what the proper roads were – at the outskirts of a city, a policeman would appear from a control booth to indicate forcefully which route should be taken. In contrast, across all of East Germany from the Baltic to the Czech border there were signs indicating the "Transit" route both before and at every intersection. Other similar examples could be given. They suggest that the systematic procedures implied by a centralized state are still more congruent with German national characteristics than with Russian ones.

In comparative terms, Russian national character can be compared with other types of contrasts to the Protestant ethic, *Gesellschaft* values, and the public virtues. The Russians and Italians both stress *Gemeinschaft* relationships. But the Italians lack "communal feeling" toward those outside the family and its allies; toward these others in the community there is an attitude of social distrust. In contrast, the Russians do show tendencies toward "communal feeling," which are in conflict with the danger that the other person may not be trusted.

Italians presume everyone else, including the state bureaucracy itself, operates according to particularistic rules. For the Russians, officials may follow universalistic rules. The individual Russians encounter this situation with some attempt to turn the interaction into a particularistic one. In this respect they show some resemblance to the French.[1] But the Russians are looking for a paternalistic relationship with implied inequality and deference, while the French are not.

For both Russians and Germans, "private" relationships clearly may extend outside the family, but the Germans tend to limit these to a comparative few, while one gets the impression, particularly in Miller's account, that even on the public streets a Russian is nearly always open for interaction involving the "private virtues."

Among our nationalities, the Russian retention of considerable communal feeling is exceptional.[2] In part, this may reflect a degree of communal feeling

---

[1] And to some extent with Americans ("Give me a break"). The Germans and the English seem the most likely to show acceptance of the legitimacy of universalistic rules.

[2] However, the German emphasis on supra-individual goals goes in the same direction.

Table 11.1. *Judgments about the Russians: summary*

Judges	Descriptive factors	
	Tight–Loose	Assertive–Unassertive
Consensus	0.72	0.33
English	0.75	0.50
Germans	0.78	0.17
French	0.57	0.53
Italians	0.83	0.37
Austrians	0.71	0.14
Finns	0.66	0.26
Greeks	0.38	0.60

in the traditional village "mir" that was exceptional, if not unique, among peasant societies. In part, it may also reflect a limitation of the present study to nationalities from Europe, all influenced by some variety of Christianity. It can be argued that Christianity generally emphasized the individual, and this tendency was accentuated by the Renaissance. Indeed, individuality and self-actualization (as opposed to individualism in achievement) has traditionally had more emphasis among Catholics such as the French and the Italians than among those influenced by Calvinism such as the Americans and the English. The more communal Russian tradition here may be more like the rest of the non-Christian world, where societies traditionally had a more communal and less individualistic emphasis.

Comparison with judgment results

We will report results for all groups of judges, but will generally comment only on the consensus results. Table 11.1 presents a summary of judgments about the Russians relative to the two major descriptive dimensions. More detailed results for the separate scales are given in Table 11.2.

The consensus judges Russians as very impulse-controlled and moderately assertive. These judgments are inconsistent with the preceding account of Russian characteristics. Nor does it seem possible to explain away much of this inconsistency. In the case of fairly similar judgments about the Germans, we tried to explain away much of any comparable inconsistency, arguing that while Germans were not ascetic, their emphasis on social rules could represent (at least the appearance of) impulse-control. But the accounts of Russian characteristics imply not only that the Russians are impulse-expressive, but that they also do not appear to be impulse-controlled except to the most superficial observation (e.g., following Miller's account, Russians might appear impulse-controlled to a visitor walking the streets of Moscow, but not

Table 11.2. Judgments about the Russians

Scales	Consensus	Judges						
		Eng.	Germ.	Fr.	Ital.	Aust.	Finn.	Greek
1a. Thrifty (+)–Extravagant (−)	1.2	1.5	1.5	1.3	0.4	1.3	1.3	−0.1
1b. Stingy (−)–Generous (+)	0.0	−1.0	0.5	0.8	−0.3	0.0	0.1	0.3
Evaluative component	+0.6	+0.2	+1.0	+1.0	+0.1	+0.6	+0.7	+0.1
Descriptive component	0.6A	1.3A	0.5A	0.3A	0.4A	0.6A	0.6A	0.2B
2a. Self-controlled (+)–Impulsive (−)	0.5	1.2	0.3	0.0	1.1	−0.3	0.6	0.8
2b. Inhibited (−)–Spontaneous (+)	−0.2	−0.7	−0.2	0.1	−0.8	−0.2	0.4	1.4
Evaluative component	+0.1	+0.2	0.0	0.0	+0.2	−0.2	+0.5	+1.1
Descriptive component	0.4A	1.0A	0.3A	0.1B	0.9A	0.1B	0.1A	0.3B
3a. Serious (+)–Frivolous (−)	1.6	2.3	1.6	1.4	2.1	1.5	0.9	1.5
3b. Grim (−)–Gay (+)	−0.4	−1.4	0.1	0.2	−1.5	0.0	0.5	0.3
Evaluative component	+0.6	+0.4	+0.8	+0.8	+0.3	+0.8	+0.7	+0.9
Descriptive component	1.0A	1.8A	0.7A	0.6A	1.8A	0.8A	0.2A	0.6A
4a. Skeptical (+)–Gullible (−)	0.8	1.0	1.4	0.6	0.8	0.8	0.5	0.3
4b. Distrustful (−)–Trusting (+)	−0.8	−0.9	−1.0	−0.5	−0.7	−0.7	−0.8	−0.9
Evaluative component	0.0	+0.1	+0.2	+0.1	+0.1	+0.1	−0.2	−0.3
Descriptive component	0.8A	1.0A	1.2A	0.5A	0.8A	0.8A	0.6A	0.6A
5a. Firm (+)–Lax (−)	1.5	2.2	1.7	1.3	1.4	0.8	1.2	1.4
5b. Severe (−)–Lenient (+)	−0.7	−2.0	−0.2	−1.0	−1.4	−0.3	0.6	−1.1
Evaluative component	+0.4	+0.1	+0.8	+0.2	0.0	+0.2	+0.9	+0.2
Descriptive component	1.1A	2.1A	1.0A	1.2A	1.4A	0.6A	0.3A	1.3A
6a. Persistent (+)–Vacillating (−)	1.4	1.9	1.4	1.5	1.7	1.3	0.6	1.5
6b. Inflexible (−)–Flexible (+)	−1.1	−1.4	−0.7	−1.2	−1.7	−1.0	−0.5	−1.0
Evaluative component	+0.2	+0.3	+0.4	+0.1	0.0	+0.2	+0.1	+0.2
Descriptive component	1.2A	1.7A	1.0A	1.4A	1.7A	1.2A	0.5A	1.2A
7a. Selective (+)–Undiscriminating (−)	0.7	0.9	0.7	0.7	1.3	−0.1	0.4	0.3
7b. Choosy (−)–Broad-minded (+)	−0.7	−0.4	−0.4	−0.6	−1.3	−0.3	−0.1	−0.3
Evaluative component	0.0	−0.2	+0.2	0.0	0.0	−0.2	+0.2	0.0
Descriptive component	0.7A	1.2A	0.6A	0.6A	1.3A	0.1A	0.2A	0.3A
8a. Cautious (+)–Rash (−)	1.3	2.1	1.6	0.3	1.7	1.2	0.9	0.7
8b. Timid (−)–Bold (+)	0.7	1.7	0.5	0.3	0.2	0.8	0.4	1.9
Evaluative component	+1.0	+1.9	+1.1	+0.3	+0.9	+1.0	+0.6	+1.3
Descriptive component	0.3A	0.2A	0.5A	0.0	0.7A	0.2A	0.3A	0.6B

9a. Calm (+)–Agitated (–)	0.7	−0.1	1.5	0.4	0.6	1.2	−0.1
b. Inactive (−)–Active (+)	1.0	1.1	0.2	1.6	1.5	0.3	1.7
Evaluative component	+0.8	+0.5	+0.8	+1.0	+1.0	+0.7	+0.8
Descriptive component	0.1B	0.6B	0.6A	0.6A	0.5B	0.4A	0.9B
10a. Peaceful (+)–Aggressive (−)	−0.2	−1.2	0.2	−0.3	−0.4	0.2	0.2
b. Passive (−)–Forceful (+)	1.1	1.6	0.9	1.2	1.3	0.5	0.2
Evaluative component	+0.5	+0.2	+0.5	+0.4	+0.5	+0.3	+0.2
Descriptive component	0.6B	1.4B	0.4B	0.7B	0.9B	0.2B	0.0
11a. Modest (+)–Conceited (−)	0.4	−0.4	1.0	0.1	0.2	1.0	0.5
b. Unassured (−)–Self-confident (+)	1.0	1.7	1.0	0.8	0.9	0.8	0.9
Evaluative component	+0.7	+0.7	+1.0	+0.5	+0.5	+0.9	+0.7
Descriptive component	0.3B	1.1B	0.0	0.3B	0.3B	0.1A	0.2B
12a. Cooperative (+)–Uncooperative (−)	0.1	−0.5	0.0	0.2	0.7	−0.6	0.5
b. Conforming (−)–Independent (+)	−0.9	−0.5	−1.0	−1.0	−1.3	−1.1	−0.4
Evaluative component	−0.4	−0.5	−0.5	−0.4	−0.3	−0.9	0.0
Descriptive component	0.5A	0.0	0.5A	0.6A	1.0A	0.3A	0.5A
13a. Tactful (+)–Tactless (−)	0.6	0.0	0.7	0.4	1.2	0.5	−0.1
b. Devious (−)–Frank (+)	0.4	0.3	0.4	0.2	0.3	0.6	−0.4
Evaluative component	+0.5	+0.2	+0.5	+0.3	+0.7	+0.5	−0.2
Descriptive component	0.1A	0.2B	0.2A	0.1A	0.4A	0.1B	0.2A
14a. Practical (+)–Impractical (−)	0.9	1.4	0.9	0.7	0.9	0.6	0.9
b. Opportunistic (−)–Idealistic (+)	0.6	1.1	0.7	1.1	0.7	0.3	1.1
Evaluative component	+0.8	+1.2	+0.8	+0.9	+0.8	+0.4	+1.0
Descriptive component	0.1A	0.2A	0.2A	0.2B	0.1A	0.2A	0.1B
15a. Admirable (+)–Deplorable (−)	0.1	−0.2	0.1	0.6	0.6	−0.7	−0.4[a]
b. Not likeable (−)–Likeable (+)	0.5	−0.4	0.8	0.9	0.1	0.7	—
Evaluative component	+0.3	−0.3	+0.5	+0.8	+0.3	0.0	—
Descriptive component	0.2B	0.1A	0.4B	0.1B	0.3A	0.7B	—
16. Hard-working (+)–Lazy (−)	1.5	2.1	1.6	1.7	1.6	0.6	1.7
17. Intelligent (+)–Stupid (−)	1.2	1.4	1.1	1.2	1.3	1.1	1.0

[a] In set 15, the Greek judges used the single scale, *desirable–undesirable*.

likely after a personal interaction with a Russian). In view of the high agreement between different groups of judges in making these judgments, we may conclude that they seem to be the clearest case of *in*accuracy in all our judgment results. (It should be noted that the judgments about Russians are made as strongly as those about other nationality "targets," so that they do not represent cases of "*recognized* unfamiliarity," as may be true, for example, for judgments about the Dutch.)

Indeed – having argued earlier that actual Russian characteristics are still basically dissimilar to the regime's ideal of the "new Soviet man" – we could say that our consensus results more resemble the latter: e.g., the Russians are judged *self-controlled* and *inhibited* (rather than *impulsive* and *spontaneous*), *firm* and *severe* (rather than *lax* and *lenient*), *persistent* and *inflexible* (rather than *vacillating* and *flexible*). Although the ideal of the new Soviet man may not yet have been successfully imposed on the average Russian, it is reflected in our judgment results!

An explanation for the inaccuracy is not hard to find. Consider our review (in Chapter 3) of the sources of information on which judgments might be based. We note that our judges are not likely to have the more useful of these sources: (a) direct contact with ordinary Russians is relatively unlikely from visitors either to or from Russia; (b) contact through literature and the media is also relatively unlikely (as compared with such information about Americans, for example), as is (c) second-hand information through others' opinions that might be based on either of the preceding. Accordingly, by default, our judges are likely to rely on inferences to national characteristics from "the character of the nation," inferences based on the official policies and attitudes of the Soviet regime. (In fact, the individuals representing these policies abroad would themselves – in contrast to average Russians – resemble the new Soviet man and our consensus results.)

In sum, we interpret the apparent inaccuracy of judgments about the Russians as a case of *un*recognized unfamiliarity that is largely based on inferences from national policy.

Some support for this interpretation can be found if we consider particular sets of outgroup judges. We will single out some nationalities who have had relatively more contact with average Russians – at least second-hand contact through the generation of the parents of our judges. In the first instance, the Finns have relatively more contact as immediate neighbors of the Russians. In the second instance, for the Germans and Austrians as well as the Finns, members of the parents' generation had contact as (invading) soldiers in World War II, and sometimes afterward as prisoners-of-war. In the area of Austria around Vienna, there were Russian occupation soldiers from 1945 to 1954.

Comparing these judges with the other standard sets of judges, we note that there is some tendency for these judges, particularly the Finnish judges, to rate Russians as less impulse-controlled. More striking – especially in view of the belligerent nature of the contact just described – these judges rate the Russians as less assertive: as *peaceful* rather than *aggressive*, as clearly *modest* (as opposed to *conceited*). This result well represents the proposed interpretation in the contrast between the assertiveness of Soviet policy, and the relative unassertiveness of average Russians.[1]

As an indication of historical change, we note that in the consensus judgments, the overall evaluative component, averaged across the 28 regular scales, was positive for Russians and the same as for Americans. This can be contrasted with the large-scale study of Buchanan and Cantril (1953) at the height of the "cold war" where judgments about Russians were overwhelmingly negative, and judgments about Americans were overwhelmingly positive.

[1] An alternative interpretation of these results could argue that these nationalities also base their judgments on Soviet policy, but see it as less aggressive than others do, perhaps because of a more immediate concern with details of that policy.

12 The Americans

> Yet in some respects this type [the other-directed man] is strikingly
> similar to *the* American, whom Tocqueville and other curious and
> astonished visitors from Europe, even before the Revolution,
> thought to be a new kind of man. Indeed, travelers' reports in
> America impress us with their unanimity. The American is said to
> be shallower, freer with his money, friendlier, more uncertain of
> himself and his values, more demanding of approval than the
> European.
>
> Riesman, 1950, pp. 19–20

In his classic study of America, Tocqueville (1954) tended to relate every characteristic of the Americans to equality. More recently, Lipset (1963) has proposed that many American characteristics can be derived from the two values of equality and achievement. Let us see how far Lipset's argument can be developed.

Equality

In Lipset's account, American equalitarianism itself derives from its history, especially the absence of a feudal tradition and the American revolution and its consequences.[1] Instead of a tradition deriving from feudalism, national identity was based on the revolution itself (in this respect similar to France) and the source of authority on the constitution.

Three aspects of "equality" need to be considered. Most important is "basic social equality." Each individual has value as a human being, and there is a tendency not to recognize qualitative differences (whether ascribed or achieved) between people that provide a categorical basis for deference. James Bryce (1891, p. 618) put it as follows: "There is no rank in America, that is to say, no external and recognized stamp, marking one man as entitled to any social privileges, or to deference and respect for others. No man is entitled to think himself better than his fellows, or to expect any exceptional consideration to be shown by them to him."

Equality combines with achievement as "equality of opportunity." This has

---

[1] Lipset makes comparisons of the United States with other "new nations" arising around 1960 in Africa and Asia, and with relatively similar countries such as Canada and Australia. Thus, Canada shares with the United States the lack of a feudal tradition, but not the history of a revolution.

some prescriptive implications ("duties") such as support for public education. Perhaps more important are the proscriptive implications ("rights") for non-interference by others, a possible meaning of both "freedom" and "individualism." These two forms of equality are not always realized in practice. In his classic study of the American Negro, Myrdal (1944) described "the American dilemma" as the conflict between the value of equality and the actuality of discrimination. A similar analysis was applied to women. Americans tend to evade recognition of such inconsistencies; the value of equality is seldom denied directly and provides a potential basis for protest – a basis utilized by blacks and then by women since the 1950s.

Equality of opportunity does not preclude "inequality of condition" as in the income and wealth that is actually achieved. This represents a conflict between equality and achievement with the latter winning.

It is revealing to consider the political consequences of these three meanings of equality, especially as regards the failure to develop a strong socialist movement as in Europe. The attitude of social equality is related to a lack of class consciousness, that elsewhere provided the basis for a socialist movement. At the same time, the lack of an aristocratic tradition leads to American conservatism supporting the traditional liberal value of equal opportunity. Thus there is an attenuation on both sides of the European political conflict of the last century between those who would preserve and those who would overturn qualitative class differences. While "inequality of condition" is not greater than elsewhere, what is striking is that the differences have not been more strongly objected to in the name of equality, as they would be by socialists elsewhere. "A European advocating equality might very well mean that all men should occupy positions that are roughly the same level in wealth, power, or enviability. But the American, with his emphasis upon equality of opportunity, has never conceived of it in this way" (Potter, 1954, p. 91). Paradoxically, the lack of class consciousness and the belief in equality of opportunity have prevented the rise of a major socialist movement that might oppose achieved inequality.

Characteristics derived from equality

What other characteristics might be derived from equality? We begin by developing Lipset's suggestions.

a. *Competition* is implied by achievement plus equality of opportunity. Success in economic competition can be validated by income and wealth. But there is also competition for general social status – "status striving."

b. *Status uncertainty* follows from basic social equality. The non-recognition of any *ascribed* social status helps to initiate status striving. But, in addition, the limited recognition of *achieved* status means that it is difficult to validate success. Several consequences follow.

c. *Conspicuous consumption* represents one way to try to convert successful economic achievement into general status. Lipset (p. 114) cites the psychologist Muensterberg: "The ability to spend was the only public sign of success at earning."

d. *"Other-directedness"* is another important consequence. Social equality implies not only status uncertainty but also that there is generally no elite group comparable to the British aristocracy that could serve to validate success in status striving by "admission to the club." Consequently Americans tend to seek validation from everyone: wanting to be liked leads to some suppression of hostility, sensitivity to approval by others leads to both kindliness and conformity. Thus, where Riesman (1950) tended to treat "other-directedness" as a largely new trend in American character, Lipset derives it from the historical American emphasis on equality.

e. *"Popular culture"* follows from the non-recognition of any elite that should establish standards. Similar "popular" influences also apply to areas that are outside of the usual meaning of "popular culture" – e.g., in education, the influence of the public in America contrasts with the British insistence on control by professionals (Lipset, p. 221), and in politics, populist tendencies include pressure for publicity as opposed to arrangements made with discreet secrecy by insiders (Lipset, pp. 219–20).

f. *Relative equality for children* has long been noted as an American characteristic. It is shown in both child–parent and child–teacher relations. (One could add for adolescents the historically distinctive American institution of "dating" – Gorer, 1948, pp. 77–8, 81–90, 93–4.)

We may add three more derivations from equality to those suggested by Lipset.

g. *"Humanitarianism"*: social equality – the tendency to consider all human beings as basically the same – allows for the *possibility* (not always realized in practice) of identifying with their plight. American activism encourages doing something about it, and American affluence has made it easier to do so. On the other hand, the value on individualism related to achievement conflicts with humanitarianism, and suggests that it be limited to those who are in distress "by no fault of their own."

A related tendency, that appears in Coleman's (1941) summary of American "traits" as the "missionary spirit," is the recurrent American belief that the world would be helped by the adoption of the specific American political or economic systems. As an illustration of its relation to belief in basic equality, Gorer (1948, p. 174) with his characteristic acerbity, cites the "one-worldly" views of Wendell Willkie and Henry Wallace during World War II, who "claimed, with apparently no feeling of incongruity, that conditions in Siberia or in Yunnan are strictly parallel with those on the American frontier a century ago."

h. *Informality* derives at least in part from social equality – since formal relations are often those between people of recognized different status. Perhaps the famous "frontier tradition" is also a factor here.

i. *Rejection of authority* derives from social equality as applied to oneself. Orders may be accepted in a functionally specific situation which one has entered voluntarily (e.g., the "boss" in one's job), but any claims to diffuse deference tend to be resisted. An illustration is provided by the military, which represents an obvious contrasting situation: a feudal heritage that includes qualitative differences as a categorical basis for privileges and diffuse deference – the very antithesis of social equality. The result is nicely summarized by Spindler's comparison of Americans with Germans in the military, which he relates to an analysis of American character centering around individualistic self-interest:

Senior officers were careful to maintain their status with appropriate ritual and rigidly maintained social distance. Junior officers somewhat guiltily accepted the implications of their role. Enlisted men completely rejected the whole business. The polls show almost unanimous resentment against the implications of the status hierarchy, and the "caste" tendencies of the system were the most violently rejected aspect of the military...

Authority and its corollary – discipline – are given low value by the Americans. The only people who consistently value it positively are those who are responsible for its execution – mostly higher ranking officers. The adjustment of the majority on the receiving end is one of constant avoidance and negation. The sparse, but emotionally laden GI vocabulary is a good barometer of attitude. There are no terms approving of authority or discipline, and at least twenty-five most foul expressions emphasizing extreme distaste. One phenomenon, the very widespread looting and black market activities of enlisted men and junior officers, deserves special mention. Though expressly and repeatedly defined in directives as a crime against military authority, it developed into big business, and openly, involving at least eighty percent of the personnel.

(Spindler, 1948, p. 278)

This last may be related to a general American tendency for "Disregard of the law," which Coleman (1941) found mentioned in all four time periods he considered.

Another comparison examined the American and British merchant marine (Richardson, 1956). Lipset (p. 269n) cites Richardson's summary:

"Comparison of British and American crews suggests that the British realize and accept the authority of competent persons and are not as fearful of the misuse of authority as Americans...British seamen are conditioned before coming to sea to accept authority..."

"Among American crews a far greater fear and suspicion of authority appears to exist. Social stratification is not widely accepted and is often denied..." Since the norms of the social structure undermine authority on American ships, there is a necessity for a "far greater formalization of the social system than [on] the British," and American ships have many more explicit rules and regulations.

In these military and quasi-military situations, tradition makes it difficult for the superordinate to adapt to American anti-authority attitudes by reducing status differences to a functionally specific minimum.[1] In other situations, such an adaptation is common. As one example, consider Goffman's (1961) description of an American surgical operating team. A striking feature is the regular informal joking led by the surgeon which tends to minimize the actual authority hierarchy. Consider the following example (Goffman, 1961, p. 118):

> CHIEF SURGEON JONES: A small Richardson please.
> NURSE: Don't have one.
> DR. JONES: O.K. then give me an Army and Navy.
> NURSE: It looks like we don't have one.
> DR. JONES (*lightly joking*): No Army or Navy man here.
> INTERN (dryly): No one in the armed forces, but Dr. Jones here is in the Boy Scouts.

The informal joking of the surgeon contributes an atmosphere where he receives a thrust from the subordinate intern. Goffman's own interpretation is that the surgeon "distances" himself from his superordinate role in order to reduce tensions. But one may question whether this would be necessary in a nationality (e.g., the Germans) that had more acceptance of hierarchical situations.

Crozier (1964), in a study of French bureaucratic organizations, includes some comparative remarks on American procedures. Both countries share a value of equalitarianism leading to resistance to authority. The French solution is to avoid face-to-face relationships involving subordination by using impersonal rules and referring decisions upward in a centralized hierarchy. The Americans in dealing with the comparable problem also use impersonal rules, but these are more often procedural than substantive. In addition there is functional specificity and decentralization of decision-making with less avoidance of face-to-face hierarchical relationships. The American bureaucratic problem is not the French one of lack of communication between isolated strata, but disputes about jurisdiction between multiple decision centers.

Achievement

In addition to equality, the second American value emphasized by Lipset (1963) is achievement. Indeed, in focusing on equality thus far, we have not

---

[1] Even so, American generals in World War II appeared without jackets and ties, and with a minimum of medals.

been able to avoid all of its complex relations with achievement.[1] Lipset's attempt to proceed using only the two values of equality and achievement – in contrast, Williams (1970) lists some 14 American values – is aided by the relation of achievement to other American values. Thus, if achievement is *required*, it must be *possible*, with implications for environmentalism (and the perfectibility of man) and optimism (the idea of "progress"). As we have seen, individualism has as two of its relevant meanings: individual responsibility for achievement, and individual rights to a minimum of interference in this undertaking. This last is a major meaning of "freedom" or "liberty." Snowman (1977) explores the complexities of these interrelationships.

Achievement is part of the Protestant ethic and will be treated in that context.

The Protestant ethic and its decline

Snowman (1977), in a comparative study of Britain and America, treats the "Puritan ethic" as central to traditional American values. He gives primary emphasis to the "worldly" rather than the "ascetic" aspects of the Protestant ethic of Weber: hard work and individual responsibility for achievement (self-reliance). He gives secondary emphasis to some other aspects: thrift, extra-marital chastity, and charity. Initially these values were supported both by Calvinism and by the severe material demands of the new world. Their preservation thereafter he relates to four historical factors: the revolution, the westward expansion, and to massive immigration and industrialization in the late nineteenth and early twentieth centuries. The effect of the "frontier" was to emphasize self-reliance and competitiveness instead of other aspects of the Protestant ethic, although the symbolic figure of the cowboy represents not only lonely self-reliance but also strict self-control. On the whole, it is consistent with Snowman's comparison of Britain and America to say that Americans emphasized more the "worldly" aspects and the British the ascetic aspects of "worldly asceticism."

Snowman suggests that in the recent period there has been a movement away from the Protestant ethic and toward the new values of what we have called the "consumption-oriented society": technique infatuation, participativeness, transitoriness, and self-indulgence.

There is widespread agreement from other authors both that traditional American national characteristics were strongly influenced by the Protestant ethic, and that there has recently been a decline in this influence. There is

---

[1] Put differently, equality and achievement can be seen as a contention between two rival philosophies: the humanitarian philosophy of the French Enlightenment emphasizing equality and the common good, and the English philosophy of laissez-faire emphasizing individualistic self-interest and freedom for achievement (Williams, 1970, p. 464).

disagreement about the evaluation of this change as good or bad, and about the direction that the change has taken. These points can be illustrated by reference to three books, all of which were popular successes: David Riesman's (1950) *The lonely crowd.* William H. Whyte's (1956) *The organization man,* and Charles Reich's (1970)*The greening of America.*

Riesman's subtle and prescient analysis remains of interest. He describes a historical sequence of social character: tradition-directed, inner-directed, other-directed. Inner-directedness bears an obvious resemblance to the Protestant ethic, but Riesman does not attribute it primarily to religious values. His own initial proposal that the historical determinant represented stages in population growth was later withdrawn. It would seem consistent with his general account to attribute the crucial change from inner-directedness to other-directedness to the change described earlier, to a consumption-oriented (and increasingly bureaucratic) economy. It is implied that the change will follow elsewhere, and appears most prominently in America only because it has reached this stage earlier.

Whyte's account is in many ways a simpler version of Riesman's. The change is referred to directly as from the "Protestant ethic" to a "social ethic," reflecting a change towards large-scale bureaucratic organizations. Whyte clearly deplores the change, while for Riesman a similar evaluation can be detected only behind a determined effort to appear neutral. Lipset (1961, 1963) objects to the suggestion of Riesman and Whyte that there has been a recent change for Americans toward conformity, and on Weberian grounds to their attempt to derive these characteristics only from materialistic causes (the organization of the economy) while neglecting the determining effect of values. He argues that conformity has always been considered a distinctive characteristic of Americans, and, as we have seen, derives other-directedness from the American value of equality. In his conclusion, however, he accepts in effect a compromise that combines both views: changes toward other-directedness over time that derive from bureaucratization of the economy and would apply to both the United States and Europe, and continued greater other-directedness by Americans deriving from the American value of equality.

In Reich's (1970) *The greening of America,* the Protestant ethic generally corresponds to what is called "Consciousness I," and something like other-directedness to "Consciousness II." Reich predicts that a further change is taking place toward hedonistic impulse-expression (Consciousness III). This change is celebrated rather than deplored. Although Reich's book is likely to have a more transient importance than Riesman's, it does represent some general tendencies: while America in the 1950s was often described as conformist, this hardly applied to the 1960s which involved tendencies toward activist public protest as well as toward individual hedonistic impulse-expression.

The conclusion is that in relating the Protestant ethic to Americans, we need to distinguish three problems: to what extent historical American characteristics corresponded to the Protestant ethic; to what extent there has been change away from this; and the nature of any such changes (e.g., whether toward conformity or toward self-expression).

The several characteristics making up the Protestant ethic will be considered in turn.

Work and achievement. In discussing the Protestant ethic, we tried to make a distinction between work as an end-in-itself (suggested by Weber's discussion of Luther's idea of work as a "calling") and work as a *means* to successful achievement. If such a distinction is made, it is not clear that the former – dedication to one's occupation and pride in its products – was ever distinctive for Americans. It *is* clear that distinctive American contributions to industrialism (interchangeable parts, the production line) would tend to go against any pride in workmanship.

Systematic "rationality" applied to work as a means to achievement can be overgeneralized to yield the restless activity described by Weber, and this appears to have been particularly characteristic of Americans.

McClelland (1961, pp. 150–1) accepts evidence for a decline in achievement motivation for Americans after a peak around 1890, but the evidence for a (further) decline between 1930 and 1950 is inconsistent. Lowenthal (1961) in a classic analysis of popular biographies, showed that there was a shift by the 1920s from "heroes of production" to "heroes of consumption." We have already cited Riesman and Whyte as suggesting a decline in the Protestant ethic by the 1950s. Albee (1977) is among those who see a major shift toward consumption-orientation by the 1970s. Against this prevailing opinion, Lipset himself argues for a more cyclical pattern, with concern about equality (and acceptance of achievement) in times of depression as in the 1930s, and concerns about achievement in times of prosperity, as in the 1950s.

Empiricism/practicality. Historically, this feature of the Protestant ethic has seemed very distinctive for Americans. Convenient illustrations can be found within philosophy and psychology, where George Miller (1962, Ch. 5) is able to argue that Americans proposed "pragmatic" theories of meaning (Pierce), truth (James), values (Dewey), and the mind (Watson). It is widely believed that within both the natural and the social sciences major theoretical ideas have tended to originate with Europeans, while the Americans have specialized in technological applications.

The general belief in technique – that, for almost any purpose, there is some method that will be relatively successful – remains characteristic of Americans. But the purposes may include not only those that are consistent with the Protestant ethic ("How to build or repair your own home"), but also those that are more or less independent of it ("How to win friends, and influence people"), and even those that are subversive of the Protestant ethic ("How to enjoy better sex"). Thus a characteristic that is somewhat peripheral to Weber's conception may retain a certain autonomy, even when it may undermine more central aspects.

Impulse-control/asceticism. Thrift is the most obvious form of impulse-control relevant to capitalism. However, even in nineteenth-century accounts about Americans, such tendencies were overcome by opposing tendencies to generosity/extravagance. This might be attributed to the relatively high level of affluence, to tendencies for conspicuous consumption, or to kindliness deriving from sympathy for the less fortunate. Gorer (1948, p. 136) writes: "The acquisition of money is very important to Americans, but its retention is relatively unimportant. Income...fixes your relative position in regard to your fellows; but [thereafter]...there is no deep emotional reason for retaining it."

On the other hand, as regards ascetic control over hedonistic pleasures, Americans were traditionally considered "puritanical." Perhaps the most dramatic example was the Prohibition of alcohol between 1919 and 1933. However, this has been interpreted (e.g., Lipset, 1963, pp. 338–40) as a last-ditch effort by nativist, non-urban fundamentalist Protestants against the increasing opposing tendencies from urbanization. These latter, together with the shift to a consumption-oriented economy, have tended to reverse the Protestant ethic especially from the 1920s onward, appearing dramatically in the 1960s with hedonistic impulse-expression involving drugs and sex. There is little doubt that hedonistic behavior has increased. Nevertheless, there are signs that residual effects of asceticism remain that continue to make this behavior conflicted rather than simply a natural part of life. While Riesman (1950) seems to have early and correctly pointed to an increasing interest in gourmet food on the part of the upper-middle class (also reported by Glyn in England) this is counteracted for the society as a whole by the spectacular spread of fast-food establishments (which meanwhile may be patronized by Frenchmen in Paris). The absence of a general interest in food might be symbolized in both America and England by the bottle of ketchup which may be poured indiscriminately on meat, fried potatoes, and cottage cheese. Sex, although widely practiced, retains some traditionally American characteristics: stimulation from the mass media (magazines such as *Playboy*), faith in technique (Snowman, 1977, p. 88, says that "for every book about love there must have been a hundred on sexual technique" and promptly lists 20 titles), the use of group arrangements (e.g., mate-swapping) for what others would consider an inherently private activity.

"Universal otherhood": public vs. private virtues. We have included in the Protestant ethic the characteristic Nelson (1969) calls "universal otherhood":

a tendency to treat everyone equally with a lack of "particularistic" relationships. This implies a lack of Dahrendorf's "private virtues" and a possible emphasis on "public virtues" instead.

Some aspects of the "public virtues" Dahrendorf describes for the English – smiling affability to all – are even more obvious for Americans. Indeed, Americans may be surprised at this description, seeing the English as relatively reserved. The difference seems to be that Americans tend to be relatively informal (and the English relatively formal) in all settings.

The difference between English formality and American informality may tend to obscure the relevant similarity. There is a lack of a sharp distinction between "public" and "private" situations and relationships. There is a tendency toward several of Parsons' "Gesellschaft" values (universalism, specificity, affective neutrality) in all settings.

In Glyn's (1970) account, the British are relatively reserved and formal even in family relationships. In contrast, Americans tend to be informal and "friendly" even in a casual social encounter. What both tend to lack are Dahrendorf's "private virtues": particularistic relationships that involve "diffuse" rights and duties, and are "intent on honesty and profoundness rather than ease and lack of friction" (Dahrendorf, 1969, p. 286).

A similar point was central to Kurt Lewin's classic comparison of Americans with Germans. Lewin proposed that for Americans the peripheral parts of personality were relatively accessible and social distance small, but the opposite holds for the central parts of personality. As a result:

Germans entering the United States notice usually that the degree of friendly and close relation, which one may achieve as a newcomer within a few weeks, is much higher than under similar circumstances in Germany. Compared with Germans, Americans seem to make quicker progress toward friendly relations in the beginning, and with many more persons. Yet this development often stops at a certain point; and the quickly acquired friends will, after years of relatively close relations, say goodbye as quickly as after a few weeks of acquaintance.

(Lewin, 1936, pp. 281–2)

Indeed, if – in Dahrendorf's account – the Germans consider the English smiling affability as "hypocritical," the American informal friendliness would seem even more misleading to others. In fact this is precisely the implication of a report on students from India (Useem and Useem, 1954). Several hypotheses are discussed as to why these students feel more sure that they know what the British are like than they do the Americans.

Still another hypothesis can be inferred from the side comments of those who say "The people are frank – but." The "but" refers to the observation that the English are hard to make out *before* a friendship is established; the Americans *after* a contact is made…

Friendships with Americans are established more quickly and either person is free to take the initiative. Although rarely rebuffed in starting a friendship, the Indian is not confident of the solidity of the bond: "You cannot assume that because Americans are friendly you are fully accepted. You still have to watch what you say." "Americans are free to talk but their freeness is a mannerism and we Indians often misunderstood." The American is described as smiling, polite, congenial, and careful not to offend. At first Indians impute from these cues more than they are intended to convey in American culture. Most of an Indian's friends take a span of time for each to test the other's involvement. The foreign returned are impressed by the rapidity with which strangers in America form friendships – and are upset when the attachments prove to be so temporary. It causes some to say, "Americans are friendly, but are they really sincere?" "Everyone is friendly – but it is hard to have a friend."

(Useem and Useem, 1954, p. 77)

Indeed, this is a repeated and nearly universal complaint about Americans. A report on Scandinavian students (Sewell *et al.*, 1954) first cites their admiration for the warm friendliness and spontaneity of Americans, but "this admiration is tempered, sooner or later, by the feeling that much of this warmth and acceptance is merely skin-deep." The superficial nature of American friendliness may itself be positively appreciated, but "on the other hand, the discovery of the seeming shallowness of friendship may come as an unpleasant shock and bring with it accusations of hypocrisy: the charge that informality is in itself merely a formality to cover up a lack of real concern for the other individual. Americans are said to have hundreds of acquaintances but no true friends" (p. 127).

For the French, American "friendliness and cordiality surpass at first what they could have expected, but the more their visit is prolonged the more they feel themselves largely deceived. They notice in effect that our cordiality at the beginning does not lead, as would probably happen in France, to a profound friendship; our friendliness remains nearly always very superficial. They even accuse us of hypocrisy because we do not behave according to our true feelings" (Wylie and Bégué, 1970, pp. 412–13).

In short, the American "public virtue" of universalistic social equality is related to difficulty in having "private" relationships with the *Gemeinschaft* qualities of particularism, diffuseness, and affectivity. These problems may appear for long-run intimate relationships with friends or within the family. Upper-middle-class American parents may have their children call them by their first names – which tends to deny that the child–parent relationship is a special one. In a study comparing American and German socialization practices cited by Lipset (1963, p. 275), American parents are less likely to accept a dependent, child-like role for the child and to respond with "parenting behavior" in the form of "affection and companionship" as well as with "direct punishment and control." Instead they put pressure on the children to achieve and to participate in semi-autonomous peer-group activity.

Americans themselves, of course, are likely to assume that spontaneous friendliness may have no deeper implications. Riesman (1950) suggests that

Americans are skeptical of being manipulated by apparent personalness ("pseudo-Gemeinschaft") as the means to some other end. He treats "false personalization" as a main obstacle to "autonomy."

If, in Lewin's terms, the central parts of Americans' personalities are relatively inaccessible for others, there may be a parallel inaccessibility for oneself. The American emphasis on "individualism" has historically meant individual responsibility for achievement, and freedom from interference, but not what we have called "individuality" – the development of the unique features of one's own personality.

The recent changes seem to have tended to retain strongly the second (laissez-faire) aspect of individualism, but give up the emphasis on responsibility for achievement in favor of more hedonistic ends. An example is the loud playing of music in college dormitories and on the public streets. Regarded more favorably, the hedonistic ends can be seen as a form of self-expression and concern for individuality. There has been a reaction against the insincerity of "self-presentation," and efforts in favor of "authenticity," "self-revelation," and personality "growth." It is striking that these efforts nevertheless have frequently taken very American forms, e.g., a search for some "technique," and the search for *individual* growth, which often uses a *group* setting as in a huge variety of "sensitivity training groups," "encounter groups," etc.

The "psycho-cultural" approach

Mead (1942) and Gorer (1948) provide related descriptions using what Gorer (p. 8) calls the "psycho-cultural" point of view. Margaret Mead was a leader in the development of the "culture and personality" approach to pre-industrial peoples – with an emphasis, influenced by psychoanalysis, on child training practices in determining adult personality, as well as in the extension of this approach to modern nations during World War II. Her book on the Americans is somewhat embarrassing in its uninhibited patriotism, but this is refreshingly balanced by Gorer's waspish thrusts. Both center their accounts around "typical" family relationships. The distinctive themes considered here are all related to loss of authority by the parents, and the father in particular, with a corresponding relative increase of female influence in child development.

Rejection of authority is related to the immigrant experience: the authority of the first-generation father, not fully assimilated, is rejected by the second-generation son; the uncertain authority of the second-generation father is rejected in turn by the third-generation son. "We are all third-generation." (Mead's emphasis on the use by the parents – especially the mother – of approval and affection as contingent on achievement, is consistent with Spindler's (1948) suggestion that this does not prepare the individual for strict obedience to authority in the military.)

Gorer also derives from mother influence the characteristic which Williams (1970) calls "moral orientation" – a tendency to evaluate conduct against ethical standards as "good" or "bad."[1] This characteristic – of "moralism" – might be included as part of the Protestant ethic. In Gorer's version the predominantly female nature of conscience meant that it need not be applied to "masculine" spheres such as business. Such exceptions are not recognized: "There is a general and concerted tendency to ignore those aspects of the universe which clash too strongly with the general ethical picture" (p. 42).

Boasting and assertiveness are related to provoking someone else to start a fight ("The chip on the shoulder") – only then will fighting be legitimate; and tendencies in the American family for children to "perform" before the parents as audience, while in the English family the parents perform with the children as audience. Similarly, Spindler's comparison of military "virility" contrasts the German "iron heart in an iron body" with American "tough-boy" aggressiveness, of the "swaggering, cocky, impudent, gang-boy" type. He suggests that this is an effort to assert masculinity against a mother-dominated family (compare the Latin-American "machismo"). Consistent with this is Gorer's emphasis on the importance of not being a "sissy" (pp. 62–3), doubts about masculinity (p. 69), and panic–fear of homosexuality (pp. 95–9) – all related to female-dominated childhood. These tendencies may have decreased recently with the increase in a more sensitive other-directedness with its suppression of aggressiveness. However, in Coleman's (1941) review of generally recognized American characteristics up to 1940 there appear: "Bragging and boasting," "Exaggeration," and "National conceit."

In any case, there is no escaping the evidence that violence is indeed as "American as apple pie." The inhibition of aggression – so striking for the English – has not been generally extended among Americans. For Americans, a tradition of violence exists side by side with a desire to be liked by everyone.

Some data

Such characteristics do not appear in Almond and Verba's (1963) comparative study in *The civic culture*. Books concerned with political democracy in the early 1960s tend to show a bland optimism about America which might be difficult to sustain today. Their American sample overwhelmingly cites the political system as what they are most proud of about their country (p. 102). Other findings support the presence of "public virtues" that plausibly favor public participation: of their five countries, Americans are the most likely to say that they could participate in school discussions (p. 333), to choose some "outgoing" (group) leisure activity (p. 263), and to say that they would organize a group if they wanted to influence the government (p. 191). They

---

[1] From this point of view, the emphasis in social psychology on the evaluative aspects of judgment, which we have been questioning here, could itself be interpreted as an American characteristic.

Table 12.1. *Judgments about the Americans: summary*

Judges	Descriptive factors	
	Tight–Loose	Assertive–Unassertive
Consensus	−0.49	0.64
English	−0.39	0.78
Germans	−0.41	0.67
French	−0.63	0.54
Italians	−0.65	0.46
Austrians	−0.34	0.74
Finns	−0.51	0.64
Greeks	0.20	0.73
Philippines	−0.30	0.65

are much the most likely (p. 131) to say positive (*c.* 67%) rather than negative (*c.* 20%) things about supporters of *opposing* political parties (the comparable figures for Italians were roughly 6% vs. 62%!), and to be indifferent as to having such a person marry into the family (p. 135).

Conflict dilemmas. The most obvious dilemma must be related to the paradox contained in Riesman's title *The lonely crowd* – a conflict between individualism and other-directedness that would be traced to Lipset's two central values of achievement and equality. Using Erikson's terms, Inkeles *et al.* (1958) propose that two critical dilemmas for Americans are those that are characteristic of adolescence: "ego-identity vs. role diffusion," and "intimacy vs. isolation." We would expect this dilemma to relate to our set *independent* (+)/*uncooperative* (−) vs. *cooperative* (+)/*conforming* (−).

Comment

We have considered a large number of American characteristics, touching on all of some 14 values cited by Williams (1970), and most of the 40 "traits" of Coleman (1941) that are relatively applicable to individuals. This extended treatment may itself be interpreted as a result of the American tendency to empiricism. Americans may not have more characteristics than our other nationalities – although the greater heterogeneity of American society would make this possible – but a list of them is more likely to have been provided.

Comparison with judgment results

We will report results for all groups of judges, but will generally comment only on the consensus results. Table 12.1 presents a summary of the results relative to the two major descriptive dimensions. The consensus judges

Table 12.2. *Judgments about the Americans*

Scales	Consensus	Judges						
		Eng.	Germ.	Fr.	Ital.	Aust.	Finn.	Greek
1a. Thrifty (+)-Extravagant (−)	−1.3	−1.5	−1.5	−1.7	−1.3	−1.0	−1.1	0.0
b. Stingy (−)-Generous (+)	1.3	−0.2	1.5	1.4	1.5	1.1	1.2	−0.2
Evaluative component	0.0	−0.1	0.0	−0.2	+0.1	+0.1	0.0	−0.1
Descriptive component	1.3B	1.3B	1.5B	1.6B	1.4B	1.0B	1.1B	0.1A
2a. Self-controlled (+)-Impulsive (−)	−0.3	−0.7	−0.2	−0.2	−0.7	0.0	0.1	0.5
b. Inhibited (−)-Spontaneous (+)	1.4	1.0	1.1	2.0	1.5	1.7	1.2	0.8
Evaluative component	+0.5	+0.2	+0.5	+0.9	+0.4	+0.7	+0.6	+0.7
Descriptive component	0.8B	0.8B	0.7B	1.1B	1.1B	0.7B	0.6B	0.2B
3a. Serious (+)-Frivolous (−)	−0.5	0.0	−0.6	−0.4	−0.8	−0.5	−0.7	−0.5
b. Grim (−)-Gay (+)	1.3	1.0	0.7	2.0	1.7	0.7	1.6	1.3
Evaluative component	+0.4	+0.5	+0.1	+0.8	+0.5	+0.1	+0.4	+0.9
Descriptive component	0.9B	0.5B	0.6B	1.2B	1.3B	0.6B	1.1B	0.3B
4a. Skeptical (+)-Gullible (−)	−0.3	0.0	0.0	−0.1	−0.7	−0.4	−0.3	0.3
b. Distrustful (−)-Trusting (+)	0.6	0.6	0.1	1.3	1.0	0.2	0.5	0.6
Evaluative component	+0.2	+0.3	0.0	+0.6	+0.2	−0.1	+0.1	+0.5
Descriptive component	0.4B	0.3B	0.1B	0.7B	0.9B	0.3B	0.4B	0.1B
5a. Firm (+)-Lax (−)	0.1	0.1	0.1	−0.3	0.0	0.2	0.4	1.5
b. Severe (−)-Lenient (+)	0.2	−0.3	−0.6	1.2	0.7	−0.5	0.6	0.3
Evaluative component	+0.1	−0.1	−0.2	+0.5	+0.3	−0.2	+0.5	+0.9
Descriptive component	0.1B	0.2A	0.4A	0.7B	0.4B	0.3A	0.1B	0.6A
6a. Persistent (+)-Vacillating (−)	0.6	1.6	0.1	0.6	0.3	0.6	0.5	1.2
b. Inflexible (−)-Flexible (+)	0.6	0.4	0.6	−0.2	1.2	1.0	0.5	−0.1
Evaluative component	+0.6	+1.0	+0.3	+0.2	+0.7	+0.8	+0.5	+0.6
Descriptive component	0.0	0.6A	0.2B	0.4A	0.5B	0.2B	0.0	0.7A
7a. Selective (+)-Undiscriminating (−)	0.5	1.3	0.0	0.6	−0.8	1.1	0.9	0.9
b. Choosy (−)-Broad-minded (+)	0.8	0.4	−0.3	1.5	1.7	0.0	1.4	0.0
Evaluative component	+0.7	+0.9	−0.1	+1.1	+0.4	+0.5	+1.2	+0.4
Descriptive component	0.1B	0.5A	0.1A	0.5B	1.3B	0.6A	0.2B	0.4A
8a. Cautious (+)-Rash (−)	−0.6	−0.6	−0.1	−0.8	−0.5	−0.3	−1.0	0.8
b. Timid (−)-Bold (+)	1.2	1.6	0.7	1.6	1.1	0.7	1.4	0.8
Evaluative component	+0.3	+0.5	+0.3	+0.4	+0.3	+0.2	+0.2	+0.8
Descriptive component	0.9B	1.1B	0.4B	1.2B	0.8B	0.5B	1.2B	0.0

9a. Calm (+)–Agitated (–)	−0.3	−0.6	0.1	−0.9	0.1	−0.2	−0.2	0.4
b. Inactive (–)–Active (+)	1.6	1.4	1.2	1.8	2.0	1.2	1.8	1.7
Evaluative component	+0.7	+0.4	+0.6	+0.5	+1.1	+0.5	+0.8	+1.0
Descriptive component	0.9B	1.0B	0.5B	1.3B	0.9B	0.7B	1.0B	0.6B
10a. Peaceful (+)–Aggressive (–)	−0.3	−1.0	−0.8	0.2	0.2	−0.4	0.1	0.5
b. Passive (–)–Forceful (+)	1.3	1.4	0.5	1.7	1.1	1.3	1.6	0.5
Evaluative component	+0.5	+0.2	−0.1	+1.0	+0.6	+0.4	+0.9	+0.5
Descriptive component	0.8B	1.2B	0.7B	0.8B	0.5B	0.8B	0.8B	0.0
11a. Modest (+)–Conceited (–)	−1.4	−1.4	−1.4	−0.6	−1.4	−1.8	−1.6	−0.3
b. Unassured (–)–Self-confident (+)	1.8	2.2	1.5	1.7	1.2	1.7	2.2	1.0
Evaluative component	+0.2	+0.4	+0.1	+0.5	−0.1	0.0	+0.3	−0.3
Descriptive component	1.6B	1.8B	1.5B	1.2B	1.3B	1.8B	1.9B	0.7B
12a. Cooperative (+)–Uncooperative (–)	0.9	0.4	0.8	1.2	1.6	0.5	1.1	0.8
b. Conforming (–)–Independent (+)	0.8	0.6	−0.5	0.8	1.4	0.8	1.8	1.0
Evaluative component	+0.9	+0.5	+0.2	+1.0	+1.5	+0.6	+1.4	+0.9
Descriptive component	0.1A	0.1B	0.7A	0.2A	0.1A	0.2B	0.4B	0.1B
13a. Tactful (+)–Tactless (–)	−0.4	−0.8	−0.7	−0.6	−0.3	−1.1	1.2	0.8
b. Devious (–)–Frank (+)	0.9	0.7	0.6	1.8	1.2	0.9	0.2	0.8
Evaluative component	+0.3	0.0	−0.1	+0.6	+0.5	−0.1	+0.7	+0.8
Descriptive component	0.6B	0.8B	0.6B	1.2B	0.7B	1.0B	0.5A	0.1B
14a. Practical (+)–Impractical (–)	1.1	0.6	0.3	1.6	2.0	1.6	0.8	0.0
b. Opportunistic (–)–Idealistic (+)	−0.2	0.4	−0.4	0.2	−0.8	−0.3	−0.5	1.9
Evaluative component	+0.5	+0.5	0.0	+0.9	+0.6	+0.6	+0.1	0.0
Descriptive component	0.7A	0.1A	0.3A	0.7A	1.4A	0.9A	0.6A	+0.9
15a. Admirable (+)–Deplorable (–)	0.3	0.1	−0.6	1.0	0.8	0.2	0.5	0.9A
b. Not likeable (–)–Likeable (+)	0.9	0.5	0.2	2.0	1.1	0.4	1.3	0.6[a]
Evaluative component	+0.6	+0.3	−0.2	+1.5	+1.0	+0.3	+0.9	—
Descriptive component	0.3B	0.2B	0.4B	0.5B	0.1B	0.1B	0.4B	—
16. Hard-working (+)–Lazy (–)	0.8	0.1	0.5	0.8	1.3	0.8	1.6	1.3
17. Intelligent (+)–Stupid (–)	0.9	0.9	0.5	1.6	0.9	0.5	1.2	0.9

[a] In set 15, the Greek judges used the single scale, *desirable–undesirable*.

Americans as quite impulse-expressive and very assertive. More detailed results are given in Table 12.2.

Assertiveness. In the consensus results, the Americans are judged in the assertive direction on all of the scales that are strongly related to the assertiveness dimension in Table 2.8, and on nearly all of these notably so (*aggressive* is the sole exception). Indeed on most of these the Americans are judged the most assertive of the six standard targets: e.g., as *bold, active, self-confident,* and *conceited.* (They are second to the Germans as *forceful* and *aggressive.*)

These results are generally consistent with accounts of American characteristics, especially as seen by others. (We would expect that in self-judgments Americans would see themselves as "calm" and "peaceful.") Americans are described as constantly active and energetic. At the same time there is an attempt (rather less successful than for the English) to avoid expressing hostility, and in American usage "aggressive" often becomes synonymous with "forceful" and "energetic."

Impulse-expression. The importance of assertiveness may also affect judgments on the Tight–Loose dimension, as represented in the first seven sets of scales. The factor analytic studies (see Appendix A) showed some secondary relation to assertiveness for the "loose" direction on the first three sets, and to the "tight" direction on the next four. It is only on the former that Americans are judged *notably* "loose" (with descriptive components larger than 0.5).

If we compare the Americans with the Italians and French – the other standard targets that are judged impulse-expressive – the Americans are judged more impulse-expressive only on the first set as *generous* (+) and *extravagant* (−). Americans are also judged notably "loose" on the next two sets, as *spontaneous* (+) and *impulsive* (−) and as *gay* (+) *and frivolous* (−).

These results seem generally consistent with accounts of American characteristics. Any asceticism derived from the Protestant ethic has clearly been reversed, with thrift replaced by *generous/extravagant.* With the weakness of formal rules, social interaction is relatively informal and "spontaneous." We should include here the judgments on set 13 of Americans as *frank* and *tactless.* This is consistent with the apparent openness of Americans (an impression which, as we have seen, is often reversed for more long-run observers). More subtle forms of residual asceticism are not well represented by our relatively general trait scales.

Americans are judged notably *trusting,* and pile up favorable evaluative components as both *persistent* and *flexible,* and as both *broad-minded* and *selective.* The basis for this last judgment is not easy to understand, and the consensus on this last pair is shared by only four of the six groups of standard judges. The *persistent–flexible* pair is a more plausible candidate as an Aristotelean virtue for Americans.

Other sets. With Americans being judged both *independent* and *cooperative* on set 12, what was anticipated as a critical conflict dilemma came out as another Aristotelean virtue.

On the other hand, Americans are not only judged *practical* (although less so than the Germans and the English) – consistent with a tradition that we have related to the Protestant ethic – but also (alone among the standard targets) *opportunistic*. This last is inconsistent with American "idealism." This result might be interpreted in relation to the moralism related to the Protestant ethic. When one of the most powerful countries typically gives moral justifications for its policies, this may be judged hypocritical and opportunistic by others who are more accustomed to "Realpolitik." We would expect such judgments to apply to the English in the nineteenth century, and to Americans since 1945.

Results by others. Karlins *et al.* (1969) provide a convenient summary of three studies with Princeton students: the original Katz and Braly results from 1933, plus replications in 1951 and 1967. Among the adjectives chosen are those suggesting assertiveness and achievement (e.g., *ambitious, aggressive, efficient*) and some of these show a decline by 1967 (e.g., *industrious, alert*). A few adjectives suggest a lack of asceticism (e.g., *pleasure-loving*) and one of these (*materialistic*) shows a notable increase. Karlins *et al.* comment that these results are not greatly at variance with judgments by non-Americans. They are also generally consistent with our own results.

Conclusion

In general, the judgments about American characteristics by ordinary people seem consistent with the accounts of American national character. At the same time, it is striking that much of the latter is not captured by the trait-adjectives. This may be in part because no limited selection of trait-adjectives can represent the great variety of characteristics in the statements of national character, and in part because some of the latter take the form of situational rules that are inherently difficult to represent as general traits.

13 North and south Italians: a regional substudy

The substudy of north and south Italians is, of course, only one example of a regional comparison. However, it is a particularly famous one. In fact, the results are perhaps the most dramatic we have found.

What expectations can we bring to this comparison? Directly applicable is the generalization of Ehrenfels (1967) about northern and southern differences within a country. According to this generalization, the northerners – as compared to the southerners – tend to be more impulse-controlled (and assertive or "potent" in Osgood's terms) but less cultured and urbane.

Not directly applicable is Weber's proposal about the "Protestant ethic." However, a modification of part of Weber's proposal might be applied: though not deriving from Protestantism, the "spirit of capitalism" has developed historically more among the north Italians than the south Italians. Crucial is the "spirit of capitalism," not capitalism as an economic system. Like Weber, Barzini's (1968) discussion of north and south Italians emphasizes psychological factors (pp. 266–7):

The fact that many southern traits and habits may be classified as typical of an "agrarian," "feudal" or "pre-capitalistic" society is only a partial and misleading, though tempting, explanation. It assumes that southerners would be northerners if only they were surrounded with the proper political and economic structures. This is not the case...The decisive reason is another: the industrial revolution was not congenial to the inhabitants of the Mezzogiorno.

Barzini elaborates his position elsewhere: the northerner thinks that the way to achieve his aims is through the acquisition of wealth. "He is...almost a pure *homo economicus*." "The southerner, on the other hand, knows that this can be done only with the acquisition of power, prestige, authority, fame" (p. 262).

When observed closely, Barzini continues, the exceptions usually confirm rather than confute the general rule. "Frequently, in fact, the northerner who seems to pursue power does so only because power will generate more money, and the southerner who apparently seeks to increase his fortune really wants the added prestige which wealth brings him...Generally speaking, southerners tend to make money in order to rule, northerners to rule in order to make money" (p. 264).

Table 13.1. *Judgments about the north and south Italians: summary*

Target	Judges	Descriptive factors Tight–Loose	Assertive–Unassertive
NORTH ITALIANS	North Italians	0.27	0.64
NORTH ITALIANS	South Italians	0.66	0.59
SOUTH ITALIANS	North Italians	−0.26	0.49
SOUTH ITALIANS	South Italians	−0.78	0.04
ITALIANS	Consensus	−0.67	0.41
ITALIANS	Italians	−0.79	0.04

It seems a fair summary of Barzini's position that, as suggested earlier, the "spirit of capitalism" has developed more among the north Italians than the south Italians. We note that Barzini's position implies greater assertiveness for the south Italians, and so is not in agreement with this part of Ehrenfels' generalization. Both proposals share an implication of more Tight impulse-control for the north Italians, more Loose impulse-expression for the south Italians.

Results and discussion

Summary results are given in Table 13.1 and detailed results in Table 13.2. For purposes of comparison, we have repeated in Table 13.1 some summary results for ITALIANS in general (from Chapter 10 above).

Table 13.1 shows that the NORTH ITALIANS are judged as having "Tight" impulse-control and the SOUTH ITALIANS as having "Loose" impulse-expression. Both of these results are relatively weak for the north Italian judges, but very strong for the south Italian judges. Thus for the south Italian judges the descriptive components for *all* of the sets 1–7 are notably in the Tight direction for NORTH ITALIANS and notably in the Loose direction for SOUTH ITALIANS. These results generally agree with the expectations discussed earlier.

A consequence is that the SOUTH ITALIANS are judged similar to ITALIANS in general. In contrast, NORTH ITALIANS are judged *dissimilar* to ITALIANS in general! Table 13.3 gives overall correlations. There is considerable agreement between the north Italian and south Italian judges in rating both the SOUTH ITALIANS ($r = 0.59$) and the NORTH ITALIANS ($r = 0.79$). However the south Italian judges give the more dramatic version of the contrast just described. As Table 13.3 shows, their self-judgments are very highly correlated with the self-judgments by Italians, but their judgments about north Italians are negatively correlated with both!

How might one explain these dramatic results? The obvious possibility

Table 13.2. *Judgments about the north and south Italians: detailed results*

Scales	NORTH ITALIANS		SOUTH ITALIANS	
Target Judges	N. Ital.	S. Ital.	N. Ital.	S. Ital.
1a. Thrifty (+)–Extravagant (−)	0.0	0.9	−0.3	−1.2
b. Stingy (−)–Generous (+)	0.0	−0.9	0.8	2.1
Evaluative component	0.0	0.0	+0.3	+0.4
Descriptive component	0.0	0.9A	0.6B	1.6B
2a. Self-controlled (+)–Impulsive (−)	0.7	1.7	−2.0	−2.2
b. Inhibited (−)–Spontaneous (+)	0.2	−0.1	0.2	0.7
Evaluative component	+0.4	+0.8	−0.9	−0.8
Descriptive component	0.2A	0.9A	1.1B	1.5B
3a. Serious (+)–Frivolous (−)	0.6	0.9	0.1	−0.4
b. Grim (−)–Gay (+)	0.4	−0.7	1.4	2.0
Evaluative component	+0.5	+0.1	+0.8	+0.8
Descriptive component	0.1A	0.8A	0.7B	1.2B
4a. Skeptical (+)–Gullible (−)	0.9	1.2	−0.1	−0.8
b. Distrustful (−)–Trusting (+)	0.2	−1.1	−0.3	0.7
Evaluative component	+0.5	0.0	−0.3	0.0
Descriptive component	0.4A	1.1A	0.1A	0.7B
5a. Firm (+)–Lax (−)	0.6	1.4	0.3	−0.7
b. Severe (−)–Lenient (+)	0.1	−1.3	−0.6	1.4
Evaluative component	+0.3	0.0	−0.1	+0.1
Descriptive component	0.3A	1.4A	0.5A	1.0B
6a. Persistent (+)–Vacillating (−)	0.5	1.7	−0.1	−1.0
b. Inflexible (−)–Flexible (+)	0.1	−1.4	−0.4	1.4
Evaluative component	+0.3	+0.2	−0.3	+0.2
Descriptive component	0.2A	1.6A	0.1A	1.2B
7a. Selective (+)–Undiscriminating (−)	0.8	1.3	−0.7	−1.7
b. Choosy (−)–Broad-minded (+)	0.6	−0.3	−0.9	0.5
Evaluative component	+0.7	+0.5	−0.8	−0.6
Descriptive component	0.1A	0.8A	0.1A	1.1B
8a. Cautious (+)–Rash (−)	0.8	1.6	−0.1	−1.2
b. Timid (−)–Bold (+)	0.3	0.3	0.4	0.8
Evaluative component	+0.5	+1.0	+0.1	−0.2
Descriptive component	0.2A	0.6A	0.3B	1.0B

9a. Calm (+)–Agitated (−)	−0.7	−0.8	0.8	0.0
b. Inactive (−)–Active (+)	0.1	−0.5	1.9	1.8
Evaluative component	−0.3	−0.7	+1.4	+0.9
Descriptive component	0.4B	0.1B	0.5B	0.9B
10a. Peaceful (+)–Aggressive (−)	−0.3	−1.5	0.1	0.6
b. Passive (−)–Forceful (+)	0.1	−0.2	1.8	1.3
Evaluative component	−0.1	−0.8	+1.0	+0.9
Descriptive component	0.2B	0.6B	0.8B	0.4B
11a. Modest (+)–Conceited (−)	−0.6	−1.2	−1.7	−0.6
b. Unassured (−)–Self-confident (+)	−0.4	0.6	1.5	1.1
Evaluative component	−0.5	−0.6	−0.1	+0.3
Descriptive component	0.1B	0.6B	1.6B	0.9B
12a. Cooperative (+)–Uncooperative (−)	0.0	−0.2	1.3	0.8
b. Conforming (−)–Independent (+)	−1.2	−1.4	0.7	0.6
Evaluative component	−0.6	−0.8	+1.0	+0.7
Descriptive component	0.6A	0.6A	0.3A	0.1A
13a. Tactful (+)–Tactless (−)	−0.5	−0.4	0.6	1.2
b. Devious (−)–Frank (+)	1.6	0.0	−0.5	0.4
Evaluative component	+0.6	−0.2	+0.1	+0.8
Descriptive component	1.0B	0.2B	0.5A	0.4A
14a. Practical (+)–Impractical (−)	0.3	0.6	2.4	2.1
b. Opportunistic (−)–Idealistic (+)	0.4	0.6	−1.6	−0.8
Evaluative component	+0.4	+0.6	+0.4	+0.7
Descriptive component	0.0	0.0	2.0A	1.4A
15a. Admirable (+)–Deplorable (−)	0.8	0.3	0.2	1.0
b. Not likeable (−)–Likeable (+)	2.1	0.9	−0.4	1.1
Evaluative component	+1.4	+0.6	−0.1	+1.0
Descriptive component	0.7B	0.3B	0.3A	0.0
16. Hard-working (+)–Lazy (−)	−0.7	−1.1	2.1	1.6
17. Intelligent (+)–Stupid (−)	1.4	1.0	0.7	1.2

Table 13.3. *Correlations for the south Italians, north Italians, and Italian self-judgments*

Judges	S. ITALIANS, ITALIANS[a]	Targets N. ITALIANS, ITALIANS[a]	S. ITALIANS, N. ITALIANS
North Italians	0.47	−0.04	0.01
South Italians	0.93	−0.52	−0.62

[a] Judgments about ITALIANS are self-judgments by the Italian judges; the other judgments are by the north Italian and south Italian judges.

would be the principle of "judgment effects relative to the stimulus context."[1] In judgments about ITALIANS, the context – explicitly or implicitly – suggests a comparison with other Europeans, including northern ones. In judgments about NORTH ITALIANS, however, the comparison suggested is with SOUTH ITALIANS. Assuming that judgments show contrast effects relative to the stimulus context, the result is that ITALIANS (like SOUTH ITALIANS) are judged relatively "Loose," but NORTH ITALIANS are judged relatively "Tight." This corresponds to the more informal observation that south Italians are like Italians only more so.

Evaluative components

It is instructive to compare the present results with those from the comparison between Chinese and Filipinos in the Philippines.[2] The data shown in Table 13.4 are excerpted from Table 5.3 above. Indeed we are here simply reconsidering points that were made more generally in connection with Table 5.3.

We accept that the comparison is not a perfect one, both because of the pro-rating of the Philippines results, and because the "primarily evaluative scales" were different in the two cases. With these limitations, we can make the following points in connection with Table 13.4.

1. The Philippines judgments are generally more positive than those by the Italian groups. (The only clear exception is that the Chinese judgments of the FILIPINOS on the primarily evaluative scales – +0.2 – are less favorable than the north Italian judgments of the SOUTH ITALIANS – +0.6.)

2. The Philippines judges consistently show larger net "ingroup effects" – shown on the last line of Table 13.4. Both these effects for the Italian groups

[1] Because the same "standard targets" were used by most groups of judges, this principle was not much tested in most of the present investigation.

[2] The Philippines results have been pro-rated (as described in Chapter 16) to be more comparable.

Table 13.4. *Evaluative indices (from Table 5.3)*

	N. ITALIANS	CHINESE	S. ITALIANS	FILIPINOS
Self-judgments (I)	+0.5/+1.0	+1.2/+1.9	0.0/+1.4	+0.4/+1.6
Judgments by outgroup (O)	+0.5/−0.1	+0.6/+0.1	−0.3/+0.6	−0.3/+0.2
Ingroup effect (I–O)	0.0/+1.1	+0.6/+1.8	+0.3/+0.8	+0.7/+1.4

Note: numbers to the left of each slash are for evaluative components on the 29 "basic scales" (these results were shown on the left side of Table 5.3). Numbers to the right of each slash are for the "primarily evaluative scales" (these results were shown on the right side of Table 5.3).

are generally larger than those for other European results in Table 5.3, so that the Philippines effects are very much larger.

3. The more "northern" groups that are judged "Tight" (i.e., NORTH ITALIANS and CHINESE) receive more favorable judgments on the standard scales. Indeed the outgroup judgments for these targets are more favorable than the ingroup self-judgments for the more "southern" groups that are judged relatively "Loose" (i.e., SOUTH ITALIANS and FILIPINOS).

4. However, the above tendency tends to be reversed on the primarily evaluative scales. While the "southern" groups may admit that they do not have the positive versions of impulse-control, they nevertheless judge themselves as *likeable, admirable,* or *desirable.*

14 Northern Europeans

This chapter – on northern Europeans – and the next – on southern and eastern Europeans – pursue relatively limited objectives. Earlier in Part II, we considered the six standard nationality "targets" in detail, comparing our own data from six sets of judges with reports about national character. In this chapter and the next, we cannot pursue either of these directions in the same detail.

In gathering our data, our policy was to use these smaller nationalities as targets only for groups of judges that were "culturally adjacent" – to reduce the problem of unfamiliarity. This means that often a nationality is judged by only one group of judges. (Admittedly, there are partial exceptions: the SWISS were judged by four groups and the DUTCH by three.) With fewer groups of judges, we cannot have the same confidence that the judgments deserve detailed consideration, either in their own right, or for comparison with statements about national character. We cannot be as sure that the judgments do not represent special views of the judges about the nationality target. Nevertheless, it is appropriate to present the results and consider them briefly.

Partly for the reason just explained, we have not attempted to discover all the literature on national character for the nationalities in these two chapters. In any case, for these smaller nationalities one would expect that to find such literature would tend to be even more difficult than it was for a larger nationality like the Italians. Nevertheless, we can develop a few general expectations.

From Weber, we should expect that insofar as northern Europeans are more often Protestant, they might have characteristics related to the "Protestant ethic." Actually, Weber's proposal would apply primarily only to nationalities with some Calvinist tradition, such as the Swiss and the Dutch, and not necessarily to other Protestants (e.g., Lutherans in Scandinavia). Indeed, Weber himself shows considerable reservations about the application to the Dutch.[1] Ehrenfels' "north–south" generalization implies that a similar set of characteristics would apply to north–south regional differences within any country. One might reasonably extend a similar generalization to north–south

---

[1] Weber implies that the Dutch upper classes represented a milder form of Calvinism (influenced – the Dutch would say – by a humanistic tolerance represented by Erasmus of Rotterdam).

Table 14.1. *Summary results: northern Europeans*

Target	Judges	Descriptive factors	
		Tight–Loose	Assertive–Unassertive
SWISS	Germans	0.78	−0.16
SWISS	French	0.84	−0.06
SWISS	Italians	0.73	0.30
SWISS	Austrians	0.87	0.00
FINNS	Finns	0.80	0.13
FINNS	Germans	0.32	−0.26
DUTCH	English	0.18	−0.23
DUTCH	Germans	0.39	−0.29
DUTCH	French	0.20	0.10
SWEDISH-FINNS	Finns	0.55	0.65
SWEDES	Finns	−0.12	0.75
IRISH	English	−0.35	0.72

differences between countries as well, resulting in a north–south gradient both within and between countries. One obvious sign of the relevant characteristics would be our measure of Tight impulse-control.

Results and discussion

The usual summary of results is presented in Table 14.1 and the detailed results in Table 14.2.

As Table 14.1 shows 10 out of 12 cases are in the "Tight" direction in the first factor.

The Swiss, for all four groups of judges, are the most clear-cut examples, along with the self-judgments by the FINNS. These five cases are generally Tight and non-assertive.

There remain five cases that are modifications of this pattern, and two cases that are exceptions in the "Loose" direction.

The German judgments of the FINNS and the judgments of the DUTCH represent one kind of modification. The loadings on the two descriptive factors are relatively small, being only mildly "Tight" and non-assertive or unassertive. In part this may be because these judgments generally have low descriptive distinctiveness (although favorable in evaluation) – a pattern suggesting unfamiliarity. But there are also indications of special combinations of descriptive characteristics – for example, the judgments of the DUTCH appear on the third factor of the inverse analysis (not interpreted previously since it is relatively small) as three of the five largest loadings (along with judgments of the AUSTRIANS by the Austrians and the Germans). This factor involves a special combination of characteristics: *peaceful* and *tactful, self-controlled*, but also *gay* – this last representing a clear departure from the "Tight" and

Table 14.2. *Judgments about north Europeans*

Scales	SWISS Germ.	SWISS Fr.	SWISS Ital.	SWISS Aust.	FINN. Finn.	FINN. Germ.	DUTCH Eng.	DUTCH Germ.	DUTCH Fr.	SWEDE-FINN. Finn.	SWEDE Finn.	IRISH Eng.
						Target Judges						
1a. Thrifty (+)–Extravagant (–)	1.7	1.6	0.5	2.0	0.9	0.9	0.7	0.8	1.2	0.5	−0.4	0.2
b. Stingy (–)–Generous (+)	−0.3	0.7	−0.4	−0.5	−0.2	0.7	1.2	0.4	1.1	−0.5	−0.3	0.1
Evaluative component	+0.7	+1.2	+0.1	+0.7	+0.4	+0.8	+1.0	+0.6	+1.2	0.0	−0.1	+0.2
Descriptive component	1.0A	0.5A	0.4A	1.3A	0.6A	0.1A	0.2B	0.2A	0.1A	0.5A	0.4B	0.1A
2a. Self-controlled (+)–Impulsive (–)	1.6	1.5	1.0	1.7	1.2	1.2	1.2	1.1	1.0	0.9	0.5	−2.2
b. Inhibited (–)–Spontaneous (+)	−0.2	0.1	0.0	0.0	−1.7	0.8	0.4	0.2	0.9	−0.3	1.0	1.1
Evaluative component	+0.7	+0.8	+0.5	+0.9	−0.3	+1.0	+0.8	+0.7	+0.9	+0.3	+0.7	−0.5
Descriptive component	0.9A	0.7A	0.5A	0.9A	1.4A	0.2A	0.4A	0.4A	0.1A	0.6A	0.3B	1.6B
3a. Serious (+)–Frivolous (–)	1.2	1.5	0.8	1.5	1.6	0.7	0.5	0.3	0.6	0.4	−0.9	−0.4
b. Grim (–)–Gay (+)	0.2	0.6	0.3	−0.1	−0.9	1.1	1.4	0.9	1.3	0.4	1.0	1.3
Evaluative component	+0.7	+1.0	+0.6	+0.7	+0.4	+0.9	+1.0	+0.6	+1.0	+0.4	+0.1	+0.4
Descriptive component	0.5A	0.5A	0.3A	0.8A	1.2A	0.2B	0.4B	0.3B	0.3B	0.0	0.9B	0.9B
4a. Skeptical (+)–Gullible (–)	0.5	0.3	0.2	1.1	0.3	1.4	0.3	0.6	0.2	0.8	0.5	0.0
b. Distrustful (–)–Trusting (+)	+0.1	0.0	−0.3	−0.3	−0.8	0.2	1.4	0.1	0.8	−0.8	−0.3	−0.7
Evaluative component	+0.2	+0.2	0.0	+0.4	−0.2	+0.8	+0.9	+0.4	+0.5	0.0	+0.1	−0.3
Descriptive component	0.3A	0.1A	0.2A	0.7A	0.6A	0.6A	0.5B	0.3A	0.3B	0.8A	0.4A	0.4A
5a. Firm (+)–Lax (–)	1.1	1.4	0.8	1.2	1.3	1.0	0.9	0.5	0.7	1.0	0.5	0.2
b. Severe (–)–Lenient (+)	0.5	0.0	0.0	0.3	0.3	0.6	0.1	0.5	0.1	−0.3	−0.4	−0.7
Evaluative component	+0.8	+0.7	+0.4	+0.7	+0.7	+0.8	+0.5	+0.6	+0.4	+0.4	0.0	−0.3
Descriptive component	0.3A	0.7A	0.4A	0.5A	0.5A	0.2A	0.4A	0.1B	0.3A	0.7A	0.5A	0.5A
6a. Persistent (+)–Vacillating (–)	1.6	1.0	1.2	1.7	1.1	1.2	0.8	0.9	1.1	0.8	0.5	1.2
b. Inflexible (–)–Flexible (+)	−1.3	−0.5	−0.1	−1.0	−1.9	0.5	0.7	0.1	−0.1	−0.7	−0.1	−0.6
Evaluative component	+0.1	+0.2	+0.5	+0.4	−0.4	+0.8	+0.8	+0.5	−0.1	0.0	+0.2	+0.3
Descriptive component	1.4A	0.8A	0.7A	1.3A	1.5A	0.3A	0.0	0.4A	0.6A	0.8A	0.3A	0.9A
7a. Selective (+)–Undiscriminating (–)	0.2	0.9	1.1	1.3	0.9	1.1	−0.3	1.1	0.4	1.3	1.5	0.3
b. Choosy (–)–Broad-minded (+)	−0.1	0.0	−0.2	0.1	−0.3	1.6	0.1	1.3	0.9	−0.6	0.6	0.1
Evaluative component	+0.1	+0.5	+0.5	+0.7	+0.3	+1.3	+0.1	+1.2	+0.6	−0.4	+1.1	+0.2
Descriptive component	0.2A	0.5A	0.7A	0.6A	0.6A	0.3B	0.2B	0.1B	0.2B	1.0A	0.4A	0.1A
8a. Cautious (+)–Rash (–)	1.7	1.6	1.3	1.7	0.5	0.7	1.3	0.9	0.5	0.4	−0.1	−1.3
b. Timid (–)–Bold (+)	−0.1	−0.2	−0.2	0.2	0.4	0.4	0.0	0.1	0.1	0.4	0.9	1.6
Evaluative component	+0.8	+0.7	+0.6	+1.0	+0.5	+0.6	+0.6	+0.5	+0.3	+0.4	+0.4	+0.2
Descriptive component	0.9A	0.9A	0.8A	0.8A	0.1A	0.2A	0.7A	0.4A	0.2A	0.0	0.5B	1.5B

9a. Calm (+)–Agitated (−)	1.7	1.8	1.0	2.0	0.7	1.6	1.6	1.3	1.1	0.6	0.4	−1.6
b. Inactive (−)–Active (+)	−0.7	0.8	1.4	−0.2	1.0	0.2	1.6	0.0	1.4	1.4	1.5	0.8
Evaluative component	+0.5	+1.3	+1.2	+0.9	+0.8	+0.9	+1.6	+0.6	+1.3	+1.0	+1.0	−0.4
Descriptive component	1.2A	0.5A	0.2B	1.1A	0.1B	0.7A	0.0	0.7A	0.2B	0.4B	0.6B	1.2B
10a. Peaceful (+)–Aggressive (−)	1.8	1.6	1.2	1.6	1.0	1.5	0.0	1.1	1.4	0.5	0.3	−1.8
b. Passive (−)–Forceful (+)	−0.5	0.7	0.9	0.6	1.3	0.5	−0.8	0.3	1.1	1.2	1.2	1.5
Evaluative component	+0.7	+1.1	+1.0	+1.1	+1.2	+1.0	+0.4	+0.7	+1.2	+0.8	+0.7	−0.2
Descriptive component	1.1A	0.5A	0.2A	0.6A	0.2B	0.5A	1.2A	0.4A	0.2A	0.3B	0.4B	1.7B
11a. Modest (+)–Conceited (−)	0.0	0.7	0.2	0.0	0.3	1.2	1.5	0.9	1.1	−1.3	−2.0	−0.7
b. Unassured (−)–Self-confident (+)	1.1	0.8	0.7	1.6	−0.1	1.1	0.7	0.8	1.0	1.3	2.0	1.0
Evaluative component	+0.6	+0.8	+0.4	+0.8	+0.1	+1.2	+1.1	+0.8	+1.1	0.0	0.0	+0.2
Descriptive component	0.5B	0.0	0.2B	0.3B	0.2A	0.0	0.4A	0.0	0.1A	1.3B	2.0B	0.9B
12a. Cooperative (+)–Uncooperative (−)	−0.3	0.7	0.7	0.3	−0.1	0.8	1.5	0.9	1.4	−0.2	0.9	−0.9
b. Conforming (−)–Independent (+)	−0.4	0.6	−0.4	0.2	0.3	1.1	0.1	0.3	0.7	0.9	1.0	0.9
Evaluative component	−0.3	+0.6	+0.2	+0.2	+0.1	+0.9	+0.8	+0.6	+1.0	+0.3	+1.4	+0.2
Descriptive component	0.0	0.1A	0.6A	0.0	0.2B	0.1B	0.7A	0.3A	0.3A	0.6B	0.5B	0.7B
13a. Tactful (+)–Tactless (−)	0.7	1.1	0.8	1.2	0.1	1.2	1.5	1.2	1.0	0.4	0.6	−1.3
b. Devious (−)–Frank (+)	0.6	1.0	0.4	1.3	1.1	1.6	0.7	1.1	1.4	0.1	−0.1	0.1
Evaluative component	+0.6	+1.0	+0.6	+1.2	+0.6	+1.4	+1.1	+1.2	+1.2	+0.3	+0.3	−0.6
Descriptive component	0.0	0.1A	0.2A	0.1B	0.5B	0.2B	0.4A	0.2B	0.2B	0.2A	0.3A	0.7B
14a. Practical (+)–Impractical (−)	1.2	1.1	1.6	1.8	1.1	1.3	1.4	0.9	1.2	1.0	1.3	−0.6
b. Opportunistic (−)–Idealistic (+)	0.1	0.4	−0.2	0.8	−0.2	0.8	0.1	−0.1	−0.3	−0.8	−0.5	−0.3
Evaluative component	+0.6	+0.7	+0.7	+1.3	+0.4	+1.0	+0.7	+0.4	+0.8	+0.1	+0.4	−0.4
Descriptive component	0.6A	0.3A	0.9A	0.5A	0.6A	0.3A	0.7A	0.5A	0.4A	0.9A	0.9A	0.2B
15a. Admirable (+)–Deplorable (−)	0.3	0.7	0.3	1.2	0.7	0.7	1.2	0.2	0.8	0.1	0.0	−0.3
b. Not likeable (−)–Likeable (+)	0.4	1.3	0.2	0.5	0.8	1.6	1.7	0.8	1.7	0.3	0.5	0.4
Evaluative component	+0.3	+1.0	+0.3	+0.8	+0.8	+1.1	+1.5	+0.5	+1.2	+0.2	+0.3	+0.1
Descriptive component	0.1B	0.3B	0.1A	0.1B	0.1B	0.4B	0.2B	0.3B	0.5B	0.1B	0.2B	0.4B
16. Hard-working (+)–Lazy (−)	1.5	1.4	1.4	2.1	1.5	1.0	1.7	1.1	1.6	1.1	1.0	0.0
17. Intelligent (+)–Stupid (−)	0.8	1.1	0.3	1.2	0.9	1.1	1.1	0.6	1.3	0.7	1.0	−0.5

non-assertive pattern. If a name were necessary, one might call this combination "Germanic gaiety" or "Gemuetlichkeit."

Another kind of modification is represented by the Finnish judgments of the once politically dominant minority of SWEDISH-FINNS. The simplest way to interpret this result is as a compromise between Finnish judgments of FINNS and of SWEDES, with which it correlates 0.59 and 0.68 respectively, although the latter correlate −0.01 with each other. In these Finnish judgments, the SWEDISH-FINNS are judged "Tight" like FINNS, and assertive like SWEDES.

The Finnish judgments of the SWEDES as assertive and somewhat "Loose" are unlike our expectation and the traditional image of "Scandinavians" generally (represented by the Finnish self-judgments). These judgments of the SWEDES are highly correlated with judgments (by most groups of judges including the Finns) about the FRENCH and particularly the AMERICANS. Perhaps for these Finnish judges (from a small city far from Helsinki) something (possibly both decadent and attractive) may be represented by present day Stockholm for the SWEDES, as more generally by New York and Paris.

The departure of the IRISH from our general expectation for northern Europe is of course not a similar surprise, since the IRISH – as a Celtic, Catholic culture – *are* an exception in a region that is generally Germanic and Protestant. In contrast to these other targets, the IRISH are judged *bold* and *rash*, *impulsive* (as well as *spontaneous*), *aggressive* (as well as *forceful*), and *agitated*. These relatively unfavorable judgments of the English about the IRISH as assertive and impulse-expressive may be temporarily enhanced by the conflict in Northern Ireland which had then already begun. However, similar judgments have been found repeatedly. The Princeton studies (Karlins *et al.*, 1969) note that a decline of percentages for "pugnacious" between 1933 and 1967 does not represent a fading of the "fighting Irish" (but, we would suggest, more about the fading of some adjectives over time): the Irish are also described as "quick-tempered," "quarrelsome," "aggressive," and "argumentative," as well as "stubborn" (cf. our set 6, *persistent/inflexible*) and "boastful" (cf. our set 10, *confident/conceited*). Two other clusters for the IRISH in the Princeton studies are not well represented by our scales: group loyalties, and the Celtic intellect (*imaginative, witty*). The decline of the latter in the Princeton studies may reflect the assimilation into American culture of Irish-Americans rather than the intellectual life of Ireland itself.

Thus, in these respects, the IRISH are only geographically "northern." However, in other respects they are more like their British neighbors than southern Catholic cultures – e.g., if not strictly ascetic, the Irish tradition is also not sensuous, with marriage (and presumably sex) often postponed until the males are in their forties or fifties.

15 Southern and eastern Europeans

This chapter – like the previous one on northern Europeans – pursues a limited objective. In contrast to the "standard" targets, we do not have data on each target from six to seven groups of judges but only from one to three groups. Partly for this reason we have also not tried to pursue the literature on national character as systematically. Accordingly, we will not attempt a full-fledged comparison between reports of national character and our data, but will limit ourselves to a more cursory view.

There are also differences with the coverage of northern Europeans. In comparison, the latter were relatively homogeneous – although ranging from the SWISS to the FINNS – allowing an exception like the IRISH to stand out. In contrast, the present coverage is more heterogeneous, ranging from the AUSTRIANS to TURKS, from SPANISH to HUNGARIANS. Partly for this reason, the results are also less consistent.

With this limitation, we can state some general expectations that are the complement of those for the northern Europeans. As regards Weber and other approaches emphasizing the legacy of religion (e.g., Peyrefitte), we note that we are considering nationalities influenced less by the Protestant Reformation than the Catholic Counter-reformation. Accordingly, we could expect less influence of the "Protestant ethic." Ehrenfels' north–south generalization about regional differences within a country may again reasonably be extended to north–south differences between countries. Both these approaches point to a greater likelihood of characteristics of Loose impulse-expression.

Results and discussion

The preceding expectations receive only inconsistent support in the data in Tables 15.1 and 15.2. In the corresponding results for northern Europeans 10/12 of the cases were in the overall direction of Tight impulse-control. But for the cases in Table 15.1, only 6/11 are in the overall direction of Loose impulse-expression. Moreover, for the two targets with more than one group of judges (i.e., the AUSTRIANS and the GREEKS), the judges disagree regarding the Tight–Loose dimension. One need not concede that these results are completely inconsistent – of the targets that are judged "Tight," several are relatively "northern" (i.e., the AUSTRIANS and the HUNGARIANS).

Indeed, the Austrians present a special case. Historically, the Austrians can

Table 15.1. *Summary results: southern and eastern Europeans*

Target	Judges	Descriptive factors Tight–Loose	Assertive–Unassertive
AUSTRIANS	Austrians	−0.12	−0.37
AUSTRIANS	Germans	0.46	−0.37
AUSTRIANS	Italians	0.67	0.68
GREEKS	Greeks	−0.39	0.65
GREEKS	Italians	0.42	−0.25
N. GREEKS	Greeks	0.17	0.54
S. GREEKS	Greeks	−0.43	0.55
TURKS	Greeks	−0.34	0.16
CZECHS	Austrians	0.62	−0.12
HUNGARIANS	Austrians	−0.25	0.47
SPANISH	French	−0.52	0.52

be seen as mediating between general German traditions and eastern Europe. What is present-day Austria formerly represented a unique double role as (a) the leading ethnic group in the Habsburg empire until 1918, which otherwise consisted of non-German nationalities from southern and eastern Europe (e.g., Hungarians, Czechs and Slovaks, Italians, Rumanians, Yugoslavs, Poles, and Ukranians); (b) a leading power until 1866 in the confederation of German states, for which – as the Holy Roman Empire – the Habsburgs generally supplied the emperor from 1438 to 1806. Moreover, the Austrians traditionally *saw* themselves as fulfilling this mediating role.

From the first point of view, the Austrians could be used in a "regional" comparison with the (north) Germans. Indeed, historically contrasts have often been proposed between the Austrians and the Germans, especially the Prussians. An example is the (Austrian) witticism: "A German says that the situation is serious but not desperate; an Austrian that the situation is desperate but not serious."

A more extensive comparison between Austrians and Prussians was given by the Austrian writer, Hoffmansthal. An excerpt of his many proposals is given in Table 15.3.

Such contrasts between Austrians and north Germans could be compared only partially with our own results for AUSTRIANS and GERMANS. Judgments about the AUSTRIANS provide an unusual result where the overall correlations are negative for the same target between different judges (e.g., for the Italian judges as opposed to the German and Austrian judges). Moreover, the AUSTRIANS are judged highly similar to the GERMANS by the Italian judges (the overall correlation is 0.96!), dissimilar by Austrians (−0.41), and somewhat similar by Germans (0.36). Thus, the Italians judge the AUSTRIANS as "Tight" and assertive like the GERMANS, while the Austrians judge themselves somewhat "Loose" and unassertive. These results would fit nicely with a principle of "contrast relative to the judges' perspective," which applied to the Italian regional differences. From an Italian perspective, the AUSTRIANS are "Tight," but not from the Austrians' own perspective.

These comparisons can be extended by focusing on the evaluative components. As judges, the Austrians were generally the most unfavorable on both evaluative indices. This negativism is also directed at themselves on the general evaluative component, but not for the primarily evaluative scales, where the Austrians judge themselves quite "sympathisch." This judgment is shared by the German judges, but emphatically not by the Italians. Indeed, the Austrians and Italians show evidence of mutual antipathy, giving each other low ratings on both evaluative indices. These judgments then have some of the properties of traditional "stereotypes." This is not surprising if one considers that the south Tyrol (Alto Adige) has been the locus of one of the few ethnic conflicts in Europe since World War II where bombs have actually exploded.[1]

Other targets

We turn now from the Austrians to the other targets considered in this chapter. The GREEKS are also judged generally "Tight" by the Italian judges but "Loose" in self-judgments. (The judgments by Italians of AUSTRIANS and GREEKS provide the only cases of overall negative correlations between judges of the same target.) The contrast between NORTHERN GREEKS and SOUTHERN GREEKS generally fits expectations from Ehrenfels (1967). (This contrast uses the same group of Greek judges, unlike the more complete design for the earlier comparison of north and south Italians.)

Dorothy Lee (in Mead, 1953) gives characteristics valued by the Greeks: individualism and independence, modesty vs. arrogance, firmness and fortitude, diligence and self-control. Our judgment results are consistent with all but the last. In addition, Friedl (1962) and Triandis (1972) emphasize tense competitiveness, which Triandis relates to the importance of the ingroup–outgroup distinction: extreme competitiveness is shown toward outgroup but cooperation within the ingroup.

The Greek judgments of the TURKS are the most extreme of all our results in the direction of traditional "stereotypes." As will be cited in Chapter 18, this case is unique in meeting all of three criteria for such stereotypes: these judgments are more evaluative than descriptive, as is true for only a small minority of cases. But where other such cases seem blandly favorable (e.g., judgments about the DUTCH), these judgments are strongly negative on both of two evaluative indices. The descriptive component seems overridden by strong negative evaluation, so that the TURKS are judged both *gullible* and *distrustful*, *lax* and *severe*, *aggressive* and *passive*, *tactless* and *devious*.

[1] Another example, of course, is between the Greeks and the Turks (see below).

Table 15.2. *Judgments about eastern and southern Europeans*

Scales	AUST. Aust.	AUST. Ger.	AUST. Ital.	GREEK Greek	GREEK Ital.	N. GREEK Greek	S. GREEK Greek	TURK Greek	CZECH Aust.	HUNG. Aust.	SPAN. Fr.
1a. Thrifty (+)-Extravagant (−)	0.3	1.1	0.5	−0.6	0.4	0.0	−0.5	−0.6	1.0	−0.3	−0.1
b. Stingy (−)-Generous (+)	0.6	0.2	−0.6	1.6	0.3	0.4	0.9	0.3	0.1	0.8	0.2
Evaluative component	+0.4	+0.7	0.0	+0.5	+0.4	+0.2	+0.2	−0.2	+0.6	+0.3	0.0
Descriptive component	0.1B	0.4A	0.6A	1.1B	0.1A	0.2B	0.7B	0.5B	0.4A	0.5B	0.2B
2a. Self-controlled (+)-Impulsive (−)	−0.3	1.1	0.7	−1.1	−0.3	−0.7	−0.5	−0.9	0.4	−0.9	−1.9
b. Inhibited (−)-Spontaneous (+)	0.1	0.2	−0.1	1.7	0.0	1.3	1.1	0.3	−0.7	0.4	c.9
Evaluative component	−0.1	+0.6	+0.3	+0.3	−0.1	+0.1	+0.3	−0.3	−0.2	−0.2	−0.5
Descriptive component	0.2B	0.4A	0.4A	1.4B	0.1B	1.0B	0.8B	0.6B	0.5A	0.7B	1.4B
3a. Serious (+)-Frivolous (−)	0.0	0.4	1.2	−0.1	1.3	0.8	0.1	−0.4	0.9	0.1	−0.7
b. Grim (−)-Gay (+)	0.7	1.0	−0.4	1.5	−0.1	0.7	1.3	−1.1	0.2	1.1	1.2
Evaluative component	+0.4	+0.7	+0.4	+0.7	+0.6	+0.8	+0.7	−0.8	+0.5	+0.6	+0.2
Descriptive component	0.3B	0.3B	0.8A	0.8B	0.7A	0.0	0.6B	0.3B	0.3A	0.5B	1.0B
4a. Skeptical (+)-Gullible (−)	−0.2	−0.1	0.7	1.2	0.4	1.1	1.0	−0.9	0.8	0.6	−0.9
b. Distrustful (−)-Trusting (+)	0.4	0.3	−0.8	−0.8	−0.2	−0.7	−0.6	−0.5	−0.8	0.4	−0.3
Evaluative component	+0.1	+0.1	0.0	+0.2	+0.1	+0.2	+0.2	−0.7	0.0	+0.5	−0.6
Descriptive component	0.3B	0.2B	0.8A	1.0A	0.3A	0.9A	0.8A	0.2B	0.8A	0.1A	0.3B
5a. Firm (+)-Lax (−)	−1.2	−0.1	1.3	0.8	0.2	1.3	0.4	−0.5	−0.2	0.3	−0.7
b. Severe (−)-Lenient (+)	1.0	−0.1	−1.3	1.0	0.2	0.0	−0.1	−0.6	−0.3	−0.2	−0.3
Evaluative component	−0.1	+0.5	0.0	+0.9	+0.1	+0.6	+0.2	−0.5	−0.3	+0.1	−0.5
Descriptive component	1.1B	0.6B	1.3A	0.1B	0.1A	0.7A	0.2A	0.0	0.0	0.2A	0.2B
6a. Persistent (+)-Vacillating (−)	−0.6	0.7	1.1	0.8	0.5	0.9	0.3	−0.2	0.3	0.0	−0.5
b. Inflexible (−)-Flexible (+)	−0.5	−0.7	−1.0	0.1	0.1	−0.6	0.4	−0.5	0.1	0.3	−1.1
Evaluative component	−0.6	0.0	0.0	+0.5	+0.3	+0.1	+0.4	−0.3	+0.2	+0.1	−0.8
Descriptive component	0.0	0.7A	1.0A	0.4A	0.2A	0.7A	0.0	0.2A	0.1A	0.2B	0.3A
7a. Selective (+)-Undiscriminating (−)	0.2	0.0	1.3	0.4	0.2	0.3	0.1	−1.2	1.2	0.5	0.1
b. Choosy (−)-Broad-minded (+)	0.0	0.0	−0.8	0.2	−0.4	0.0	0.3	0.2	0.3	0.0	−0.8
Evaluative component	+0.1	0.0	+0.2	+0.3	−0.1	+0.1	+0.2	−0.5	+0.8	+0.2	−0.4
Descriptive component	0.1A	0.0	1.1A	0.1A	0.3A	0.1A	0.1B	0.7B	0.5A	0.3A	0.2A

Item											
8a. Cautious (+)-Rash (−)	0.7	1.1	1.0	0.0	0.8	0.8	0.3	−0.8	1.1	0.7	−0.3
b. Timid (−)-Bold (+)	−0.3	−0.2	0.6	1.8	0.0	1.6	1.4	−0.1	0.2	0.6	0.6
Evaluative component	+0.2	+0.5	+0.8	+0.9	+0.4	+1.2	+0.9	−0.4	+0.7	+0.7	+0.2
Descriptive component	0.5A	0.6A	0.2A	0.3B	0.4A	0.4B	0.6B	0.4B	0.4A	0.1A	0.5B
9a. Calm (+)-Agitated (−)	0.3	1.5	−0.1	−0.1	0.9	1.0	−0.1	−0.5	0.5	−0.5	−1.5
b. Inactive (−)-Active (+)	0.0	0.2	1.4	1.4	0.4	1.1	0.7	−0.9	0.5	1.3	0.1
Evaluative component	+0.2	+0.8	+0.7	+0.6	+0.7	+1.0	+0.3	−0.7	+0.5	+0.4	−0.7
Descriptive component	0.2A	0.6A	0.8B	0.7B	0.2A	0.0	0.4B	0.2A	0.0	0.9B	0.8B
10a. Peaceful (+)-Aggressive (−)	1.3	1.4	−0.6	0.2	1.1	0.0	0.1	−1.4	0.7	−0.7	−1.2
b. Passive (−)-Forceful (+)	−0.6	−0.7	1.5	1.1	0.1	0.7	0.5	−0.8	−0.1	0.3	−0.3
Evaluative component	+0.4	+0.4	+0.5	+0.6	+0.6	+0.3	+0.3	−1.1	+0.2	−0.2	−0.8
Descriptive component	1.0A	1.0A	1.1A	0.4B	0.5A	0.4B	0.2B	0.3B	0.4A	0.5B	0.5B
11a. Modest (+)-Conceited (−)	0.1	0.7	−0.5	0.5	0.4	1.3	0.4	−0.7	0.9	0.7	−0.7
b. Unassured (−)-Self-confident (+)	0.0	0.6	1.1	1.4	−0.2	0.8	0.3	−0.3	0.0	0.7	0.1
Evaluative component	0.0	+0.6	+0.3	+0.9	+0.1	+1.1	+0.3	−0.5	+0.4	+0.7	−0.3
Descriptive component	0.0	0.0	0.8B	0.5B	0.3A	0.2A	0.0	0.2B	0.5A	0.0	0.4B
12a. Cooperative (+)-Uncooperative (−)	0.7	0.5	0.7	0.3	−0.1	0.9	0.7	−0.8	0.2	−0.2	−0.1
b. Conforming (−)-Independent (+)	−0.1	−0.1	−0.6	1.7	−0.8	0.4	0.9	0.0	0.0	−0.3	0.1
Evaluative component	−0.1	−0.1	+0.1	+1.0	−0.4	+0.6	+0.8	−0.4	+0.1	−0.2	0.0
Descriptive component	0.8A	0.6A	0.6A	0.7B	0.3A	0.2A	0.1B	0.4B	0.1A	0.0	0.1B
13a. Tactful (+)-Tactless (−)	0.4	1.3	0.5	−0.3	1.0	0.3	−0.1	−1.2	0.7	1.2	−1.0
b. Devious (−)-Frank (+)	0.5	0.8	0.2	−0.1	0.6	1.0	−0.3	−1.0	0.2	0.5	−0.2
Evaluative component	+0.4	+1.0	+0.4	−0.2	+0.8	+0.7	−0.2	−1.1	+0.5	+0.9	−0.6
Descriptive component	0.0	0.2A	0.2A	0.1B	0.2A	0.3B	0.1A	0.1B	0.2A	0.3A	0.4B
14a. Practical (+)-Impractical (−)	−0.1	0.4	1.1	1.6	−0.4	1.0	0.8	−0.3	0.8	0.0	−0.5
b. Opportunistic (−)-Idealistic (+)	−0.1	0.0	0.2	−0.2	1.6	0.3	0.3	−1.2	0.6	−0.6	0.3
Evaluative component	−0.1	+0.2	+0.7	+0.7	+0.6	+0.6	+0.6	−0.8	+0.7	−0.3	−0.1
Descriptive component	0.0	0.2A	0.5A	0.9A	1.0B	0.3A	0.3A	0.4A	0.1A	0.3A	0.4B
15a. Admirable (+)-Deplorable (−)	0.5	0.4	0.3	1.5[a]	0.5	(1.4)	(1.3)	(−1.5)	−0.9	−0.1	−0.1
b. Not likeable (−)-Likeable (+)	1.1	0.9	−0.8	—	0.6	—	—	—	0.8	1.2	0.4
Evaluative component	+0.8	+0.6	−0.3	—	+0.5	—	—	—	−0.1	+0.5	+0.1
Descriptive component	0.3B	0.2B	0.5A	—	0.1B	—	—	—	0.7B	0.6B	0.2B
16. Hard-working (+)-Lazy (−)	−0.1	0.8	1.1	0.6	−0.1	1.3	0.5	−1.3	0.9	0.5	0.1
17. Intelligent (+)-Stupid (−)	0.8	0.6	0.8	1.4	0.9	0.9	1.6	−1.1	0.8	0.5	−0.1

[a] In set 15, the Greek judges used the single scale, *desirable–undesirable*.

Table 15.3. *Some Prussian and Austrian characteristics*

Prussian	Austrian
Confidence and egocentrism	
self-assured & self-assertive	self-irony
self-righteous & didactic	embarrassed, vain, witty
fights for rights	lethargic
lacks understanding of others	excessive empathy
Systematization	
determined & ambitious	play-acting & pleasure-seeking
pushes things to crises	avoids crises
efficiency in execution	quicker to catch on
follows regulations	uses cleverness
abstract reasoning & logical consistency	more adaptable
emphasizes public roles	emphasizes private roles, social relationships & individuality

Source: Hoffmansthal (1924).

The TURKS also received the most negative judgments of any target from Americans in the Princeton studies. The similarity with our results for Greek judges seems largely superficial. The Princeton subjects show indications of uncertainty about their judgments: consensus was very low, and "nearly 20% of the subjects refused to cooperate entirely" (Karlins *et al.*, 1969, p. 15). The 1933 subjects may have responded (e.g., with *cruel*) to a fragmentary impression based on the 1914 persecution of the Armenian minority; American children in the 1940s who had not eaten all the food on their plates were still told to "remember the starving Armenians." The Greek judges are unlikely to have felt any such uncertainty: their response is not vaguely negative, but the result of centuries of group conflict that still continues.

The CZECHS do not represent a serious exception to any expectation: they could as well have been grouped with northern as with southern Europe. Our results are in good agreement with a classic portrait like the good soldier Schweik, made more serious by the years of Communism: *skeptical* and *distrustful*, *cautious*, *peaceful* and *passive*.

The HUNGARIANS as judged by the Austrians present only a damped down version of the traditional impulse-expressiveness represented in Viennese operettas. They are still judged distinctively "Loose" on sets 1–3 and assertive on set 9.

The SPANISH are judged by the French as more clearly "Loose" and assertive. The judgments are most highly correlated (0.92) with French judgments of Italians, but with less favorable evaluations. Thus these judgments do little to convey the differences between the Spanish and Italians, and emphasis on personal honor of the Spanish tradition. Instead, the French judgments of the SPANISH resemble the north Italians' judgments of SOUTH ITALIANS. Indeed, these two cases have traditional expressions that are similar: "Africa begins at the Pyrenees" and "Africa begins south of Rome." One recalls that the Austrian minister Metternich said that "The Orient begins at the Landstrasse" (i.e., at the eastern edge of Vienna). In each case, European civilization is seen as ending at the southern or eastern boundary of one's own ethnic group.

16 The Philippines results revisited

The study of group judgments in the Philippines – first reported in Peabody (1968) – served as a pilot study for the much larger European investigation reported in the previous chapters. It is instructive to reexamine the earlier Philippines data within the context of the present larger study.

As regards theories about national character, it would have been more obvious to have proceeded the other way around and to have begun with European nationalities. At the time when the Philippines research was done, the trait inference research had disclosed the large descriptive dimensions called Tight impulse-control versus Loose impulse-expression, and it had been noted that this dimension resembled the generally recognized differences between northern and southern Europeans and the "Protestant ethic" described by Weber. It would have been natural to have done next the study of European nationalities that is reported here.

Instead, I found myself in the summer of 1967, with a mandate to carry out some social science research, in the Philippines – the only country in Asia that is predominantly Christian, but Catholic – and indeed at a Jesuit university. Preliminary inquiries indicated that there were judged differences between Filipino ethnic subgroups and that these tended to fit the "northern" vs. "southern" characteristics described by Ehrenfels (1967) – for example, the northernmost Ilocanos – the group of President Marcos.

However, it seemed more promising to compare the Filipinos as a whole with the minority of Chinese origin. Weber argued that the Chinese did not have the exact combination of characteristics needed to originate modern capitalism. But it is clear that the Chinese are well adapted to capitalism once it is introduced. Although the Chinese minority in the Philippines is smaller (perhaps 5% of the population) than in other countries of southeast Asia, they nevertheless play a disproportionate role in the economy (by one estimate they then controlled around 45%, along with 50% for Americans!).

Ironically, then, one had to explain to the (largely American) Jesuit professors that a study was planned concerning Filipino-Chinese differences but theoretically related to the "Protestant ethic." What this incident illustrates is that we are here using the "Protestant ethic" in a looser sense to summarize characteristics that would be common among Catholic Jesuits and among the Chinese – more so than among the average of nominal "Protestants."

Table 16.1. *Philippines results (pro-rated): summary*

Target	Judges[a]	Descriptive factors Tight–Loose	Assertive–Unassertive
CHINESE	Chinese	0.66	0.00
CHINESE	Filipinos	0.70	0.20
FILIPINOS	Filipinos	−0.19	−0.16
FILIPINOS	Chinese	−0.44	0.11
AMERICANS	Philippines	−0.30	0.65
JAPANESE	Philippines	0.43	0.66

[a] The Chinese and Filipino judges are used separately for judgments of each other, but combined for judgments of the outgroup AMERICANS and JAPANESE.

Results and discussion

To compare Philippines results with the others, it is necessary to "pro-rate" the former since they had originally used a different response scale. (The Philippines response scale could be scored -5, -3, -1, $+1$, $+3$, $+5$. In contrast the scales used otherwise are scored -3, -2, -1, 0, $+1$, $+2$, $+3$. We have used the simple method of multiplying the Philippines results by 3/5 to make the potential ranges comparable. This may or may not succeed in making the results wholly comparable. However, it would be equally debatable to use a more complex method – e.g., equalize the mean and standard deviation between the Philippines and European data.)

The pro-rated results are used for the summary in Table 16.1 and the detailed results of Table 16.2.

The evidence indicates that there are two major differences between the Philippines and the European results. Appendix A (see Table A.2) outlines an analysis of the relative variance contributed by the evaluative and descriptive components. In the European results the descriptive components are generally more important than the evaluative components. However, if this analysis is applied to the Philippines results, the evaluative components are more important than the descriptive ones.

The greater role of evaluation also appears in another major difference. In the comparisons between the Filipinos and the Chinese, there was not only agreement between the ingroup and outgroup judges about the descriptive components of each target, but also systematic differences about the evaluative components, with the ingroup judges being more favorable on every pair of scales. These are the first two judgment principles discussed in Chapter 3: *Descriptive convergence* and *Ingroup self-evaluation*. In contrast, while the overall European results reviewed in Chapter 5 showed continued support for descriptive convergence, they did *not* generally support ingroup self-evaluation.

Table 16.2. *Philippines study: detailed results (pro-rated)*

Scales	Targets Judges	CHI. Chi.	CHI. Fil.	FIL. Chi.	FIL. Fil.	AMER. Chi. + Fil.
1a. Thrifty (+)-Extravagant (−)		2.2	1.6	−1.7	−0.5	−1.2
b. Stingy (−)-Generous (+)		1.2	−0.4	0.6	1.4	1.7
Evaluative component		+1.7	+0.6	−0.6	+0.5	+0.2
Descriptive component		0.5A	1.0A	1.2B	1.0B	1.4B
2a. Self-controlled (+)-Impulsive (−)		2.0	0.9	−1.2	0.3	0.7
b. Inhibited (−)-Spontaneous (+)		0.6	0.1	0.4	0.5	1.3
Evaluative component		+1.3	+0.5	−0.4	+0.4	+1.0
Descriptive component		0.7A	0.4A	0.8B	0.1B	0.3B
3a. Serious (+)-Frivolous (−)		2.0	1.2	0.3	1.2	1.6
b. Grim (−)-Gay (+)		0.1	−0.2	1.3	1.4	0.9
Evaluative component		+1.0	+0.5	+0.8	+1.3	+1.2
Descriptive component		1.0A	0.7A	0.5B	0.1B	0.3A
4a. Skeptical (+)-Gullible (−)		0.4	0.3	−1.2	−0.3	0.5
b. Distrustful (−)-Trusting (+)		0.8	−0.5	−0.4	0.9	1.2
Evaluative component		+0.6	−0.1	−0.8	+0.3	+0.9
Descriptive component		0.2B	0.4A	0.4B	0.6B	0.3B
5a. Firm (+)-Lax (−)		1.3	0.7	−0.9	0.1	1.3
b. Severe (−)-Lenient (+)		0.3	−0.3	0.4	0.9	0.8
Evaluative component		+0.8	+0.2	−0.3	+0.5	+1.1
Descriptive component		0.5A	0.5A	0.6B	0.4B	0.3A
6a. Persistent (+)-Vacillating (−)		1.8	1.4	−0.1	0.4	1.4
b. Inflexible (−)-Flexible (+)		1.0	0.7	0.8	0.9	1.4
Evaluative component		+1.4	+1.0	+0.4	+0.7	+1.4
Descriptive component		0.8A	0.3A	0.5B	0.2B	0.0
7a. Selective (+)-Undiscriminating (−)		1.7	0.9	−0.5	1.2	1.4
b. Choosy (−)-Broad-minded (+)		0.2	−0.5	−0.6	−0.1	1.1
Evaluative component		+1.0	+0.2	−0.5	+0.5	+1.3
Descriptive component		0.8A	0.7A	0.0	0.6A	0.2A

8a. Cautious (+)–Rash (−)	2.1	1.1	−0.5	0.1	0.5
b. Timid (−)–Bold (+)	1.0	0.6	0.0	0.0	1.7
Evaluative component	+1.6	+0.9	−0.3	+0.1	+1.1
Descriptive component	0.5A	0.2A	0.2B	0.1A	0.6B
9a. Peaceful (+)–Aggressive (−)	2.1	0.7	−0.9	0.7	0.1
b. Passive (−)–Active (+)	0.4	0.2	−1.4	−0.4	1.5
Evaluative component	+1.3	+0.5	−1.2	+0.1	+0.8
Descriptive component	0.8A	0.3A	0.3A	0.5A	0.7B
10a. Modest (+)–Conceited (−)	1.4	1.1	0.0	1.2	−0.5
b. Unassured (−)–Self-confident (+)	1.5	0.7	0.1	0.3	2.0
Evaluative component	+1.4	+0.9	0.0	+0.7	+0.8
Descriptive component	0.1B	0.2A	0.1B	0.4A	1.2B
11a. Cooperative (+)–Uncooperative (−)	1.4	0.0	0.6	1.3	1.7
b. Conforming (−)–Independent (+)	1.2	0.7	−2.1	−1.4	2.1
Evaluative component	+1.3	+0.4	−0.7	0.0	+1.9
Descriptive component	0.1A	0.4B	1.3A	1.3A	0.2B
12a. Tactful (+)–Tactless (−)	1.3	0.7	0.1	1.3	1.5
b. Devious (−)–Frank (+)	0.1	0.0	−0.1	−0.5	2.4
Evaluative component	+0.7	+0.4	0.0	+0.4	+2.0
Descriptive component	0.6A	0.4A	0.1A	0.9A	0.5B
13a. Practical (+)–Impractical (−)	1.2	1.1	0.4	0.6	2.1
b. Opportunistic (−)–Idealistic (+)	1.3	−0.1	−0.8	0.6	0.7
Evaluative component	+1.3	+0.5	−0.2	+0.6	+1.4
Descriptive component	0.1B	0.6A	0.6A	0.6	0.7A
14a. Calm (+)–Agitated (−)	1.0	0.8	−0.4	0.3	0.3
b. Inactive (−)–Active (+)	1.9	1.9	−0.4	0.3	2.0
Evaluative component	+1.5	+1.4	−0.4	+0.3	+1.2
Descriptive component	0.4B	0.6B	0.0	0.0	0.9B
15. Desirable (+)–Undesirable (−)	1.9	0.1	0.2	1.5	1.6
16. Hard-working (+)–Lazy (−)	2.8	2.2	−0.9	0.4	1.6
17. Intelligent (+)–Stupid (−)	2.0	1.4	0.7	1.7	1.9
18. Honest (+)–Dishonest (−)	2.1	−0.2	−0.3	0.8	1.6

There was no such average effect in the basic scales (where the Philippines results gave systematic effects) but only on the special evaluative scales.

Thus, in the Philippines judgments evaluation plays a larger role. According to the pro-rated results, the mean ratings across all six targets are almost twice as positive as for the European results. This evidence for a greater "leniency" or "positivity" effect is consistent with other findings that Oriental judges show major tendencies to make favorable and "acquiescent" judgments. In the deferential Orient, this includes in particular judgments about influential foreigners – both the Americans and the Japanese were military conquerors in recent history and strong economic influences today. The Philippines judgments about AMERICANS and JAPANESE, together with the Chinese self-judgments, represent three cases (out of the 76) with the most favorable evaluative components. On the other hand the Chinese judgments of the FILIPINOS resemble the north Italian judgments of SOUTH ITALIANS, but are not as negative as the Greek judgments about the TURKS.

As regards the descriptive aspects of the results, the judgments about AMERICANS (as assertive and Loose) are very similar to those by European judges.

The CHINESE are judged Tight and non-assertive, the JAPANESE Tight and assertive (and so resemble results for the SWISS and the GERMANS respectively). In the detailed results, for sets 1–7 the descriptive component is in the "Tight" direction in 19/21 instances. The Princeton studies generally gave similar results for American judges: the CHINESE were judged "industrious," "quiet," "reserved" (and "deceitful"); the JAPANESE "industrious," "aggressive," "ambitious" (and "shrewd," "sly"). This is consistent with the other evidence for economic achievement by the Japanese and the overseas Chinese, which suggests that the characteristics we have loosely called the Protestant ethic can today be found prominently among Asians.

That the FILIPINOS are less clearly "Loose" (as well as non-assertive) is due to being atypically "Tight" on certain scales. If we combine the two groups of Philippines judges, the FILIPINOS would be significantly "Loose" on all of the present sets 1–6 (though less distinctively so than the ITALIANS or FRENCH). But, at least in their self-judgments, the FILIPINOS are distinctively in the "Tight" direction on such characteristics as *selective/choosy* and *tactful/devious*.[1] The original report commented: "The Filipinos were not always judged as pure examples of impulse-expression on a 'latin' or 'mediterranean' model" (Peabody, 1968, p. 298).

[1] We note that the Oriental targets are all judged in the *tactful/devious* direction. Comparable results were uncommon for European targets, and in particular did not appear for targets (such as ITALIANS and AUSTRIANS) where they might be expected. It seems that the Oriental judges were more ready to recognize such differences in interpersonal subtlety.

Part III
Conclusions

17 Conclusions:
national characteristics

In search of comparative issues

The accounts of national character that we have considered in the previous chapters generally suffer from the lack of a comparative approach. Each nationality tends to be described on its own terms, and of course this has advantages as well as disadvantages. Given the preponderance in numbers of Americans in social science, a particular nationality is often compared – implicitly if not explicitly – with Americans, who serve as a kind of standard for comparison. This procedure can be misleading: an account of the French may imply that they are distinctive in differing from Americans in a certain respect; and an account of the Germans may indicate that *they* are distinctive and differ from Americans in a certain respect. But a broader comparative view might show that these respects were basically similar, and that it may be the Americans who are distinctive and differ from most of the rest of the world.

We considered earlier a limited number of existing approaches that provide schemes for a comparative approach. The present chapter will try to supplement these schemes by inducing comparative issues from the separate accounts of national character. This effort is in the spirit of the plea by Inkeles and Levinson (1969, p. 447) about the need for a set of "standard analytic issues" to permit comparative analysis. They tentatively proposed three such issues: relations to authority, conceptions of the self, and primary dilemmas or conflicts, and ways of dealing with them. The five issues that we have been able to induce from our materials are not the same as those proposed by Inkeles and Levinson, but they are not unrelated to them.

1. *Social relationships*

The first issue concerns the relations between people in social interaction. This issue is related to all of the comparative schemes considered earlier. Starting with the variables of Lipset and Parsons, we may distinguish three types where there are predominantly *Gemeinschaft* relationships, predominantly *Gesellschaft* relationships, and a "mixed" type where there is a clear separation between "public" *Gesellschaft* relationships and "private" *Gemeinschaft* relationships.[1] This "mixed" type will be discussed first.

The "mixed" type. In this "mixed" type, the distinction between "public" and "private" relationships parallels, at least roughly, the verbal distinction in pronouns of address (Brown, 1965, Ch. 2) – e.g., the distinction between "vous" and "tu" or between "Sie" and "Du", when used reciprocally.

Private relationships with the family and close friends tend to have the *Gemeinschaft* qualities of particularism, diffuseness, affectivity, etc. They tend to call for Dahrendorf's "private virtues" which are "immediate, not domesticated by general rules, intent on honesty and profoundness rather than ease or lack of friction."

Similar standards apply in relationship to oneself. This type tends to involve the greatest emphasis on the development of one's unique qualities – an emphasis that may be called "individuality" or "self-actualization." The individual tends to distinguish clearly between his public role and his "real self."

In contrast to the "private" sphere, there is a public one where relationships tend to have the *Gesellschaft* qualities of universalism, specificity, affective neutrality, etc. Such relationships are also accorded some normative legitimacy. Among the nationalities on which we have focused, the Germans and French seem to come closest to this mixed type.

Predominance of Gemeinschaft *relationships.* In contrast to this mixed type would be one where *Gemeinschaft* relationships are predominant. (In an idealized "Gemeinschaft" one would expect in addition positive communal feelings and solidarity between members – see the earlier discussion on terminology in Chapter 6.) With this predominance, all relationships will tend to be particularistic and diffuse. There is not the same clear separation of distinct "public" and "private" spheres. Nor is there the same emphasis on the development of "individuality."

It is clear that none of our large nations match this type. However, both the Italians and the Russians resemble it in part, but in quite different ways. According to the accounts, the Italians *do* make a sharp distinction between the family and its close allies (toward whom there are positive feelings and solidarity) as opposed to everyone else (toward whom there is an attitude of social distrust). However, these latter relationships are not really *Gesellschaft* ones, but (negatively toned) *Gemeinschaft* relationships that are still very particularistic. It is not expected that others (including officials of the state) will in fact act on other than a particularistic basis. Similarly, the individual himself acts particularistically. Confronted by someone, such as an official,

[1] These proposals were already introduced during discussion of Parsons' "pattern variables" in Chapter 6.

who claimed to be following universalistic rules, the individual would not believe this and assume that some way must be found to appeal to the official's particularistic interests. In this sense, the adoption in Italy of the forms of the modern state – which seem to imply universalistic rules – could be called a form of "pseudo-Gesellschaft."

Overall, the Italians seem to show a combination of features: not only the predominance of *Gemeinschaft* relationships, but also features of the "mixed" type (e.g., emphasis on "individuality"). The latter features should be expected given the general similarity between the Italians and the French. The difference is that the Italians did not develop a sphere where *Gesellschaft* values were primary.

The Russian case is different. The Russian peasant village of a generation or so back may still have come very close to a true "Gemeinschaft." Some tradition of communal feeling and solidarity remains. On first migrating to an industrial area, the Russian peasant may have had no basis for dealing with the *Gesellschaft* relationships demanded. Later, expectations would develop that officials may follow universalistic rules. However, the individual's own behavior will still tend to be particularistic, seeking special treatment on a paternalistic basis with implied inequality and deference.[1]

The various cases considered thus far all emphasize the importance of private relationships, but there are interesting differences between them. For the Italians and the French such relationships tend to center primarily within the family. Both the Germans and the Russians tend in addition to have private relationships outside the family. For the Germans, these tend to be relatively few, and the transition is likely to receive explicit attention (e.g., in the decision to say "Du" to each other) and even be marked by ritual (e.g., in the "brotherhood" ceremony, the two parties drink together using locked arms). In contrast, the Russians are portrayed as open to private relationships virtually at any moment.

Predominance of Gesellschaft *relationships.* In contrast to the preceding types is the predominance of *Gesellschaft* relationships. In comparison to the "mixed" type, the distinction between "public" and "private" spheres is less clear cut. There is a tendency for all relationships to emphasize Dahrendorf's "public virtues" – ease and lack of friction rather than honesty and profoundness. All relationships tend to become specific and universalistic – what Nelson (1969) called "universal otherhood." This type can thus be related to all of the comparative schemes considered earlier: the Protestant ethic, Lipset's *Gesellschaft* values, and Dahrendorf's public virtues.

The English and the Americans seem to come closest to this type. The

---

[1] The French and the Americans also show some tendency to try to convert such a situation into a particularistic one, but with less acceptance of inequality. The Germans and the English seem the most likely to accept that they should not be treated as an exception.

similarity between the English and the Americans is obscured by a difference in the nature of what the universalized relationships are like: the English tend to be relatively reserved and formal not only in public but also in private – in Glyn's (1970) description even with members of the family. In contrast, the Americans are relatively informal and "spontaneous" even in public settings. In this respect, the Americans are more misleading, their immediate "friendliness" suggesting the possibility of "private" relationships that are never forthcoming. This tends to be a nearly universal complaint about Americans. Americans themselves are aware of the possibility of what Riesman (1950) calls "pseudo-Gemeinschaft" tendencies, where apparent personalness may be used as a means to some other end.

Relationships with others have parallels in the relation to oneself. Individualism takes the forms of individual responsibility for achievement and individual freedom from interference by others, but there is traditionally less concern with the development of "individuality" with the Americans and the English than, for example, with the Germans and the French. In contrast to Montaigne's sharp distinction between his public role and his "real self," for many Americans self-identity is defined primarily by their occupational role.

Change is always with us. Since the 1960s there has been a countertrend among Americans in favor of "authenticity" and "self-revelation" toward others, and of "growth" and "self-actualization" for oneself. (However, as noted earlier, these efforts often take peculiarly American forms: seeking "authenticity" and "individuality" by relying on the application of some technique and often in large-group settings.) Dahrendorf (1969, p. 290) also suggests changes for the English: in the last decades the Germans discovered the public virtues and the English the private ones.

Nevertheless, it is plausible to conclude that "private" relationships remain less common among the English and the Americans than among other Europeans. The strength of such a conclusion may depend on what one selects as the crucial criterion for "private relationships." Dahrendorf's "private virtues" suggest a criterion related to "self-revelation" (especially of negative feelings). Another and perhaps preferable criterion would consider the "diffuseness" (vs. "specificity") of long-run duties and rights, which may be virtually unlimited in a "private" relationship. Suppose one compares Americans with the "private relations" for some of the more taciturn nationalities of Europe (e.g., the Swiss and the Swedes). Then it is not so clear that the Americans would show less self-revelation as that they would tend to less diffuse obligations. The American encounter-group weekend may be symbolic: it fosters self-revelation and at the same time avoids any long-run "commitment."

Obviously, the three types we have considered can be arranged in a logical order, with the "mixed" type intermediate between *Gemeinschaft* and *Gesellschaft* predominance. On the assumption that there has been a historical shift from *Gemeinschaft* to *Gesellschaft*, this order could also be considered a historical sequence. It seems that there is some truth in such a sequence, without assuming that it is either completely inevitable, or desirable.

This order (or sequence) has some curvilinear properties – e.g., the distinction between "public" and "private" and the emphasis on individuality seem to reach a maximum in the intermediate, "mixed," case. Even with the simplified three types used here, there are still two separate differences or transitions. Many treatments have considered only one of these. Thus, Cuddihy (1974) makes a plausible case that the assimilation of Jews in western Europe represented a belated, accelerated, and therefore peculiarly difficult transition from predominantly *Gemeinschaft* relationships into "modernization":[1]

The emergence of cities, multiplying strangers...enables us to live with unknown others without transforming them into either brothers or enemies. Initiation into the social interaction rituals of civility equips us "to deal with strangers routinely" in urban public space...In the nineteenth century, the peasant or the "young man from the provinces" comes to Paris or London or Dublin...For the first time, perhaps, he must differentiate relations in private places from decorum in public places. Acquiring this private–public differentiation is a "great transition", neglected in sociology...

(Cuddihy, 1974, p. 12)

In our terms, Cuddihy is concerned with the transition from a predominance of *Gemeinschaft* relationships to the "mixed" type where public and private relationships are sharply separated. In contrast, Dahrendorf (1969) is concerned with the difference from such a "mixed" type to the predominance of *Gesellschaft* relationships (with emphasis on "public virtues" at the expense of "private virtues" and a truly "universal otherhood") where the private–public distinction would again become less important.

2. Social rules

Formal and official rules shade off into informal implicit rules for social interaction. Two related aspects of these rules will be considered here: emphasis on rules of procedure and on general principles vs. more specific substantive rules; the degree that rules are "internalized" and considered "legitimate."

The English and American patterns emphasize rules of procedure, and – beyond these – relatively general principles or ends. More specific substantive applications are left to be worked out in the concrete case. (This is consistent with the tradition of practicality/empiricism.) In contrast, the other nationalities generally have more specific substantive rules, with the Germans being

[1] We need not consider here the plausibility of Cuddihy's provocative argument that this transition was central to the genesis of such theories as Freud and Marx.

the most striking case. An illustration comes from an Austrian colleague[1] who has conducted sensitivity training groups (T-groups) with a variety of nationalities. He reported that in this relatively unstructured situation the English and the Americans typically try to agree on a relatively few rules and then get on with the discussion, while the continental Europeans try to set up a more detailed set of rules. It is as if the latter were trying to establish the counterpart of the detailed legal code of their societies.

The preceding issue, of *what* rules are emphasized, obviously affects the second issue: the degree that the rules are internalized or considered legitimate. Internalization and legitimacy are related but not identical concepts: internalization is a psychological concept implying that the individual has accepted the rule as his/her own – this need not necessarily be a conscious process. Legitimacy is a concept from the social sciences implying that the individual accepts the rules as normatively valid.

It is probably the Germans who belong at one end of this dimension: a large number of substantive rules are internalized and treated as part of the "legitimate order." The English may show a comparable degree of internalization and legitimacy for their rules of procedure and general principles, but this leaves more of the substantive details to be worked out in practice.

The Italians seem to be at the other end of this dimension. Internalization and legitimacy are generally not accorded to public rules, but only to those governing "private" relationships. Relations with others are affected by social distrust, and – in the absence of social rules – there is a tendency to act on utilitarian grounds of immediate self-interest. This can lead to anarchic tendencies.

The French situation is partly similar, but differs because of the effective centralized state and its universalistic rules, which are granted some degree of legitimacy. However, there is also a tendency to try to get around the official system, possibly by the use of particularistic connections: "Wherever there is a queue, there is someone being let in the back way."

The Russian situation is somewhat similar to the French, and for similar reasons. The centralized system is granted some legitimacy, but evokes tendencies to get around its regulations (e.g., through particularistic connections – "blat" – and the "left-hand" counter-economy). The American case is necessarily different, since there are fewer rules and a lower degree of centralized control. Nevertheless, when placed in a comparable situation, as in the army, the American reaction is not that different from the French and Russian ones to a situation of centralized control and the possibly unrealistic demands resulting from it. Under these circumstances, the American "scrounging" becomes the counterpart of the French "système D" and the Russian

---

[1] T. Lindner, personal communication.

"left-hand" arrangements – all unofficial procedures to get around the demands of the official rules.

3. *Control of hostility*

The control of hostility could be considered an important special case of social rules. From a more individual point of view, it is also a special case of impulse-control, to be discussed below. It is obviously important because of the threat to disrupt social relationships. Here again, we find several contrasting alternatives.

The Anglo-American alternative is to avoid public hostility by following Dahrendorf's "public virtues": getting along with others without friction by smiling affably. From an American point of view, it may seem strange to find that the English are criticized (e.g., by the Germans in Dahrendorf's account) for smiling, since the English tend to strike Americans as reserved. But, if we take smiling (and joking) even in limited public interaction as an index of the "public virtues," this simply shows that Americans are even more extreme on this dimension than the English. Of our other nationalities, only the Italians might tend to smile in public, for quite different reasons. For the other nationalities – the French, the Russians, and the Germans – the absence of public smiling is explicitly mentioned. For the Russians this is ascribed to the general tendency to express feelings directly (in this case boredom). And it is on similar grounds that the Germans regard the public smiling of the English as hypocritical.

Another alternative is represented by the "Latin" model for the French and Italians. Here public hostility is avoided by a code of formal politeness, which is recognized as having the function of avoiding social friction. We have seen that Americans regard these polite forms as hypocritical, preferring greater spontaneity. On the other hand, the French join everyone else in regarding the American spontaneous friendliness as superficial and so hypocritical.

In the absence of both "public virtues" and a code of politeness, public life may have a certain abrasiveness. This seems to be the German case which Hellpach, reflecting the contrast with the Latin formal code, calls "rejection of formality." The Russians may also come closest to this alternative (e.g., the offhanded bumping in public settings).

4. *Impulse-control*

Accounts of the French and Italians are basically similar and may be treated as a "Latin" model of impulse-expression. Impulse-expression is not considered ascetically as wrong in principle. Impulses are not subjected to suppression by internalized inhibitions. Instead, they are likely to be consciously recognized, as in Leites' (1969) long list of child-like impulses recognized by the French and deliberately opposed by a Cartesian standard. There is deliberate, "rational" choice of the circumstances for impulse-expression, based on more pragmatic grounds. In Freudian terms there is more ego-control and less super-ego and repression. At the same time, there tend to be systems of external controls, such as the traditional chaperone system.

In contrast, for the English and Americans we may find in the problem of impulse-control a persistent effect of the Protestant ethic, which in its ascetic aspect generally proscribed impulse-expression. The impulse-control tended to be highly internalized. If these internalized inhibitions are strong enough, impulses may never be consciously recognized, and so never require deliberate renunciation (as in the Latin model). Insofar as this system of internalized controls is effective, it is possible to dispense with both deliberate rational control, and with systems of external control, such as the chaperone system. The relative absence of these alternatives means that any lessening of internalized controls (as may have occurred in the 1960s) will be more noticeably displayed.

Consider sexual attraction.[1] On the Latin model, such attractions will be generally recognized, and a deliberate choice made as to how far to pursue this impulse. On the traditional Anglo-American model, the presumption is the other way around: no attraction may be recognized unless or until it is established that both parties are open to such a possibility. An even more clear-cut example is the suppression of hostility especially among the English.

For the Germans, there is no general ascetic rule against impulse-expression, but a collection of more specific ones. For activities where few specific rules are established (e.g., automobile driving), a Hobbesian situation may be approached.

In the account of Russian modal personality, there is less emphasis on individual impulse-supervision and more reliance on the group and on authority. In Freudian terms, instead of the deliberate ego-control of the Latin model, or the internalized super-ego of the Anglo-American one, we have more of an "externalized" super-ego.

The degree of internalization is a general theme which relates particularly to the present topic of impulse-control, but appears under the other headings as well. In one alternative, the degree of internalization is strong. What is internalized may include rules of procedure and general principles or ends, together with control over hostility and other impulses (as for the English and the Americans), or more specific substantive rules (as for the Germans). All of these cases have the effect of prescribing certain options and ruling out

---

[1] It is noteworthy that sex is given relatively minor attention in most accounts of national characteristics. This seems an unfortunate kind of diffidence. Quite aside from the argument that sex is generally important, we have found that the social rules related to sex often provide excellent illustrations of general national differences.

others, which – with strong internalization – may not be recognized as options at all.

The contrasting alternative – a weaker degree of internalization – is more common among the French and Italians, and, in different respects, among the Russians. Options are less often ruled out in principle by internalized control, and therefore depend on deliberate "rational" choice or on external control. Impulse-expression will occur if circumstances seem to permit. Thus, one may have the paradox of greater impulse-expression together with greater explicit emphasis on impulse-control – an emphasis that is less necessary where inhibitions are more internalized.

5. *Authority and hierarchical relations*

On this issue – in contrast to the others – we do not find a pairing of the Americans and the English. Instead this issue seems to relate to the value of equality resulting from an anti-aristocratic revolutionary tradition, and so pairs the Americans and the French.

To summarize the French–American comparison: in French society the actual status differences are fairly obvious, in this comparable to the English or the Germans. Hence the French value of equality leads to resentment and avoidance by the subordinates. In contrast, for Americans status differences are actually attenuated in several ways, and tend not to be recognized.

Based on Crozier's (1964) analysis, the American version includes: rejection of inequality with emphasis on impersonal rules, especially rules of procedure, and on functional specificity with decentralization of decision-making. The main bureaucratic problem is disputes about jurisdiction between the many decision-making centers. Americans will accept face-to-face subordinate relationships provided the subordination is minimized by informality, and is functionally specific and so does not involve claims to more diffuse deference.

In the French version, on the other hand, resistance to inequality involves formality and avoidance of face-to-face subordinate relationships, with emphasis on impersonal rules – more often substantive as well as procedural than for Americans – as a substitute for personal authority, and on referring disputes up the centralized hierarchy of the state. There is strong emphasis on equality within groups and a lack of cooperative activities ("negative solidarity"), leading to some isolation for the individual for whom this represents at the same time a zone of autonomy. The system of impersonal rules derived from a centralized authority allows for avoiding dependence on the whims of another individual, and at the same time for rationality and even an absolutism of authority that is thought to be necessary. The bureaucratic problems for the French are lack of communication between strata and inflexibility with respect to change with a resulting alternation of routine and crisis.

For the Italians, we have not found as explicit a statement concerning attitudes to authority and subordination. From what is available, one can infer that there is not the same rejection of subordination as for the Americans and the French, but acceptance of subordination within a particularistic relationship (as in a protector–protégé relation); at the same time, there is little internalized acceptance of official authority.

Much of English history can be interpreted as a struggle about equality in particular domains. In the much-quoted formulation of Marshall (1950, p. 14) one can ascribe the development of "civil rights to the eighteenth, political to the nineteenth, and social to the twentieth" centuries. But this process has stopped short of a demand for complete social equality comparable to the Americans or the French. The English are inclined to accept general status differences and diffuse deference to status superiors. Richardson's (1956) study of the merchant marine shows that this has the advantage of cutting down the number of rules needed to reduce conflict. On the other hand, Crozier (1964, p. 236) suggests that the English deferential patterns have their own disadvantages of constraint and rigidity.

Russian "modal personality characteristics" include a need for dependence on authority to provide rules for impulse-control and guidance of achievement. What is important about authority is that it shows a paternal concern with the individual's welfare, and not its preservation of rules of procedure. Crozier (1964, pp. 228–31) compares the American and Soviet alternatives to the dilemma of French bureaucracy where the centralized decision-makers are isolated from the relevant information. The American alternative is to decentralize decision-making, to give power to those who have the necessary information. The Soviet alternative is to maintain centralized decision-makers and to accept their intrusive efforts to gather information. This tends to lead to multiple networks of informants to check on each other, and to the dilemma of trust vs. mistrust which is a central one for the Russians.

Finally, the Germans are said not only to accept authority, but even to prefer a hierarchical arrangement with clearly designated superordinates and subordinates.

Comment

We have now considered five "comparative issues": (1) social relationships; (2) social rules; (3) control of hostility; (4) impulse-control; (5) authority and hierarchical relations. It is noteworthy that these generally come less close to representing traits of the individual than to rules for interaction in different situations – although these rules tend to be "internalized" by the individuals.

Part of the explanation may be that writings on national characteristics tend to be from a sociological and social science point of view, rather than a psychological one. These accounts often are of institutional arrangements.

The effort here to translate these into individual terms may have proceeded only part-way as far as stating rules for (individual) interaction, and simply not have managed the further step of formulating these as characteristics of the individual.

But in part, the explanation may be that a formulation in terms of interaction rules is often more natural and appropriate than one in terms of individual traits. This issue is not peculiar to national characteristics, but is part of the recent general debate in personality and social psychology concerning the relative advantages of formulations using situational rules as an alternative to individual traits.[1] Certainly the preceding issues provide excellent illustrations of the arguments against the formulation of personality in terms of consistent "traits" on the grounds that this does not recognize sufficiently variation between situations. For example, how are we to judge the trait of "openness" as between Americans (who show a relatively high degree of openness in "public" situations but relatively little increase for "private" ones), and all those (e.g., Germans, French, and Italians) who show more situational variability, with a relatively low degree of openness in "public" situations, and a high degree in "private" ones?

Insofar as such a situational criticism of a trait formulation is justified, it follows that the reliance of our empirical judgments on trait-adjectives must necessarily only be partially adequate for describing national characteristics. National characteristics would need to be formulated in terms of situational rules of interaction rather than only in terms of trait-adjectives.

Conclusion

A deliberate effort was made to apply a comparative approach to the accounts of national characteristics, which tend to treat each nationality on its own terms. Using this "inductive" approach, we have been able to propose five comparative issues. These issues tend to be consistent with, and to complement, the few comparative approaches we were able to discover in advance: Weber's formulation of the "Protestant ethic"; Lipset's "value patterns"; Dahrendorf's proposals concerning rules of procedure and "public" vs. "private" virtues.

On four of the five issues considered above, we find the English and Americans paired as similar. Some kind of similarity might be expected from the fact that the English colonists established the original American cultural traditions. But the nature of the similarities seems related to the significance of a Calvinist tradition in both cultures.

On many of the issues we also find a pairing for the French and the Italians. This suggests the significance of Catholic and Latin traditions, different in many ways from the Calvinist ones.

[1] See the discussion of situationism in Chapter 2.

The remaining two nationalities, the Germans and the Russians, are not paired with such a clear similarity. In part they are paired only by default – e.g., as traditions that are not Calvinist or Latin. However, this allows for the possibility of some real similarities – e.g., the German emphasis on supra-individual goals involves a degree of communal feeling and solidarity, like the Russians.

A limitation of the present study is its concentration on traditions that are European and Christian. With a broader comparative perspective we would expect that these issues would generally apply but with some shift in the distribution of examples (e.g., the small communities studied by anthropologists – now disappearing – would supply some examples closer to a pure *Gemeinschaft* type). We would also expect some major additional issues to emerge.

18 Conclusions: judgments about national characteristics

This chapter considers three questions regarding judgments about national characteristics: (I) the most important summary features of these judgments; (II) comparison between these judgments and reports about "national character"; (III) comparison between these judgments and the traditional concept of "stereotypes."

I. Judgments about groups: summary features

Some basic analyses were summarized in Chapter 5.[1] The summary included three conclusions: (1) differences between nationality targets are much more important than differences between groups of judges; (2) the descriptive aspects of judgment are more important than the evaluative aspects; (3) three major dimensions summarize much of the results: (a) a descriptive dimension called "Tight vs. Loose" control over impulse-expression; (b) a descriptive dimension called self-assertiveness; (c) a general evaluative dimension.

Of the judgment principles considered in Chapters 3 and 5, the principle that was most clearly supported was that called "descriptive convergence": different judges tend to agree about the descriptive aspects of judgments about national characteristics.

The preceding points suggest that the most important summary of our empirical results is to consider different nationality targets according to the descriptive aspects summarized by the dimensions of Tight–Loose and Assertive–Unassertive. The inverse ("Q") analysis provides a convenient summary of these dimensions[2] for all 76 cases. We have so far made use of this analysis piece-meal at the beginning of each chapter in Part II, as a convenient summary for each nationality considered. We now present the entire analysis in Table 18.1.

To complete the record, Table 18.1 also includes two evaluative indices in the third and fourth columns: (a) the mean evaluative component across the 28 basic scales. This is a measure of the general evaluative dimension; (b) an evaluative index based on the "primarily evaluative scales."[3] These

---

[1] These analyses are considered in detail in Appendix A.

[2] As explained in Appendix A, this analysis provides two large factors which can be identified with the Tight–Loose and Assertive–Unassertive dimensions.

[3] In most cases, this index is the mean evaluative component on the two scales *admirable* (+) vs. *deplorable* (−) and *likeable* (+) vs. *non-likeable* (−). For the Greek and Philippine judges, this index is the score on the scale *desirable* (+) vs. *undesirable* (−).

Table 18.1. *Summary indices for 76 targets*

	Judges	Descriptive indices[a]		Evaluative indices[b]	
		Tight–Loose	Assertive–Unassertive	Basic scales	Evaluative scales
"Tight" targets					
ENGLISH	Consensus	0.69	0.18	+0.6	+0.8
	English	0.37	0.16	+0.7	+1.2
	Germans	0.80	−0.07	+0.7	+0.9
	French	0.72	0.12	+0.5	+0.8
	Italians	0.84	0.39	+0.6	+0.3
	Austrians	0.71	0.20	+0.6	+0.4
	Finns	0.72	0.28	+0.8	+1.0
	Greeks	0.85	0.30	+0.6	(+0.5)
RUSSIANS	Consensus	0.72	0.33	+0.4	+0.3
	English	0.75	0.50	+0.4	−0.3
	Germans	0.78	0.17	+0.5	+0.5
	French	0.57	0.53	+0.4	+0.8
	Italians	0.83	0.37	+0.3	+0.3
	Austrians	0.71	0.14	+0.3	+0.0
	Finns	0.66	0.26	+0.5	+0.6
	Greeks	0.38	0.60	+0.4	(−0.4)
GERMANS	Consensus	0.56	0.58	+0.5	+0.3
	Germans	0.79	0.10	0.0	0.0
	English	0.58	0.75	+0.6	+0.4
	French	0.53	0.55	+0.6	+1.1
	Italians	0.66	0.67	+0.5	−0.3
	Austrians	0.31	0.80	+0.3	−0.3
W. GERMANS	Finns	0.47	0.62	+0.7	+1.0
E. GERMANS	Finns	0.77	0.26	+0.4	+0.5
GERMANS	Greeks	0.64	0.63	+0.5	−0.4
SWISS	Germans	0.78	−0.16	+0.5	+0.3
	French	0.84	−0.06	+0.8	+1.0
	Italians	0.73	0.30	+0.5	+0.3
	Austrians	0.87	0.00	+0.8	+0.8
CHINESE	Chinese	0.66	0.00	+1.2	(+1.9)
	Filipinos	0.70	0.20	+0.6	(+0.1)
JAPANESE	Philippines	0.43	0.66	+0.9	(1.0)
CZECHS	Austrians	0.62	−0.12	+0.3	−0.1
FINNS	Finns	0.80	0.13	+0.3	+0.8
	Germans	0.32	−0.26	+1.0	+1.1
SWEDISH-FINNS	Finns	0.55	0.65	+0.3	+0.2
N. ITALIANS	N. Italians	0.27	0.64	+0.5	+1.0
	S. Italians	0.66	0.59	+0.5	−0.1
DUTCH	English	0.18	−0.23	+0.8	+1.4
	Germans	0.39	−0.29	+0.7	+0.5
	French	0.20	0.10	+0.8	+1.2
AUSTRIANS	Austrians	−0.12	−0.37	+0.1	+0.8
	Germans	0.46	−0.37	+0.4	+0.6
	Italians	0.67	0.68	+0.3	−0.3

Table 18.1 (cont.)

| | | Descriptive indices[a] | | Evaluative indices[b] | |
	Judges	Tight– Loose	Assertive– Unassertive	Basic scales	Evaluative scales
GREEKS	Greeks	−0.39	0.65	+0.6	(+1.5)
	Italians	0.42	−0.25	+0.3	+0.5
N. GREEKS	Greeks	0.17	0.54	+0.6	(+1.4)
"Loose" targets					
	Consensus	−0.67	0.41	−0.1	+0.5
ITALIANS	Italians	−0.79	0.04	+0.1	+1.8
	English	−0.71	0.55	+0.1	+0.2
	Germans	−0.58	0.57	+0.1	+0.4
	French	−0.55	0.67	−0.1	+0.4
	Austrians	−0.65	0.50	−0.3	0.0
	Finns	−0.74	0.14	−0.2	+0.3
	Greeks	−0.83	−0.07	+0.1	(+0.9)
FRENCH	Consensus	−0.60	0.52	+0.2	+0.9
	French	−0.23	0.77	−0.1	+0.4
	English	−0.63	0.61	+0.2	+0.7
	Germans	−0.60	0.60	+0.5	+1.1
	Italians	−0.85	0.11	+0.4	+1.1
	Austrians	−0.58	0.58	+0.2	+0.9
	Finns	−0.68	0.45	+0.3	+1.0
	Greeks	−0.16	0.55	+0.5	(+1.0)
AMERICANS	Consensus	−0.49	0.64	+0.4	+0.6
	English	−0.39	0.78	+0.4	+0.3
	Germans	−0.41	0.67	+0.1	−0.2
	French	−0.63	0.54	+0.6	+1.5
	Italians	−0.65	0.46	+0.5	+1.0
	Austrians	−0.34	0.74	+0.3	+0.3
	Finns	−0.51	0.64	+0.6	+0.9
	Greeks	0.20	0.73	+0.7	(+0.6)
	Philippines	−0.30	0.65	+1.1	(+1.6)
S. ITALIANS	S. Italians	−0.78	0.04	0.0	+1.4
	N. Italians	−0.26	0.49	−0.3	+0.6
S. GREEKS	Greeks	−0.43	0.55	+0.4	(+1.3)
SPANISH	French	−0.52	0.52	−0.3	+0.1
HUNGARIANS	Austrians	−0.25	0.47	+0.2	+0.5
TURKS	Greeks	−0.34	0.16	−0.6	(−1.5)
IRISH	English	−0.35	0.72	−0.1	+0.1
SWEDES	Finns	−0.12	0.75	+0.4	+0.3
FILIPINOS	Filipinos	−0.19	−0.16	+0.4	(+1.5)
	Chinese	−0.44	0.11	−0.3	(+0.2)

Note: for the relevant targets, a dashed line is used after results for the six standard judges (which are those averaged to provide the Consensus).
[a] The descriptive indices are loadings on the first two unrotated factors of the inverse analysis.
[b] The evaluative indices are for mean evaluative components for the 28 basic scales and for the primarily evaluative scales.

evaluative indices have already been used in considering the overall results in Chapter 5, and will be used again in the last section of this chapter. However, the present section will comment only on the *descriptive* summary indices shown in the first two columns of Table 18.1.

Comments on the inverse analysis

The Tight–Loose dimension. In Table 18.1, nearly all the nationalities have a clear direction on the Tight–Loose dimension. In general, this direction is agreed on by different groups of judges. The only exceptions are for the AUSTRIANS and the GREEKS; in both cases the directions of self-judgments is "Loose," and the outgroup judgments "Tight." (These cases include the *only* two instances where there is a negative correlation – across the 28 scales – between different judges of the same target – i.e., between the outgroup Italian judges and the Austrian and Greek self-judgments.)

The Assertive–Unassertive dimension. On the Tight–Loose dimension the nationalities tended to divide fairly evenly into those judged "Tight" and "Loose." The results for Assertiveness are different. Here most nationalities – including all the standard targets except the ENGLISH – are clearly judged Assertive (as indicated by substantial positive loadings on the second factor). But there are no nationalities that are as clearly Unassertive (as would be indicated by equally substantial negative loadings). Instead of a contrast between Assertive and Unassertive, we have more a contrast between high and low Assertiveness, or – one might say – between nationalities judged Assertive and *Non*-Assertive.

The nationalities that are judged relatively Non-Assertive, are generally also judged "Tight": e.g., the ENGLISH, SWISS, CHINESE, FINNS, DUTCH. Cases judged both Loose and Non-Assertive are few. In these cases, the Non-Assertiveness is often only for *some* of the groups of judges (e.g., the ITALIANS are judged Non-Assertive by Italians, Finnish, and Greek judges, but Assertive by four other groups of judges). Indeed, there are no cases with two or more groups of judges where these groups agree that a target is both Loose (e.g., a negative loading larger than -0.20 on the first factor) and Non-Assertive (e.g., no positive loading larger than 0.20 on the second factor).

Is this situation likely to be universally true? We speculate that such a conclusion would be premature. The non-industrialized cultures studied by anthropologists often appear to be both impulse-expressive and unassertive – in what might be called a "South Sea Island" model. (It is granted that anthropologists would be able to argue that such an appearance is over-simplified.) This model is represented by none of our targets, and is approached perhaps only by the Filipinos.[1]

---

[1] It was pointed out in the original report of the Philippines study (Peabody, 1968, p. 298) that the Filipinos were not judged as "pure examples of impulse-expression on a 'latin' or 'mediterranean' model."

It seems conceptually possible for relatively clear-cut cases of Unassertiveness to exist,[1] although they did not appear in our results.

II. Judgments and national character

This section compares national characteristics in our group judgments and in reports of national character. (In traditional terminology, we consider the relation between "national stereotypes" and "national character.") This relation was considered *separately* for the different nationalities in the chapters of Part II. Here we consider the overall comparison.

For this purpose we may treat the reports of national character as a criterion, without assuming that they are entirely valid. In relation to this criterion, we would suggest two conclusions about our group judgments: first, judgments by ordinary people about national characteristics (traditionally "stereotypes") are *generally* more similar than dissimilar to reports about national character; however, secondly, these judgments do not represent the more complex and subtle features of national character.

The first conclusion has implications for the traditional problem of accuracy, suggesting that the judgments are more often accurate than inaccurate. The conclusion is an impression derived from the separate chapters of Part II. It might be possible to go through these chapters and make a tally of the number of cases of correspondence and of non-correspondence. However, to avoid the possibility of bias by the present author, such a tally should better be made by someone who can be considered more detached.

Certainly relevant to this issue is what we have called "descriptive convergence": the similarity between different judges about the characteristics of the same nationality. The traditional implication that judgments about groups are *generally* false "illusions" should have to explain why this illusion is shared. (Indeed, this fact – especially the agreement between *self*-judgments and outgroup judgments – has always been a weakness of the stereotypes tradition.)

More interesting than the sheer question of accuracy or inaccuracy is the tendency of our judgment results to follow cognitive principles. From these principles the accuracy *or* inaccuracy of the judgments would follow. For example, the "descriptive convergence" between different groups of judges was systematically reduced for self-judgment. But several of the judgment principles imply precisely such differences between self-judgments and those by outgroups.

As another example, consider the most clear-cut instance of non-correspondence between judgments and national character: the RUSSIANS are consistently judged as representing "Tight" impulse-control, but the

[1] Another possible example would be the traditional female sex role which was relatively impulse-expressive and unassertive. In the currently popular scales of masculinity–femininity–androgyny, the masculinity items represent mostly Assertiveness.

reports about national character suggest that ordinary Russians are impulse-expressive. But as regards the possible basis on which judgments could be made, it is about ordinary Russians – among the standard targets – for whom the least adequate information was available to our judges. The judges are accordingly more likely to be reduced to inferences derived from Soviet policy – inferences which are inaccurate in this instance. Thus, a clear-cut instance of non-correspondence between judgments and national character (with the implication that the judgments are not accurate) can be explained by general principles of cognition (e.g., that cognitions are necessarily based on the information possessed by the judge).

Thus, the judgments traditionally called "national stereotypes" are more similar than dissimilar to reports on "national character," and – presumptively – more accurate than not.

The second conclusion is that judgments about national characteristics do not represent the more complex and subtle features of our national character. There are two general reasons for this. First, the cognitions of ordinary people, such as our student judges, simply do not include many of the more complex and subtle features that are included in the cognitions of expert observers. Secondly, our methods would limit the possibility for any observer to *express* the complex and subtle features of national characteristics. The first point is obvious, and we will concentrate on the second.

Trait-adjectives left out

As explained in Chapter 2 and – in more detail – in Appendix B, our representation of trait-adjectives deliberately left out certain classes of them, in particular those related to the "interpersonal virtues" or affiliation, and those related to the "impersonal virtues" or achievement. Some of these characteristics are of obvious importance for differences in national character-istics – for example, the Protestant ethic tends to emphasize achievement at the expense of affiliation.

Nevertheless, this point would seem to be only a minor limitation on our method. Recent research (Peabody, 1984) shows that the classes of adjectives that were left out are generally related to adjectives that were included. Thus, while a relative emphasis on achievement vs. affiliation is not represented directly, it can appear as a general difference in Tight impulse-control vs. Loose impulse-expression.

The use of trait-adjective scales

More serious is the fact that our results could only be expressed on scales defined by trait-adjectives. In this respect our results are basically similar to other "stereotypes" research, and in some respects a definite improvement on these. Nevertheless, any judgments using trait-adjectives cannot really express some of the more complex and subtle features in accounts of national character. The clearest cases all involve the coexistence of *contrasting* characteristics, a coexistence which cannot be represented by a single judgment with trait-adjectives. We will consider three varieties.

Appearance vs. underlying situation. Some of these cases (e.g., the first example below) may reflect the judgment principle of "behavior" (available to outgroups) vs. "conscious experience" (available to self-judgments). The French (and Italians) appear impulse-expressive, but are themselves conscious of efforts at deliberate ("rational") impulse-control. The Italians appear credulous and trusting, but are said to be pessimistic and distrustful. The Americans superficially appear friendly, but are said to avoid real friendships.

Situational differences. In the previous example, the Americans are informal and open in "public" relationships with previously unknown others, as well as in "private" relationships – and indeed, tend not to make a sharp distinction between the two. In contrast, the European nationalities tend to make a sharp distinction, and their overall degree of formality or openness could not be represented by a single judgment.[1]

Conflict dilemmas. The conflict dilemmas emphasized by Erik Erikson involve a conflict between contrasting tendencies. Thus, Inkeles *et al.* (1958) suggest that Erikson's dilemma of *basic trust* vs. *mistrust* is important for Russians (but not for Americans) while the dilemmas of *identity* vs. *role diffusion* and *intimacy* vs. *isolation* are important for Americans (but not for Russians).

Single judgments on a trait-adjective scale cannot well represent such a conflict, and might in fact take several forms. (1) The judgments may be identical to neutral ones, with the two conflicting tendencies in effect being treated as cancelling each other. (2) The judgments may emphasize one tendency and not the other – if for example the first tendency is stronger or, at least, more obviously apparent. For example, Hellpach implies that for Germans there is a conflict between persistent $(+)$/inflexible $(-)$ and vacillating $(-)$/flexible $(+)$, but it is only the former characteristics that appear in the results. (3) The judgments may reflect both tendencies, one on each of the paired scales; if both scales are evaluatively favorable, the results will look like an Aristotelean virtue. For example, Americans may have a conflict between cooperative $(+)$/conforming $(-)$ and uncooperative $(-)$/independent $(+)$, but are judged both *cooperative* and *independent*.

In summary, we have considered a number of ways that our trait-adjective scales would not permit our judges to express some of the more subtle and complex features of national character. More open-ended methods would

---

[1] Alternatively, following the European norms the Americans are inconsistent in not making a sharp distinction between the two types of situations.

allow for this expression. But in any case, we assume that the cognitions of our student judges would include fewer of these features to begin with.

III. Where are the stereotypes of yesteryear?

Finally, we must consider how our judgments about groups relate to traditional group "stereotypes." The basic answer is that our judgments generally do *not* correspond to this tradition.

Why is this so? *Part* of the answer is that traditional stereotypes were largely presumed rather than demonstrated. In the Katz and Braly tradition, if a subject checks some characteristic for a nationality, it is assumed that this judgment is exceptionless, undifferentiated, and inflexible (see Chapter I). But there is generally no evidence for this assumption, and indeed evidence suggests that the judgments are usually probabilistic ones. Thus, traditional "stereotypes" represented, to a considerable degree, the assumptions of the researchers rather than evidence about the judges.

Does this mean that judgments about national characteristics have never corresponded to traditional "stereotypes"? It would be reckless to assume that this is true. Instead, we shall look to see whether there is any evidence in our own data that resembles traditional stereotypes, in however limited a degree. In doing so, we need to select criteria for traditional stereotypes that are adapted to our own method of analysis. For this purpose, we select the implication that traditional stereotypes represent *primarily* the expression of (typically negative) affect or evaluation. This suggests three criteria for traditional stereotypes.

1. The evaluative components should be more important than the descriptive components (in the analysis of the scale variances described in Appendix A). This criterion is met by 13 of the 76 cases.

For the other two criteria, the relevant indices were included in Table 18.1.

2. The mean evaluative component should be negative on the 28 basic scales. This criterion is met by 9 of the 76 cases.

3. The means evaluative component should be negative on the primarily evaluative scales. This criterion is met by 12 of the 76 cases.

Table 18.2 summarizes the situation while Table 18.3 gives a listing of the relevant cases. Two-thirds of the 76 cases meet *none* of the criteria. One case meets all three criteria. We will consider briefly the cases that meet *any* of the criteria.

a. *Evaluative components are more important, but are positive* (7 cases). These cases might correspond to a traditional *ingroup* stereotype, with judgments representing primarily the expression of *positive* effect. One case fits this interpretation: the self-judgments by the Chinese in the Philippines which have large positive evaluative components both on the regular scales ($+1.2$)

Table 18.2. *Number of cases meeting three criteria for traditional stereotypes*

Type	Criteria met	No. of cases
	None	50
(a)	(1) only	7
(b)	(3) only	10
(c)	(2) only	3
(d)	(1) & (2)	4
(e)	(2) & (3)	1
(f)	(1), (2), & (3)	1
Total		76

Note: the three criteria are as follows.
(1) In the analysis of scale variances, the evaluative components are larger than the descriptive components.
(2) The mean evaluative component is negative for the 28 regular scales.
(3) The mean evaluative component is negative for the primarily evaluative scales.

and on the primarily evaluative scale ($+1.9$). The remaining six cases are not self-judgments and include some variety. The Philippines judges give very positive evaluations to both the foreign outgroups: the AMERICANS and the JAPANESE. These positive evaluations may reflect an Oriental tendency to be diplomatic, and the small descriptive variance some relative unfamiliarity with these nationalities. This latter may also apply to other cases: the DUTCH judged by the French; the FINNS judged by the Germans; the AMERICANS judged by the Greeks. There remains as an apparent exception the HUNGARIANS judged by the Austrians; even here the "Iron Curtain" may produce relative unfamiliarity with average Hungarians.

b. *Mean evaluative component is negative on the primary evaluative scales* (10 cases). In these cases the evaluative components on the *basic* scales are positive, and their variance is generally smaller than the overall average. In all but one of these cases the target is judged "Tight" on impulse-control. On the two primarily evaluative scales, targets such as the RUSSIANS and the GERMANS may be judged "not likeable" but not equally "admirable." In considering self-judgments in Chapter 5 we noted a complementary tendency for "Loose" judges (e.g., the south Italians) to rate themselves more favorably on the primarily evaluative scales than on the regular scales. Here the same judges rate targets seen as "Tight" less favorably on these scales.

c. *Mean evaluative components on the basis scales are negative* (3 cases). These cases have above average variances for both the evaluative components and the (still larger) descriptive components. In contrast to most of the other cases

Table 18.3. *Three criteria for traditional stereotypes: examples*

Target	Judges	(1) Evaluative variance/ Total	(2) Evaluative component Regular scales	(3) Evaluative component Special scales
No criteria met (averages for 50 cases)		0.25	+0.5	+0.8
(a) Criterion (1) only				
CHINESE	Chinese	0.68	+1.2	(+1.9)[a]
JAPANESE	Philippines	0.62	+0.9	(+1.0)
AMERICANS	Philippines	0.72	+1.2	(+1.6)
AMERICANS	Greeks	0.67	+0.7	(+0.6)
FINNS	Germans	0.64	+1.0	+1.1
DUTCH	French	0.73	+0.9	+1.2
HUNGARIANS	Austrians	0.55	+0.2	+0.5
(b) Criterion (3) only				
GERMANS	Germans	0.38	+0.5	−0.0
GERMANS	Austrians	0.30	+0.3	−0.3
GERMANS	Italians	0.10	+0.5	−0.3
GERMANS	Greeks	0.18	+0.5	(−0.4)
RUSSIANS	English	0.19	+0.4	−0.3
RUSSIANS	Greeks	0.44	+0.4	(−0.4)
N. ITALIANS	S. Italians	0.19	+0.5	−0.1
AUSTRIANS	Italians	0.08	+0.3	−0.3
CZECHS	Austrians	0.21	+0.3	−0.1
AMERICANS	Germans	0.27	+0.1	−0.2
(c) Criterion (2) only				
IRISH	English	0.35	−0.1	+0.1
ITALIANS	Finns	0.40	−0.3	+0.3
ITALIANS	French	0.42	−0.1	+0.4
(d) Criteria (1) & (2)				
FILIPINOS	Chinese	0.60	−0.3	(+0.2)
S. ITALIANS	N. Italians	0.82	−0.3	+0.6
SPANISH	French	0.69	−0.3	+0.1
FRENCH	French	0.57	−0.1	+0.4
(e) Criteria (2) & (3)				
ITALIANS	Austrians	0.37	−0.3	−0.0
(f) All criteria				
TURKS	Greeks	0.84	−0.6	(−1.5)

[a] Parentheses are used for the Greek and Philippine (which include the Chinese) judges, where the special scale is *desirable–undesirable*. For all other judges the special scales were *admirable–deplorable* and *likeable–not likeable*.

considered in this section, these are thus primarily clear-cut descriptive judgments. They seem to represent the complement of the previous category: here for targets seen as "Loose" (and Assertive) the evaluative components are slightly negative on the basic scales (but positive on the primarily evaluative scales): the ITALIANS judged by the French and the Finns; the IRISH judged by the English.

d. *Evaluative components are more important, and negative on the basic scales* (4 cases). Thus far, except for the Chinese self-judgments, we have hardly found any cases with a dramatic resemblance to traditional "stereotypes." In this category some suggestive evidence appears. Two of these cases involve close ingroup–outgroup contact within the same country, where relatively "Tight" judges rate a relatively "Loose" target with negative evaluative components on the basic scales: the FILIPINOS judged by the Chinese, and the SOUTH ITALIANS judged by the north Italians. A third case – the SPANISH judged by the French – fits part of this description. However, the fourth case is the French self-judgments! This does not contribute to any simple interpretation. (Admittedly, the negative component in this case is a marginal −0.1.)

e. *Mean evaluative component is negative on the basic scales and on the primarily evaluative scales* (1 case). In this case – the ITALIANS judged by the Austrians – the latter component is *very* marginally negative. Here we have another case of close contact and of conflict since World War II based on nationality (conflict regarding the ethnic Austrians in the "south Tyrol" or "alto Adige").

f. *All three criteria* (1 case). This case – the TURKS judged by the Greeks – comes closest to the traditional "stereotype" toward outgroups. The judgments overwhelmingly reflect evaluative components which are large and negative both on the basic scales (−0.6 where the largest other value is −0.3) and the primarily evaluative scale (−1.5).

Conclusion

Evidence having resemblance to traditional stereotypes appears in only a very few cases, which have only a few repeated features. On the one hand, the two groups may be in close contact, with conflict presumed between them. There may be two groups within the same country (such a comparison was included in our design only for the Filipinos and Chinese in the Philippines, and for the north and south Italians, both of which appear here as examples). In this situation, we will presume conflict. Alternatively, there may be groups from adjacent countries, with a political conflict related to nationality *since* World War II of an intensity extending to violence – e.g., bombs in the south Tyrol; the Turkish occupation of Cyprus. (The conflicts of World War II have been largely compensated for in our results – e.g., the French and Germans both give more favorable judgments to each other than to themselves.)[1]

[1] Moreover, the effects of the "cold war" are not a major factor in our results. Thus, the mean evaluative component on the basic scales is the same (+0.4) for consensus judgments about the RUSSIANS and the AMERICANS. In contrast, Buchanan and Cantril (1953) found large differences, with positive characteristics for AMERICANS and negative ones for RUSSIANS.

A secondary feature is that "Tight" judges judging "Loose" targets are more likely to produce negative evaluations on the basic scales. ("Loose" judges with "Tight" targets are more likely to produce negative evaluations on primarily evaluative scales.)

For comparative purposes, we have already mentioned in Chapter 5 the study of groups within countries in East Africa by Brewer and Campbell (1976). Their results come much closer to traditional "stereotypes." In contrast to our results, they found highly consistent tendencies for all outgroups to be judged unfavorably relative to the ingroup. Their detailed discussion indicates that negative judgments were strongest toward outgroups considered relatively "uncivilized" (presumably less impulse-controlled) as compared with the opposite case. Their situation generally fits the features we have just described.

If the suggested features needed for traditional stereotypes are correct, we can reach the following conclusions: not only can traditional stereotypes exist, but it would be possible to pin-point when they were common in the past, and where they are likely to be found today. But in contemporary Europe they have largely vanished.

Two explanations suggest themselves for this difference in results: an actual decline in "cold war" polarization between the early 1950s and 1970; a greater tendency to express such sentiments for the national sample of Buchanan and Cantril than for our student judges.

Appendix A
Basic analyses

This appendix considers some basic analyses, the conclusions of which were reported at the beginning of Chapter 5. Section I considers analyses of the variances of the 14 pairs of scales. Section II considers analyses of the relationships between the scales. At the end these analyses are compared to those for comparable scales from the trait inference study.

I. Analyses of the scale variances

The method used here is analogous to, but not identical with, the familiar analysis of variance. We are concerned with a data matrix of 28 scales by 76 "cases" (or some portion of these) of a group of judges rating a nationality. The entries in the matrix are means for the group of judges on each scale.

Proceeding as in the analysis of variance, one could separate the total variance of the data matrix into two terms: (a) the variations of each scale mean around the grand mean, and (b) the variances for each scale around its mean.

Term (a) would correspond to a "main effect due to scales" in the analysis of variance. The problem is that for the present data this term depends on the direction in which the scales are scored. The present study has systematically given a high score to the favorable evaluative direction, so that a high score is given to *thrifty* on the scale *thrifty–extravagant*, and to *generous* on the scale *generous–stingy*. However, psychologists often use a different scoring convention with two variables that are meant to reverse each other. They choose to score both variables in the same *descriptive* direction; in the previous example they might then give a high score to *stingy* on the scale *generous–stingy*. This would of course affect the value of the mean on this scale (and so the deviation of this mean around the grand mean).[1]

In general, relatively arbitrary decisions about the direction of scoring may affect term (a) as described above, but not term (b). Accordingly the present analyses consider only the latter: the variances of each scale around its mean. With this amendment the analysis can proceed much as in the analysis of variance. One can compute the variance on any scale (or all scales) due to any selection of cases.

Targets vs. judges

The most obvious application is to select the 36 cases representing the six standard judges and the six standard targets. As in the analysis of variance, one can compute

---

[1] The details of the mathematical development relevant to this section are reduced to a minimum here. Any interested reader may obtain them by writing to the author.

Table A.1. *Variance of scales analyzed by targets and judges (6 standard judges, 6 standard targets, 28 scales)*

	Average value	Proportion
Targets	0.96	0.63
Judges	0.13	0.09
Targets X judges	0.43	0.28
Total	1.52	1.00

for each target and each judge the squared deviations from each scale mean and average these across all scales. The results are shown in Table A.1.

Table A.1 shows that the variation in the scales is predominantly due to differences between the targets, secondarily to interaction between targets and judges, and only to a small extent to differences between judges. This supports the first conclusion, stated in Chapter 5: *differences between nationality targets are much more important than differences between groups of judges.*

Analysis into evaluative and descriptive components

This analysis takes advantage of the use of pairs of scales to separate evaluative and descriptive components. As was shown in Chapter 4, one can use scores on any pair of scales to estimate evaluative and descriptive components. Proceeding the other way around, one can express the scores on any pair of scales (a and b) in terms of the evaluative and descriptive components (E and D). We begin by simply repeating equations (4.1) from Chapter 4 as (A.1):

$$a = E + D$$
$$b = E - D. \tag{A.1}$$

We can then express the variance of each scale in terms of the two components, using the basic formula for the variance of any sum or difference:

$$s^2 a = s_E^2 + s_D^2 + 2 \text{ covariance } (E, D)$$
$$s^2 b = s_E^2 + s_D^2 - 2 \text{ covariance } (E, D). \tag{A.2}$$

If the two equations in (A.2) are added together, the covariance terms cancel:

$$s_a^2 + s_b^2 = 2(s_E^2 + s_D^2). \tag{A.3}$$

Equation (A.3) shows that the sum of the variances of the two scales is equal to twice the sum of the variances of the evaluative and descriptive components. On this basis, one can analyze any pair of scales in terms of the two components. In the applications below, we are concerned only with the relative size of the two components.

Table A.2 begins in the left-hand column with the results from Table A.1 for the 36 cases classified by targets and judges. To the right, these results are expressed in terms of the two components. The lower part of Table A.2 adds results for the other cases.

Table A.2. *Variance of scales analyzed by components*

	Mean value	E	D	%E	%D
Targets	0.96	0.19	0.77	20%	80%
Judges	0.13	0.07	0.06	51%	49%
Targets X judges	0.43	0.15	0.29	34%	66%
Total (36 cases)	1.53	0.40	1.12	26%	73%
Other European (34 cases)	1.21	0.45	0.76	37%	63%
Philippines (6 cases)	1.57	0.89	0.68	57%	43%
Average (76 cases)	1.41	0.46	0.94	33%	67%

In Table A.2 the results for the 36 cases show that the descriptive variance is much more important than the evaluative variance. This conclusion applies especially to the differences between targets. It does not apply to the smaller differences between judges, where the evaluative variance is slightly more important than the descriptive variance.

If we compare the totals for the 36 cases with the other cases, we note an increase in the importance of evaluation relative to description. This is for two different reasons. For the 34 "other European" cases the major change is a decrease in the size of the descriptive variance. We would interpret this as due to the inclusion among the non-standard targets of several that were relatively unfamiliar. (For the Greek judges, who were not included among the 36 cases, the change occurred only on the "non-standard" targets.)

In contrast, in the results for the Philippines judges, the major further change is an increase in the size of evaluative variance. We suggested earlier that the Philippines results show polite favorableness toward foreigners, and hostility toward domestic outgroups wherein they come closer to traditional "stereotypes."

Overall, the results in Table A.2 show that evaluation represents about one-third and description two-thirds of the total. Hence for the present results, one can state the second conclusion given in Chapter 5: *the descriptive aspects of judgment are more important than the evaluative aspects.*

This conclusion is subject to a qualification. The results here are based on scales (from "sets of four") selected to unconfound evaluative and descriptive aspects of judgment. They do not represent other trait-adjectives (from "sets of two" and "sets of three"). Appendix B considers what would happen if such scales had been used, based on the recent completion of the trait inference study. These results show that the addition of these other scales would increase the relative importance of evaluation. The implication is that the disadvantage of evaluation in the preceding analysis here would be reduced if all types of trait-adjective scales had been used for judgments about national groups.

Further applications

In principle one could apply the preceding method to each scale (across some selection of cases) to any selection of cases (averaged across the scales). For example, within the six standard judges and six standard targets, it could be shown that the Italians have the largest variances both as judges and as targets. Thus the Italian judges make more clear-cut judgments than other judges, and the ITALIANS as a target are judged in a more clear-cut way than the other standard targets. The preceding method was applied separately to each of the 76 cases (across the 28 scales). There were only 12 cases where the evaluative components were larger than the descriptive ones. This analysis was used in Chapter 18, where a predominance of (negative) evaluation or affect was used as one of the criteria for the traditional conception of "stereotypes."

II. Relationships between the scales

This section considers relationships between the scales. It is thus concerned with what is "common" to the several scales, in the factor analytic sense. The previous section considered in addition what may be relatively "specific" to each scale or each pair of scales. It seemed appropriate to begin in this way, since one would expect that evaluation would be relatively "general," while descriptive aspects could be relatively "specific." The descriptive aspects might be decisive for specific judgments, but underestimated by an analysis considering only common factors. For the present data, however, it turns out that while evaluation is indeed very general, the descriptive aspects appear on large common factors, and more specific descriptive aspects seem not to be of major importance.

We will proceed by successive stages, first examining the evaluative and descriptive components separately. The previous section showed that these components represented 33% and 67% of the overall scale variances. Unless otherwise specified, all analyses are for the 28 scales across the 76 cases, and use the method of principal components and Varimax rotation. For reasons that will be explained as we proceed, we generally examine the unrotated factors instead of following the traditional procedure and considering only the rotated factors.

Evaluative components

Analysis of the evaluative components provided three factors, with the first factor representing 51% of the variance of the evaluative components, plus two smaller factors representing 12% and 8% of this variance. The first factor is a "general" factor, since the loadings on all 14 sets of scales are positive and substantial. Thus the analysis of the evaluative components gives evidence for a dimension of general evaluation. As one would expect, the Varimax rotation redistributes the general factor across the three rotated factors, all of which have only positive loadings and thus represent varieties of general evaluation as combined with the two smaller unrotated factors. None of these have any obvious theoretical interpretation.

Descriptive components

Analysis of the descriptive components provided two large factors (representing 43.4% and 21.1% of the variance of the descriptive components) and two smaller factors (representing 8.2% and 7.8% of this variance). Table A.3 presents results for the first two factors, as well as any substantial loadings (larger than 0.40) on the other two factors.

Table A.3. *Factor analysis of descriptive components: unrotated factors*

A	Descriptive contrast vs.	B	I	II[a]
1a. Thrifty (+)		Extravagant (−)	0.90	0.06
b. Stingy (−)		Generous (+)		
2a. Self-controlled (+)		Impulsive (−)	0.91	0.20
b. Inhibited (−)		Spontaneous (+)		
3a. Serious (+)		Frivolous (−)	0.92	0.00
b. Grim (−)		Gay (+)		
4a. Skeptical (+)		Gullible (−)	0.77	−0.25
b. Distrustful (−)		Trusting (+)		
5a. Firm (+)		Lax (−)	0.80	−0.44
b. Severe (−)		Lenient (+)		
6a. Persistent (+)		Vacillating (−)	0.86	−0.23
b. Inflexible (−)		Flexible (+)		
7a. Selective (+)		Undiscriminating (−)	0.79	−0.35
b. Choosy (−)		Broad-minded (+)		
8a. Cautious (+)		Rash (−)	0.70	0.55
b. Timid (−)		Bold (+)		
9a. Calm (+)		Agitated (−)	0.45	0.68
b. Inactive (−)		Active (+)		
10a. Peaceful (+)		Aggressive (−)	−0.01	0.91
b. Passive (−)		Forceful (+)		
11a. Modest (+)		Conceited (−)	0.08	0.74
b. Unassured (−)		Self-confident (+)		
12a. Cooperative (+)		Uncooperative (−)	0.10	0.47
b. Conforming (−)		Independent (+)		
13a. Tactful (+)		Tactless (−)	0.39	0.20
b. Devious (−)		Frank (+)		
14a. Practical (+)		Impractical (−)	0.38	−0.25
b. Opportunistic (−)		Idealistic (+)		
		% Total variance	43.4	21.1

Additional factors
III (8.2% of variance): 12 (0.78); 13 (−0.43)
IV (7.8% of variance): 12 (−0.63); 14 (0.54)
[a] The direction of this factor can be "reflected."

The two large factors can be identified clearly with the two large descriptive dimensions found in the trait inference study: "Tight vs. Loose control over impulse-expression" and "Self-Assertiveness." (The second factor would need to be reversed in direction – "reflected" – since as it stands it represents Unassertive vs. Assertive.) The first factor has very large loadings on sets 1 through 8. The second factor has substantial loadings on sets 8 through 12. The two smaller factors are relatively specific. The third factor has substantial loadings on sets 12 and 13, and the fourth factor on sets 12 and 14.

The rotation procedure generally would tend to break up these factors and spread the variance across the several rotated factors. In the present case, the first factor is "robust" enough to be little changed by rotation. The second factor retains sets 8 through 11 but loses set 12 to the third rotated factor.

In summary, separate analyses of the evaluative and descriptive components do disclose the three dimensions of general evaluation, Tight–Loose, and Assertive–Unassertive. The interpretations of the results in the text generally rely on these components (rather than results for the single scales). Hence one may conclude that there is justification for interpretations in terms of these three dimensions.

Analyses of scales

It is another question as to how easily these dimensions can be identified in analyses of the scales themselves. It has been argued previously (Peabody, 1978, 1984) that such unconfounded dimensions will certainly not appear in the factors resulting from Varimax rotation – since such rotations align the factors close to some of the scales, which themselves involve the confounding of evaluative and descriptive components. On the other hand, the *unrotated* factors might or might not approach unconfounded dimensions. For example, in the analysis of the complete trait inference data (Peabody, 1984), the unrotated factors from the analysis of scales were confounded ones. However, it was possible to make a deliberate rotation of these factors to the unconfounded dimensions of Evaluation, Tight–Loose, and Assertive–Unassertive.

With this introduction, we may now consider the analysis of scales. The results are presented in Table A.4. There are three larger factors (representing 38%, 15%, and 14% of the variance). The first factor is close to the Tight–Loose dimension, but slightly confounded with evaluation – i.e., on sets 1–7 the positive loadings on the "a" scales ("Tight and good") are consistently larger than the negative loadings on the "b" scales ("Loose and good"). The second factor is largely general evaluation (there are only two tiny negative loadings), but it is slightly confounded with the "b" scales for "Loose and good." It seems clear that a deliberate rotation of these two factors could put them close to the unconfounded dimensions. The third factor is close to the Assertive–Unassertive dimension (note the large loadings on sets 9–11).

We generally expect the factors from Varimax rotation to be more confounded than the unrotated ones. In the first rotated factor, however, the Tight–Loose dimension is largely preserved, now slightly confounded the other way with evaluation (i.e., light on the "a" scales for "Tight and good"). General evaluation is now spread over the second and third factors, for both of which the negative loadings are few and generally small. The third rotated factor confounds evaluation and Assertiveness. The second rotated factor confounds evaluation and what is left over – Tight and Unassertive.

In sum, it is possible (with some effort) to identify the three dimensions even in the scale analysis.

Analysis of objects of judgment ("Q-analysis")

Unconfounded dimensions are unlikely to emerge from analyses of scales because these include both evaluative and descriptive aspects which are likely to get confounded with each other. The situation is quite different if one considers analyses of correlations between the objects of measurement across the scales. As has been noted previously (Peabody, 1970, 1978, 1984) such correlations tend to eliminate general evaluation in advance. (These correlations are taken *around* the means for each object of measurement – across the scales. But these means represent the effect of general

Table A1.4. Factor analyses of scales: group judgment study

Scales	Unrotated factors			Rotated factors		
	I	II	III	I	II	III
1a. Thrifty (+) / Stingy (−)	0.81	−0.05	−0.32	0.71	0.50	−0.04
b. Generous (+) / Extravagant (−)	−0.69	0.46	0.00	−0.78	−0.18	−0.14
2a. Self-controlled (+) / Inhibited (−)	0.87	0.32	−0.15	−0.56	0.70	0.27
b. Spontaneous (+) / Impulsive (−)	−0.72	0.28	0.40	−0.81	−0.28	0.27
3a. Serious (+) / Grim (−)	0.89	−0.01	−0.18	0.80	0.33	0.02
b. Gay (+) / Frivolous (−)	−0.84	0.32	0.08	−0.89	−0.19	−0.07
4a. Skeptical (+) / Distrustful (−)	0.82	0.09	0.10	0.59	0.40	0.46
b. Trusting (+) / Gullible (−)	−0.45	0.69	−0.11	−0.66	0.13	−0.13
5a. Firm (+) / Severe (−)	0.89	0.06	0.21	0.73	0.20	0.39
b. Lenient (+) / Lax (−)	−0.59	0.54	−0.37	−0.78	0.31	−0.24
6a. Persistent (+) / Inflexible (−)	0.88	0.09	0.17	0.70	0.25	0.43
b. Flexible (+) / Vacillating (−)	−0.66	0.51	−0.02	−0.81	0.04	−0.12
7a. Selective (+) / Choosy (−)	0.71	0.19	0.34	0.42	0.39	0.63
b. Broad-minded (+) / Undiscriminating (−)	−0.49	0.60	−0.01	−0.77	0.20	0.21
8a. Cautious (+) / Timid (−)	0.89	0.04	−0.27	0.71	0.57	0.08
b. Bold (+) / Rash (−)	0.16	0.02	0.70	0.11	−0.44	0.63
9a. Calm (+) / Inactive (−)	0.71	0.38	−0.46	0.42	0.76	0.01
b. Active (+) / Agitated (−)	0.22	0.31	0.64	0.04	−0.06	0.47
10a. Peaceful (+) / Passive (−)	0.27	0.64	−0.58	−0.10	0.86	−0.12
b. Forceful (+) / Aggressive (−)	0.45	0.15	0.69	0.34	−0.18	0.63
11a. Modest (+) / Unassured (−)	0.31	0.23	−0.57	0.18	0.44	−0.40
b. Self-confident (+) / Conceited (−)	0.38	0.25	0.71	0.12	0.03	0.88
12a. Cooperative (+) / Conforming (−)	0.08	0.69	0.11	−0.23	0.32	0.13
b. Independent (+) / Uncooperative (−)	0.02	0.52	0.56	−0.32	0.15	0.75
13a. Tactful (+) / Devious (−)	0.51	0.49	−0.25	0.11	0.83	0.17
b. Frank (+) / Tactless (−)	0.19	0.61	−0.09	−0.07	0.21	0.11
14a. Practical (+) / Opportunistic (−)	0.66	0.41	0.26	0.39	0.27	0.46
b. Idealistic (+) / Impractical (−)	0.08	0.06	−0.14	−0.02	0.06	0.01
% Total variance	38	15	14	31	16	15

Additional unrotated factors
IV (5% of variance): 13b (0.75); 8b (0.43); 10a (0.41)
V (5% of variance): 13b (0.46)
VI (4% of variance): 14b (0.53); 12b (−0.43)

Additional rotated factors
IV (8% of variance): 12b (0.85); 13a (0.48); 11a (0.81); 4b (0.46)
V (7% of variance): 14b (0.81); 11a (0.65)
VI (6% of variance): 13b (0.89); 10a (0.48)

Table A.5. *Proportions of variance*

	Evaluative	Descriptive	
A. Components	0.33 (0.23)	0.67 (0.77)	
	General evaluation	Tight vs Loose	Assertive vs. Unassertive
B. Within separate components	0.51 (0.71)	0.43 (0.54)	0.21 (0.28)
Multiply: A × B	0.16 (0.16)	0.30 (0.41)	0.15 (0.21)
Scale analysis	0.15 (0.17)	0.38 (0.43)	0.14 (0.23)
FANOVA analysis	0.16 (0.16)	0.34 (0.43)	0.14 (0.23)

Note: numbers in parentheses are for comparable scales from the trait inference results.

evaluation.) These correlations therefore provide relatively clear definitions of unconfounded descriptive factors.

The trait inference study had the special feature that the "objects of measurement" were the same trait-adjectives (used singly) that defined the scales. Accordingly it was possible to interpret the factors from the factor loadings on these traits. For the present data the "objects of measurement" are the 76 cases of nationality targets rated by groups of judges. There were two large factors (representing 34.2% and 22.5% of the variance) and 10 small factors (representing 7.4% to 1.4% of the variance). The factor loadings for the 76 cases on the two large factors were presented in Table 18.1 and used for the various nationalities as convenient summaries of the two descriptive dimensions. However the *identification* of these factors as the descriptive dimensions of Tight–Loose and Assertive–Unassertive cannot be made from these factor loadings, but from the factor *scores* on the 28 scales. (For the first factor, the factor scores for the scales specified as "+" in Table 2.7 average 1.08; for the scales specified as "−" the average is −1.36. For the second factor, the comparable averages are 1.52 and −1.62.)

Review

It is possible to relate most of the analyses in this appendix to each other. The relevant results are collected in Table A.5.

Section I presented an analysis of the scale variances, which showed that the evaluative components represented 0.33 and the descriptive components represented 0.67 of the total. These values are shown on the top row ("A") of Table A.5.

Section II began with factor analyses for the two components separately. This analysis showed that the general evaluative dimension represented 51% of the variance *within* the evaluative components. The dimensions of Tight vs. Loose and Assertive vs. Unassertive represented 43% and 21% of the variance *within* the descriptive components. These proportions are shown on the second row ("B") of Table A.5.

Logically, it should be possible to multiply the top two rows to arrive at a projection of the proportion of the combined scale variance that would be represented by each of the three dimensions. The products of this multiplication are shown on the third row of Table A.5.

Section II presented factor analyses of the scales. The largest unrotated factors could be identified only fairly well with the three unconfounded dimensions. The percentages of scale variance for these factors are shown on the fourth row of Table A.5. If these proportions are compared with the projected ones in the third row, it can be seen that the correspondence is reasonably close.

Gollob's FANOVA analysis

In the attempt to identify unconfounded evaluative and descriptive dimensions, the analysis of scales was certainly not elegant. And yet with traditional procedures, this is where we would have started: trying to interpret the rotated factors from the analysis of scales.

In contrast, Gollob (e.g., 1968) has proposed a method that is elegant but untraditional. This method combines features of the analysis of variance (ANOVA) and of factor analysis, from which the name "FANOVA." In this procedure differences between the means for the measures and for the objects of measurement are removed first as "main effects,"[1] whose magnitude can be estimated – as in the analysis of variance. The remaining "interactions" can then be analyzed by methods like those of factor analysis.

As we saw earlier, in our own data, differences between the means for the objects of measurement represent general evaluation. In comparison with our own earlier analyses, FANOVA resembles the inverse ("Q") analysis in removing these differences in advance, and so reducing the likelihood of confounding in the later analysis. But in FANOVA this is not done inadvertently but deliberately – so that the magnitude of the "main effect" can be estimated.

Through the assistance of Dr Gollob, it was possible to carry out FANOVA analyses with our data. The "main effect" corresponding to general evaluation represented 16% of the total variance. There were two large "interaction factors" and several small ones. The two large factors (representing 34% and 14% of the total variance) could be identified with the Tight–Loose and Assertive–Unassertive dimensions. In general, the FANOVA results – included as the last row of Table A.5 – confirm the other analyses.

Through all the various analyses considered, it remained possible to identify the three major dimensions. There we may state the third conclusion given in Chapter 5. *Three major dimensions summarize much of the results: a descriptive dimension that we have called "Tight vs. Loose control over impulse-expression"; a descriptive dimension that we have called "Self-assertiveness"; a general evaluative dimension.*

[1] Alternatively the data can be "standardized" with respect to *either* the measure or the objects of measurement, and the remaining differences between the other means removed as a single "main effect." This alternative is followed here: the scales were standardized and the differences between objects of measurement were removed as a main effect.

Comparison with the trait inference study

It is of interest to compare the present results for judgments about national groups with the trait inference study. In the terminology of Wiggins (1973) the trait inference study is an example of "internal" structure – cognitions about the relationships between traits. In contrast, "external" structure would apply to judgments about actual people – traditionally individuals, but in the present case groups of people.

It will be recalled that the present 28 scales are revisions of scales from the trait inference study. For present purposes we therefore consider the subset of the trait inference data involving the comparable 28 scales and 56 traits.[1]

All of the preceding analyses were carried out on the comparable trait inference data. The results are summarized in Table A.5 by the values in parentheses. In general, the trait inference data had larger variance and a still higher proportion of descriptive variance, and the three dimensions represent still more of the total (e.g., for the scale analyses 85% instead of 67%).

What is the explanation for this difference? Two features (not unrelated) of the trait inference study suggest themselves. First, the objects of measurement (other trait-adjectives) seem to have a very high relevance to the measures (trait-adjective scales) that is unlikely to be equalled by "external" objects of measurement (individuals or, as here, groups of persons). Secondly, there is evidence (Peabody, 1984) that internal structure involves fewer and larger factors than external structure.

However, the present results compare favorably with other, more traditional, studies of external structure – i.e., ratings by others or self-reports for individuals. Few of these studies approach accounting for 67% of the variance with three factors. At least part of the explanation is that we have combined groups of judges (typically 40 to 50) so that each data entry represents the mean for many individual judgments. Few studies of ratings by others have as many as a dozen judges for each target, and of course for self-report data there is only a single judge. Hence, the present study, by combining (aggregating) many individual judgments, has allowed for increased reliability in the results and so permitted larger factors to emerge.

[1] Of the 56 trait-adjectives, 16 were revised. The only notable change was for scale 9a where *calm–agitated* was considered a revision of *relaxed–tense*; *tense* had been "Tight," but *agitated* was "Loose" and "Assertive."

Appendix B
Characteristics of persons

This appendix is a supplement to Chapter 2, which proposed that the possible characteristics of persons could be represented by trait-adjectives. Trait-adjectives normally confound evaluative and descriptive aspects. To meet this problem, sets of trait-adjectives were classified according to a scheme for separating evaluative and descriptive aspects. Various sets represented four, three, and two of the four possible combinations.

A study of inferences between trait-adjectives (Peabody, 1967) represented sets of four and sets of three, but the sets of two were omitted since they could not be used to unconfound evaluative and descriptive aspects. For similar reasons, in the present study of group judgments, the sets of three were omitted as well. This raises a question: to what extent may these omissions have affected the present results?

It is possible to provide some evidence on this question, since the trait inference study was recently completed by adding representatives of the sets of two that had been omitted earlier (Peabody, 1984). Only a brief summary is given here. Most of the scales that were added fell into two broad classes: "impersonal virtues" relating to achievement, and "interpersonal virtues" relating to affiliation. The scales representing these two classes are listed in Table B.1.

These two classes have obvious relevance for national characteristics. For example, Weber's theory of the Protestant ethic implies an emphasis on the impersonal virtues of achievement at the expense of the interpersonal virtues of affiliation. Thus their omission could be a serious problem for the present study.

This problem is reduced by the results of the study. The added traits did not introduce any important new factors. In particular, the new scales of achievement and affiliation had high relations to evaluation and to the descriptive Tight–Loose dimension. They could to a considerable extent be summarized as combinations of these two dimensions: achievement as "Tight" and good (like *thrifty–extravagant*); affiliation as "Loose" and good (like *generous–stingy*).

Thus one may conclude that while the omission of scales for achievement and affiliation is a disadvantage of the present study, this disadvantage is reduced because they involve dimensions that *are* well represented. One may hope that much of what they would provide is represented indirectly through these dimensions.

The previous discussion concerns the omission in the present study of sets of two. Some comment should be added on the omission of sets of three. The major content represented primarily in the sets of three involves intelligence and related cognitive traits. In the trait inference study they were most strongly related to Tight impulse-control. But in studies of judgments about actual people, intelligence may be at least partly separated from impulse-control and achievement. This problem is somewhat reduced by the inclusion of *intelligent–stupid* as one of the extra scales.

Table B.1. *Scales for achievement and affiliation*

Achievement	Affiliation
hard-working–lazy	unselfish–selfish
ambitious–unambitious	kind–unkind
responsible–irresponsible	warm–cold
organized–disorganized	sociable–unsociable
capable–incompetent	good-natured–irritable

Table B.2. *Percentages of total variance for different types of scales*

			Percent total variance	
	No. of scales	Evaluation	Tight/Loose	Assertive/Unassertive
Sets of four	30	23%	37%	15%
Sets of three	10	39%	19%	19%
Sets of two	15	42%	23%	14%
Total	55	31%	30%	16%

Source: derived from Peabody (1984).

Thus if one first considers scales from sets of four, then the addition of the other scales did not change the presence of the three major dimensions. It did, however, affect their relative importance, increasing the importance of general evaluation relative to the descriptive dimensions. In Table B.2 the results for the completed trait inference study (Peabody, 1984) are separated for the different kinds of sets.

Table B.2 shows that the relative importance of evaluation is smaller for the sets of four than for the other sets. Indeed, it was anticipated earlier that the latter traits would be more related to evaluation – this was the reason why they could not be successfully unconfounded, but remained partly or wholly confounded with evaluation. These results show that for the sets of four by themselves the importance of evaluation is smaller as compared with the use of all types of scales.

What are the implications of these results for the present study? The preceding results became available only recently, after the completion of the present study of national characteristics. The present study used only revised scales from the sets of four, where one could unconfound evaluative and descriptive aspects. The results and interpretations apply to the data that were actually obtained with these scales.

One could, however, ask the hypothetical question: what might be changed, if one *had* used scales representing all types of trait-adjectives? From the results of the completed trait inference study, one could infer that some interpretations would not have to be qualified, while others would have to be qualified in degree, although not so many in their general direction. For example, consider two of the conclusions stated in Chapter 5 and supported in Appendix A. One conclusion was that much of the results can be summarized by the three dimensions of Tight–Loose, Assertive–Unassertive and general evaluation. As we have just seen, in the completed trait inference study these same dimensions remain and no important new factors appear. This implies that this conclusion would not have to be qualified.

A second conclusion is that the descriptive aspects of judgment are more important than the evaluative ones. This conclusion is supported in Appendix A, where an analysis of the variances of the scales showed that 33% represented evaluative components and 67% descriptive components. As we have just seen, in the trait inference study the relative importance of evaluation was increased if other scales were added to those from sets of four. This implies that the disadvantage of evaluation would be reduced if all types of scales had been represented in the present study.

Appendix C
Translating the scales

Dora Capozza, Willem Doise, Georg Wieser, and Dean Peabody

The procedure for translation of the scales was described briefly in Chapter 4. In each case there were several informants whose first language was that of the translation, and also fluent in English. They were instructed to follow the classification scheme of Table 2.1, and aim not only at translations of the separate English terms, but also to try to preserve the descriptive and evaluative relations between the four terms in each set.

Table C.1. *Scales in German*

Descriptive direction A–B

1a.	sparsam (+)–verschwenderisch (−)
b.	geizig (−)–freigiebig (+)
2a.	beherrscht (+)–unbeherrscht (−)
b.	gehemmt(−)–unbefangen (+)
3a.	ernst (+)–albern (−)
b.	mürrisch (−)–heiter (+)
4a.	skeptisch (+)–leichtgläubig (−)
b.	misstrauisch (−)–vertrauend (+)
5a.	bestimmt (+)–lax (−)
b.	unerbittlich (−)–milde (+)
6a.	beharrlich (+)–wankelmütig (−)
b.	starr (−)–flexibel (+)
7a.	kritisch (+)–kritiklos (−)
b.	intolerant (−)–tolerant (+)
8a.	vorsichtig (+)–unvorsichtig (−)
b.	ängstlich (−)–kühn (+)
9a.	ruhig (+)–aufgeregt (−)
b.	inaktiv (−)–lebhaft (+)
10a.	friedlich (+)–aggressiv (−)
b.	passiv (−)–energisch (+)
11a.	bescheiden (+)–eingebildet (−)
b.	unsicher (−)–selbstsicher (+)
12a.	zur Zusammenarbeit bereit (+)–eigensinnig (−)
b.	konformistisch (−)–unabhängig (+)
13a.	taktvoll (+)–taktlos (−)
b.	unaufrichtig (−)–offen (+)
14a.	realistisch (+)–unrealistisch (−)
b.	opportunistisch (−)–idealistisch (+)
15a.	bewundernswert (+)–beklagenswert (−)
b.	unsympatisch (−)–sympatisch (+)
16.	fleissig (+)–faul (−)
17.	intelligent (+)–dumm (−)

Table C.2. *Scales in French*

Descriptive direction A–B
1a. économe (+)–gaspilleur (−) b. mesquin (−)–généreux (+)
2a. maître de soi (+)–impulsif (−) b. contracté (−)–spontané (+)
3a. sérieux (+)–frivole (−) b. lugubre (−)–gai (+)
4a. sceptique (+)–crédule (−) b. soupçonneux (−)–confiant (+)
5a. ferme (+)–négligent (−) b. sévère (−)–indulgent (+)
6a. tenace (+)–versatile (−) b. entêté (−)–souple (+)
7a. sélectif (+)–sans discernement (−) b. tatillon (−)–large d'idées (+)
8a. prudent (+)–téméraire (−) b. timide (−)–hardi (+)
9a. calme (+)–agité (−) b. inerte (−)–actif (+)
10a. paisible (+)–agressif (−) b. passif (−)–énergique (+)
11a. modeste (+)–prétentieux (−) b. mal assuré (−)–sûr de soi (+)
12a. coopératif (+)–non coopératif (−) b. conformiste (−)–indépendant (+)
13a. plein de tact (+)–indiscret (−) b. cachotier (−)–franc (+)
14a. pratique (+)–sans esprit pratique (−) b. opportuniste (−)–idéaliste (+)
15a. admirable (+)–déplorable (−) b. antipathique (−)–sympathique (+)
16. travailleur (+)–paresseux (−)
17. intelligent (+)–stupide (−)

Naturally there was great variation in the degree of convergence between informants on the translation of different terms. In cases of disagreement, final selections were made by a senior investigator for each language. The process of translation is inherently a task for professionals. However, ideally one would like some check with a wider sample on how well the intended evaluative and descriptive reactions were preserved across the translations. We carried out a special study on a crucial part of this question: the relative evaluations of the two terms used to define each scale.

For this study, special questionnaires (usually 32) were prepared for the translations into German, French, and Italian. These translations are presented in Tables C.1., C.2, and C.3. Since the number of questionnaires prepared for the main group judgment study was limited (usually to 48), and the total group of subjects (e.g., students from a class) was never exactly this large, additional members of the group were given the much briefer special questionnaire. These were supplemented when necessary (e.g.,

Table C.3. *Scales in Italian*

Descriptive direction A–B

1a. parsimonioso (+)–prodigo (−)
  b. avaro (−)–generoso (+)
2a. autocontrollato (+)–impulsivo (−)
  b. inibito (−)–spontaneo (+)
3a. serio (+)–frivolo (−)
  b. cupo (−)–allegro (+)
4a. critico (+)–credulone (−)
  b. diffidente (−)–fiducioso (+)
5a. fermo (+)–cedevole (−)
  b. rigoroso (−)–indulgente (+)
6a. persistente (+)–incostante (−)
  b. rigido (−)–flessibile (+)
7a. selettivo (+)–facilone (−)
  b. pignolo (−)–de larghe vedute (+)
8a. prudente (+)–avventato (−)
  b. timoroso (−)–intrepido (+)
9a. calmo (+)–agitato (−)
  b. inattivo (−)–attivo (+)
10a. pacifico (+)–aggressivo (−)
  b. passivo (−)–energico (+)
11a. modesto (+)–presuntuoso (−)
  b. insicuro (−)–sicuro (+)
12a. dotato di spirito di cooperazione (+)–
    privo di spirito di cooperazione (−)
  b. conformista (−)–indipendente (+)
13a. discreto (+)–privo di tatto (−)
  b. subdolo (−)–franco (+)
14a. pratico (+)–privo di senso pratico (−)
  b. opportunista (−)–idealista (+)
15a. ammirevole (+)–spregevole (−)
  b. antipatico (−)–simpatico (+)
16. laborioso (+)–pigro (−)
17. intelligente (+)–stupido (−)

if the total group was less than 80) by giving the special questionnaire afterwards to subjects in the main study who were the first to finish. For the usual reasons (minor errors of administration) the number of usable special questionnaires varied from 29 to 32 for the three samples.

In the special questionnaire itself, subjects were given the pairs of translated terms used to define each of the 32 scales. They were asked to mark "+" beside one of the two terms as more favorable in evaluation, or "−" beside the term that was more unfavorable. In analyzing the results, we consider whether or not subjects made this choice in the direction "intended": the direction of the scale that was scored as positive vs. negative, based on the version in English. Table C.4 presents the number of subjects who chose the "unintended" direction – as if the translation was in "error" in this respect.

The totals for Table C.4 show that 10% of the total choices were "errors" – in the

Table C.4. *Relative evaluations of traits defining scales: number of choices in unintended direction*

Descriptive contrast		French N = 32	Italian N = 30	German[a] N = 28	Total N = 90
A	B				
1a. Thrifty (+)	Extravagant (−)	5	11	2	18
1b. Stingy (−)	Generous (+)	1	1	—	2
2a. Self-controlled (+)	Impulsive (−)	1	6	1	8
2b. Inhibited (−)	Spontaneous (+)	—	2	—	2
3a. Serious (+)	Frivolous (−)	6	2	3	11
3b. Grim (−)	Gay (+)	1	3	—	4
4a. Skeptical (+)	Gullible (−)	4	—	—	4
4b. Distrustful (−)	Trusting (+)	10	11	10	31
5a. Firm (+)	Lax (−)	1	3	1	5
5b. Severe (−)	Lenient (+)	11	10	4	25
6a. Persistent (+)	Vacillating (−)	—	4	1	5
6b. Inflexible (−)	Flexible (+)	11	5	—	16
7a. Selective (+)	Undiscriminating (−)	9	1	—	10
7b. Choosy (−)	Broad-minded (+)	1	1	1	3
8a. Cautious (+)	Rash (−)	15	3	—	18
8b. Timid (−)	Bold (+)	3	5	1	9
9a. Calm (+)	Agitated (−)	8	2	—	10
9b. Inactive (−)	Active (+)	—	—	—	—
10a. Peaceful (+)	Aggressive (−)	11	12	4	27
10b. Passive (−)	Forceful (+)	1	—	1	2
11a. Modest (+)	Conceited (−)	5	5	1	11
11b. Unassured (−)	Self-confident (+)	1	1	—	2
12a. Cooperative (+)	Uncooperative (−)	3	2	—	5
12b. Conforming (−)	Independent (+)	4	3	1	8
13a. Tactful (+)	Tactless (−)	2	2	—	4
13b. Devious (−)	Frank (+)	—	1	—	1
14a. Practical (+)	Impractical (−)	2	2	1	5
14b. Opportunistic (−)	Idealistic (+)	5	12	7	24
15a. Admirable (+)	Deplorable (−)	3	—	—	3
15b. Not likeable (−)	Likeable (+)	2	—	—	2
16. Hard-working (+)	Lazy (−)	1	3	2	6
17. Intelligent (+)	Stupid (−)	—	—	—	—
	Total "errors"	127	113	41	281
	Total cases	1,024	960	896	2,879
	% "− errors"	12%	12%	5%	10%

[a] The translation into German used Austrian subjects.

"unintended" direction – so that 90% were in the "correct" or intended direction. This shows that the translations were generally successful in preserving the evaluative direction of the scales.

However, these overall totals do not represent the varying results for the individual scales. In every case, the majority of subjects chose the intended direction. However, in statistical terms this direction of choice is not "significant" when the number of subject errors is 10 or larger. For the great majority of scales, the choice of the intended direction *is* significant, but it is non-significant for 5/32 scales for the French and Italian translations, and for one scale with the German translation.

However, most of our interpretations are made by comparing the two scales in a set, rather than interpreting the single scales. Here the outlook is even more encouraging: even in cases where the single scale is not significantly in the intended direction, the pair of scales tends to be. Consider the "worst" example in our results: for the French translation of *cautious* vs. *rash* (*prudent* vs. *téméraire*) only a bare majority of 17 subjects chose "prudent" as more favorable, while 15 subjects did not. However, the evaluative component for this set is estimated by *averaging* this scale with the translation of the scale *bold* vs. *timid*. On this latter scale only three subjects chose in the unintended direction (two of them had done so on the first scale as well). In interpreting the average of the two scales as the evaluative component, we would be "right" for 16 subjects; "wrong" for 2 subjects; "half-right" and "half-wrong" for 14 subjects. The direction of this interpretation would be significant (using the sign test).

We conclude that the translations were not completely successful (as anticipated), and limit the interpretation of some individual scales. But in general the basic direction of the scales has been successfully preserved across translation.

References

Adorno, T. W., Frenkel-Brunswik, E., Levinson, D. T. and Sanford, R. N. (1950). *The authoritarian personality*. New York: Harper.

Albee, G. W. (1977). The protestant ethic, sex and psychotherapy. *American Psychologist*, **32**, 150–61.

Allport, G. W. (1954). *The nature of prejudice*. Cambridge, Mass.: Addison-Wesley.

Allport, G. W. and Odbert, H. S. (1936). Trait names: a psycho-lexical study. *Psychological Monographs*, **47** (Whole No. 211).

Almond, G. A. and Verba, S. (1963). *The civic culture*. Princeton, NJ: Princeton University Press.

Asch, S. E. (1952). *Social psychology*. New York: Prentice-Hall.

Bailey, G. (1972). *Germans, biography of an obsession*. New York: Avon.

Banfield, E. C. (1958). *The moral basis of a backward society*. Glencoe, Ill.: Free Press.

Barzini, L. C. (1968). *The Italians*. Harmondsworth: Penguin Books/H. Hamilton.

Bauer, R. A., Inkeles, A. and Kluckhohn, C. (1956). *How the Soviet system works: cultural, psychological, and social themes*. Cambridge, Mass.: Harvard University Press.

Benedict, R. F. (1934). *Patterns of culture*. Boston, Mass.: Houghton Mifflin.

Brandt, R. B. (1959). *Ethical theory*. Englewood Cliffs, NJ: Prentice-Hall.

Brewer, M. B. and Campbell, D. T. (1976). *Ethnocentrism and intergroup attitudes*. New York: Halsted/Wiley.

Brigham, J. C. (1971). Ethnic stereotypes. *Psychological Bulletin*, **76**, 15–38.

Brown, R. (1958). *Words and things*. Glencoe, Ill.: Free Press.

(1965). *Social psychology*. New York: Free Press.

Bruner, J. S. and Perlmutter, H. V. (1957). Compatriot and foreigner; a study of impression formation in three countries. *Journal of Abnormal and Social Psychology*, **55**, 253–60.

Bryce, J. (1891). *The American commonwealth*, Vol. 2. Toronto: The Copp Clark Publ. Co., Ltd.

Buchanan, W. and Cantril, H. (1953). *How nations see each other*. Urbana: University of Illinois Press.

Campbell, D. T. (1967). Stereotypes and the perception of group differences. *American Psychologist*, **22**, 817–29.

Campbell, D. T. and Fiske, D. W. (1959). Convergent and discriminant validation by the multitrait-multimethod matrix. *Psychological Bulletin*, **56**, 81–105.

Coleman, L. (1941). What is America? A study of alleged American traits. *Social Forces*, **19**, 492–9.

Craig, G. A. (1982). *The Germans*. New York: Putnam's.

Crankshaw, E. (1948). *Russia and the Russians*. New York: Viking.

Crozier, M. (1964). *The bureaucratic phenomenon*. Chicago: University of Chicago Press.

Cuddihy, J. M. (1974). *The ordeal of civility*. New York: Basic Books.

Dahrendorf, R. (1969). *Society and democracy in Germany*. Garden City, New York: Doubleday.

Dicks, H. (1952). Observations on contemporary Russian behavior. *Human Relations*, 5, 111–75.

Duijker, H. C. J. and Frijda, N. H. (1960). *National character and national stereotypes*. Amsterdam: North Holland Publishing Co.

Ehrenfels, U. R. (1967). Nord-Sued-Polarisation als ganzheitliches Phaenomen. *Zeitschrift fuer Ganzheitsforschung*, 11, 129–38.

Eiser, J. R. (ed.) (1984). *Attitudinal judgment*. New York: Springer-Verlag.

Eiser, J. R. and Stroebe, W. (1972). *Categorization and social judgment*. London, New York: Academic.

Erikson, E. H. (1950). *Childhood and society*. New York: Norton.

Friedl, E. (1962). *Vasilika; a village in modern Greece*. New York: Holt, Rinehart and Winston.

Fromm, E. (1941). *Escape from freedom*. New York: Farrar and Rinehart.

Gambino, R. (1974). *Blood of my blood: the dilemma of Italian-Americans*. Garden City, New York: Doubleday.

George, C. and George, K. (1968). Protestantism and capitalism in pre-revolutionary England. In S. N. Eisenstadt (ed.), *The protestant ethic and modernization*. New York, London: Basic Books. (Reprinted from *Church History*, 1958, 27, 351–72.)

Gilbert, G. M. (1951). Stereotype persistence and change among college students. *Journal of Abnormal and Social Psychology*, 46, 245–54.

Ginsberg, M. (1945). German views of the German mind. In G. P. Gooch *et al.*, *The German mind and outlook*. London: Chapman and Hall.

Glyn, A. (1970). *The British*. New York: Putnam's.

Goffman, E. (1961). *Encounters*. Indianapolis: Bobbs-Merrill.

Goguel, F. (1954). The idea of democracy and political institutions. In S. K. Padover (ed.), *French institutions, values and politics*. Stanford, CA: Stanford University Press.

Gollob, H. F. (1968). Confounding of sources of variation in factor-analytic techniques. *Psychological Bulletin*, 70, 330–44.

Gorer, G. (1948). *The American people, a study in national character*. New York: Norton. (1955). *Exploring English character*. New York: Criterion Books.

Gorer, G. and Rickman, J. (1949). *The people of great Russia; a psychological study*. London: Cresset Press.

de Gramont, S. (1969). *The French: portrait of a people*. New York: Putnam's.

Guilford, J. P. (1936). *Psychometric methods*. New York: McGraw-Hill.

Hamilton, D. L. (1979). A cognitive-attributional analysis of stereotyping. In L. Berkowitz (ed.), *Advances in experimental social psychology*, Vol. 12. New York: Academic Press.

Hartz, L. (1955). *The liberal tradition in America: an interpretation of American political thought since the revolution*. New York: Harcourt, Brace.

Hellpach, W. (1954). *Der deutsche Charakter*. Bonn: Athanaeum.

Hoffmansthal, H. H. (1924). *Gesammelte Werke*. Berlin: S. Fischer.

Hooykaas, R. (1972). *Religion and the rise of modern science.* Edinburgh: Scottish Academic Press.

Inkeles, A. (1955). Social change and social character: the role of parental mediation. *Journal of Social Issues,* 11, 12–23. Reprinted in Y. Cohen (ed.), *Social structure and personality.* New York: Holt, 1961.

Inkeles, A., Hanfmann, E. and Beier, H. (1958). Modal personality and adjustment to the Soviet socio-political system. *Human Relations,* 11, 3–22. Reprinted in Y. Cohen (ed.), *Social structure and personality.* New York: Holt, 1961.

Inkeles, A. and Levinson, D. J. (1969). National character: the study of modal personality and sociocultural systems. In G. Lindzey and E. Aronson (eds.), *The handbook of social psychology,* Vol. 4 (2nd edn). Cambridge, Mass.: Addison-Wesley.

Jespersen, O. (1968). *Growth and structure of the English language.* New York: Free Press.

Jones, E. E. and Nisbett, R. E. (1972). The actor and the observer: divergent perceptions of the causes of behavior. In Jones, E. E. *et al., Attribution: perceiving the causes of behavior.* New York: General Learning Press.

Jones, R. A. and Ashmore, R. D. (1973). The structure of intergroup perception: categories and dimensions in views of ethnic groups and adjectives used in stereotype research. *Journal of Personality and Social Psychology,* 25, 428–38.

Karlins, M., Coffman, T. L. and Walters, G. (1969). On the fading of social stereotypes: studies in three generations of college students. *Journal of Personality and Social Psychology,* 13, 1–16.

Katz, D. and Braly, K. W. (1933). Racial stereotypes of one hundred college students. *Journal of Abnormal and Social Psychology,* 28, 280–90.

(1935). Racial prejudice and racial stereotypes. *Journal of Abnormal and Social Psychology,* 30, 175–93.

Kluckhohn, C. (1958). Have there been discernible shifts in American values during the past generations? In E. E. Morrison (ed.), *The American style: essays in value and performance.* New York: Harper.

La Piere, R. T. (1934). Attitudes vs actions. *Social Forces,* 13, 230–7.

Leites, N. (1969). *The rules of the game in Paris.* University of Chicago Press. (Originally, *La règle de jeu à Paris,* Amsterdam: Mouton, 1966.)

Levine, R. A. and Campbell, D. T. (1972). *Ethnocentrism: theories of conflict, ethnic attitudes and group behavior.* New York: Wiley.

Lewin, K. (1936). Some social psychological differences between the United States and Germany. *Character and Personality,* 36, 265–93. Reprinted in K. Lewin, *Resolving social conflicts.* New York: Harper, 1948.

Lipset, S. M. (1961). A changing American character? In S. M. Lipset and L. Lowenthal (eds.), *Culture and social character: the work of David Riesman reviewed.* Glencoe, Ill.: Free Press.

(1963). *The first new nation.* New York: Basic Books.

Lowenthal, L. (1961). *Literature, popular culture, and society.* Palo Alto, CA: Pacific Books.

Ludwig, E. (1943). *The Germans: double history of a nation.* Boston: Little, Brown.

Luethy, H. (1964). Once again: Calvinism and capitalism. *Encounter,* 22, 26–38. Reprinted in S. N. Eisenstadt (ed.), *The protestant ethic and modernization.* New York: Basic Books, 1968.

McClelland, D. C. (1961). *The achieving society*. Princeton: Van Nostrand.

McClelland, D. C., Sturr, J. F., Knapp, R. H. and Wendt, H. W. (1958). Obligations to self and society in the United States and Germany. *Journal of Abnormal and Social Psychology*, **56**, 245–55.

de Madariaga, S. (1928). *Englishmen, Frenchmen, Spaniards*. London: Oxford University Press.

Mann, T. (1945). *Germany and the Germans*. US Library of Congress.

Marshall, T. H. (1950). *Citizenship and social class*. Cambridge: Cambridge University Press.

Mead, M. (1942). *And keep your powder dry; an anthropologist looks at America*. New York: W. Morrow.

(1953). *Cultural patterns and technical change*. Paris: UNESCO.

Merton, R. K. (1957). *Social theory and social structure*. Glencoe, Ill.: Free Press.

(1970). *Science, technology and society in seventeenth century England*. New York: Harper. (Originally published in 1938.)

Miller, G. A. (1962). *Psychology: the science of mental life*. New York: Harper and Row.

Miller, W. (1960). *Russians as people*. New York: Dutton.

Mischel, W. (1968). *Personality and assessment*. New York: Wiley.

Morsbach, H. (1977). Some characteristics of Japanese interpersonal relations – a westerner's viewpoint. Paper presented at the Conference of the British Psychological Society, December.

Mosse, G. L. (1964). *The crisis of German ideology*. New York: Grosset and Dunlap.

Myrdal, G. (1944). *An American dilemma*. New York: Harper.

Nelson, B. (1969). *The idea of usury from tribal brotherhood to universal otherhood*. Chicago: University of Chicago Press. (Originally published in 1949.)

Norman, W. (1967). *2800 personality trait descriptors: normative operating characteristics for a university population*. Ann Arbor, Mich.: Department of Psychology, University of Michigan.

Osgood, C. E., Suci, G. J. and Tannenbaum, P. H. (1957). *The measurement of meaning*. Urbana: University of Illinois Press.

Ostrom, T. M. and Upshaw, H. S. (1968). Psychological perspective and attitude change. In A. G. Greenwald, T. C. Brock and T. M. Ostrom (eds.), *Psychological foundations of attitudes*. New York: Academic Press.

Parsons, T. (1951). *The social system*. Glencoe, Ill.: Free Press.

(1960). Pattern variables revisited: a response to Robert Dubin. *American Sociological Review*, **25**, 467–83.

Peabody, D. (1967). Trait inferences: evaluative and descriptive aspects. *Journal of Personality and Social Psychology Monographs*, **7** (Whole No. 644).

(1968). Group judgments in the Philippines: evaluative and descriptive aspects. *Journal of Personality and Social Psychology*, **10**, 290–300.

(1970). Evaluative and descriptive aspects in personality perception: a reappraisal. *Journal of Personality and Social Psychology*, **16**, 639–46.

(1978). In search of an evaluative factor: comments on De Boeck. *Journal of Personality and Social Psychology*, **36**, 622–7.

(1984). Personality dimensions through trait inferences. *Journal of Personality and Social Psychology*, **46**, 384–403.

Peyrefitte, A. (1976). *Le mal français*. Paris: Plon.

Pitts, J. R. (1963). Continuity and change in bourgeois France. In S. Hoffman *et al.*, *In search of France*. New York: Harper and Row.

Potter, D. M. (1954). *People of plenty*. Chicago: Univ. of Chicago Press.

Reich, C. (1970). *The greening of America*. New York: Random House.

Richardson, S. (1956). Organizational contrasts on British and American ships. *Administration Science Quarterly*, 1, 189–207.

Riesman, D. (1950). *The lonely crowd*. New Haven, Conn.: Yale University Press.

Rosenberg, S. and Sedlak, A. (1972). Structural representations of implicit personality theory. In L. Berkowitz (ed.), *Advances in experimental social psychology*, Vol. 6. New York: Academic Press.

Sanford, R. N. (1956). The approach of the authoritarian personality. In J. L. McCary (ed.), *Psychology of personality: six modern approaches*. New York: Logos.

Sewell, W. H., Morris, R. T. and Davidsen, O. M. (1954). Scandinavian students' images of the United States: a study in cross-cultural education. *American Academy of Political and Social Science, Annals*, No. 295, 127–35.

Sherif, M. and Hovland, C. I. (1960). *Social judgment: assimilation and contrast effects in communication and attitude change*. New Haven, Conn.: Yale University Press.

Smith, H. (1976). *The Russians*. New York: Quadrangle/NY Times Book Co.

Snowman, D. (1977). *Britain and America*. New York: New York University Press.

Spindler, G. D. (1948). American character as revealed by the military. *Psychiatry*, 11, 275–81. Reprinted in Y. A. Cohen, *Social structure and personality*. New York: Holt, Rinehart and Winston, 1961.

de Stael-Holstein, A. L. G. (1859). *Germany*. Translated by O. W. Wright. Boston: Houghton Mifflin.

Sumner, W. G. (1906). *Folkways*. New York: Ginn.

de Tocqueville, A. (1954). *Democracy in America*. New York: Vintage Books.

Tresselt, M. E. (1948). The effect of experience of contrasted groups upon the formation of a new scale. *Journal of Social Psychology*, 27, 209–16.

Triandis, H. C. (1972). *The analysis of subjective culture*. New York: Wiley-Interscience.

Useem, R. H. and Useem, J. (1954). Images of U.S. and Britain held by foreign-educated Indians. *American Academy of Political and Social Science, Annals*, No. 295, 73–82.

Virtanen, R. (1967). French national character in the twentieth century. *American Academy of Political and Social Science, Annals*, No. 370, 82–92.

Weber, M. (1930). *The protestant ethic and the spirit of capitalism*. Translated by Talcott Parsons. London: G. Allen & Unwin; New York: Scribner's, 1958. (Original 1904–5.)

  (1946). The protestant sects and the spirit of capitalism. In H. H. Gerth and C. W. Mills, *From Max Weber: Essays in sociology*. New York: Oxford University Press.

Whyte, W. H. (1956). *The organization man*. New York: Simon and Schuster.

Wiggins, J. S. (1973). *Personality and prediction: principles of personality assessment*. Reading, Mass.: Addison-Wesley.

Williams, R. J. (1970). *American society; a sociological interpretation*, 3rd edn. New York: Knopf.

Wylie, L. and Bégué, A. (1970). *Les Français*. New York: Prentice-Hall.

Subject index

Index of names